Museums and Public Value

Museums and Public Value

Creating Sustainable Futures

EDITED BY CAROL A. SCOTT

ASHGATE

Published by
Ashgate Publishing Limited
Wey Court East
Union Road
Farnham
Surrey, GU9 7PT
England

Ashgate Publishing Company
110 Cherry Street
Suite 3-1
Burlington, VT 05401-3818
USA

www.ashgate.com

British Library Cataloguing in Publication Data
Museums and public value : creating sustainable futures.
   1. Museums--Public relations. 2. Museums and community.
   I. Scott, Carol.
   069.1-dc23

The Library of Congress has cataloged the printed edition as follows:
Museums and public value : creating sustainable futures / [edited] by Carol Scott.
      pages cm
   Includes bibliographical references.
   ISBN 978-1-4094-4643-9 (hardback) -- ISBN 978-1-4094-4644-6 (ebook) 1. Museums--
Public relations. 2. Museums--Social aspects. 3. Social values. 4. Museums--Public relations--
Case studies. 5. Museums--Social aspects--Case studies. I. Scott, Carol, 1946-
      AM124.M87 2013
      069--dc23

2012044658

ISBN 9781409446439 (hbk)
ISBN 9781409446446 (ebk – PDF)
ISBN 9781472402356 (ebk – ePUB)

Reprinted 2015

MIX
Paper from
responsible sources
FSC
www.fsc.org   FSC® C013985

Printed in the United Kingdom by Henry Ling Limited,
at the Dorset Press, Dorchester, DT1 1HD

Contents

List of Figures and Tables

Notes on Contributors

Dr Carol A. Scott works with museums to build public value. She is Chair of ICOM UK and an executive member of ICOM Marketing and Public Relations Committee. Her articles on museums and value have been published in *Curator: The Museum Journal*, *Museum Management and Curatorship*, *Cultural Trends* and the *International Journal of Arts Management*. Formerly Head of Evaluation and Audience Research at Sydney's Powerhouse Museum, she is now based in London where she runs an international consultancy, Carol Scott Associates.

Professor Mark L. Weinberg directs the Ohio University Voinovich School and teaches public value and strategy in the MPA and Executive Leadership programmes. He co-authored a recent article on this topic for the *Museum Management and Curatorship Journal*. He is the current President of the Southern Consortium for Public Service Organizations and has served on boards of the National Business Incubation Association and Ohio Tuition Trust. From 2002 to 2005 he was the Whisman Scholar for the Appalachian Regional Commission.

Kate Leeman is a Senior Research Associate at Ohio University's Voinovich School of Leadership and Public Affairs and has a background in economic development, nonprofit management, community education and anti-poverty work. Over the last 12 years, she has been actively involved in programme evaluation and strategic planning as well as coordinating activity related to the Voinovich Scholars and Visiting Fellows Programs, the Executive Leadership Institute and the Nonprofit Alliance.

Randi Korn is Founding Director of Randi Korn & Associates, Inc., a company that helps museums plan their strategic work around achieving impact. Randi presents at conferences, writes for journals, and lectures at Johns Hopkins University, The Corcoran College of Art and The George Washington University. She is a board member of the Visitor Studies Association and on the editorial board for *Museums & Social Issues*. Her recent publication, 'The Case for Holistic Intentionality', underscores her commitment to intentional practice to achieve desired results.

Mary Ellen Munley has 30 years' experience as a museum educator, evaluator and administrator. She is principal of MEM and Associates, a consulting firm dedicated to enhancing the role of museums in the lives of people and communities. Recent clients include the National Museum of Natural History, Science Museum of Minnesota and the US Capitol Visitor Center. She received the American Association of Museums' award for excellence in museum education, is widely published, and speaks at national and international conferences.

Mike Houlihan is the Director of Te Papa Tongarewa, the National Museum of New Zealand. He was previously Director General of Amgueddfa Cymru – National Museum Wales and was the first Chief Executive of the National Museums and Galleries of Northern Ireland. He has been Deputy Director at the Horniman Museum in London and began his museum career at the Imperial War Museum. Prior to leaving the UK, Mike was Chairman of ICOM UK and Chair of the Collections Trust.

Ben Garcia is Head of Interpretation and Education at the Phoebe A. Hearst Museum of Anthropology. His extensive experience as a museum educator encompasses early childhood, informal, social justice, arts education, lifelong learning and professional development. He has spoken nationally and internationally on informal learning, the arts and social change. Garcia guest-edited the spring 2010 issue of the *Journal of Museum Education* on public value. He was named Pacific Region Museum Educator of the Year by the National Art Education Association in 2010.

David Spence is Director of Programmes for the Museum of London, the UK's largest social history museum. He was formerly Director, Museum of London Docklands. Spence is Visiting Professor to the School of Art & Design History for Museum & Gallery Studies at Kingston University, London. He has been an adviser on the development of a new Museum of Slavery in Qatar and museums in the Caribbean Leeward Islands. Prior to joining the museum he was Director of Exhibitions and Display at the National Maritime Museum in Greenwich's UNESCO World Heritage site.

Dr Tom Wareham is Curator of Community and Maritime History at the Museum of London Docklands. He was co-lead curator, with Dr Caroline Bressey, of the *London, Sugar and Slavery Gallery* at the Museum of London Docklands, and co-author of *Reading the London, Sugar and Slavery Gallery* (2010). He has curated several temporary exhibitions, including *Londoners at Work* and *Pirates: The Captain Kidd Story*. He is the author of several books and studied Museum Studies at University College, London.

Dr Caroline Bressey is Lecturer in Human Geography at University College London and the founding director of the Equiano Centre (www.ucl.ac.uk/equianocentre/). Her research focuses upon recovering the historical geographies of the black community in Victorian Britain, especially London. Parallel to this are her interests in ideas of early anti-racist activism and identity in Victorian society. In addition she explores the connections between contemporary identities and the representation of British history at heritage sites. She has collaborated with the National Portrait Gallery, London and the Museum of London Docklands.

Dr June Bam-Hutchison has worked in the field of heritage transformation over the past two decades in Southern Africa, Rwanda and Nigeria and in Europe. She has led on major projects at the British Museum and co-curated a popular exhibition on cricket at the International Museum of Slavery in Liverpool. June served on the Council of Iziko Museums (15 national museums in South Africa). Currently, she is a Visiting Research Fellow at the Institute for the Public Understanding of the Past, York University and with Kingston University's Faculty of Business and Law.

Annette Day is the Head of Programmes at the Museum of London where she is responsible for the museum's exhibitions, informal adult events and community collaboration and inclusion. She is leading the *Many East Ends* programme to create a new contemporary history gallery at Museum of London Docklands. She was previously Senior Curator of Oral History and Contemporary Collecting, during which time she was the museum's lead on a partnership project called the Refugee Communities History Project which resulted in the major exhibition *Belonging: Voices of London's Refugees*.

Lisa Conolly is Director of Rural and Regional Statistics for the Australian Bureau of Statistics (ABS). Lisa has been with the ABS for over 10 years and previously managed the National Centre for Culture, Recreation and Migrant Statistics. Prior to the ABS, Lisa worked for 10 years in local government in a variety of roles. Lisa has also worked in universities on various research projects, predominantly in the social sciences. Lisa has an Executive Masters degree in Public Administration from the Australian and New Zealand School of Government, and an Honours degree in Psychology from Macquarie University, Sydney.

Marsha L. Semmel is Director, Office of Strategic Partnerships, at the Institute of Museum and Library Services, a federal agency based in Washington, DC. She has been president and CEO of Conner Prairie, a living history museum near Indianapolis, Indiana, and Women of the West Museum, in Denver. She worked at the National Endowment for the Humanities (NEH) for 12 years, where, from 1993 to 1996, she directed the NEH Division of Public Programs. This chapter was written in Ms Semmel's personal capacity. The views expressed are her own and do not necessarily represent the views of the Institute of Museums and Library Services, or the United States Government.

Dr David O'Brien is a Lecturer in Cultural and Creative Industries at City University London. He specialises in public policy, cultural value and urban cultural policy issues. He has a PhD in Sociology from the University of Liverpool. His first book, *Cultural Policy: Value, Management and Modernity in the Creative Industries*, will be published by Routledge in 2013. His work on cultural value includes the report 'Measuring the Value of Culture', which followed a secondment to the UK's Department for Culture Media and Sport, along with several conference papers and forthcoming research articles on this topic.

Sharon Heal is Head of Publications and Events for the Museums Association, the membership organization that represents people who work in museums and galleries in the UK. She is the editor of *Museums Journal*, the association's monthly news magazine, and has responsibility for *Museum Practice* online, the association's best practice publication.

Sharon is responsible for the Museums Association's annual conference, the largest event for museum, gallery and heritage professionals in Europe. Sharon's background is in journalism and editing with previous work on local and national newspapers and in book publishing.

Joanne Orr is CEO of Museums Galleries Scotland, the strategic development body for museums and galleries in Scotland. A graduate of the MLI 2010 (Museum Leadership Institute) funded by the Getty Foundation Joanne also has an MBA from Durham University Business School and academic degrees in history, industrial archaeology and museum studies. Joanne is the founding Chair of the UNESCO Scotland Committee and is passionate about the role of culture in international development and has considerable consultancy experience both in the UK and abroad.

Preface

Introduction

Public Value speaks to our time – to the role that museums can play in creating civil societies, to the challenges involved in using limited assets strategically, to the demand for results that make a difference and to the imperative that we build the kind of engagement that sustains our futures.

This book interrogates the concept of public value from the perspective of museums. It will interest museum professionals who want their work to make a positive difference in the lives of individuals and communities. It will be of particular interest to those who have the authority to lead change that is coherent, focused, and which aims to build positive relationships with decision-makers and the public. It argues that public value as a theory, model and practice addresses management issues central to our ongoing sustainability as a sector including:

1. Adaptability

   Contemporary museum leadership must be adaptable. Museums operate in a dynamic environment where systemic change is the norm. Identifying emerging issues and responding to them is crucial to creating ongoing value and maintaining relevance. Public value begins with this dynamic environment and provides practical guidance for navigating within it.

2. Accountability

   Accountability, particularly in the publically subsidized museums' sector, is a requirement of our professional practice. Governments, policy-makers and other funders require evidence that there is a return on their investment. But in an economic climate where the total amount of public funding is declining, museums in many countries find themselves fighting to maintain a position as essential public goods in competition with other necessary services. We are no longer just accounting for public monies. Providing evidence that museum work results in public benefit is now crucial to our survival.

3. Audiences

   Audiences are demanding a new relationship with museums. Increasingly, people expect to author their own experiences and to engage in agenda setting. This implies a role as co-producers with significant implications for the ways that museums think about and engage with the public. Successful strategies for engagement that put the public at the centre can build loyal supporters.

4. Assets

In these constrained economic times, museums need to ensure that they are using their assets (collections, intellectual resources, ideas, partnerships, mission, purpose and unique capabilities) and increasingly scarce funding allocations in strategically focused ways to ensure results that build capacity and ensure the ongoing future of the institution.

5. Advocacy

How we articulate the role of museums in the twenty-first century, what value we create and how we measures that value are all subjects which form part of a wider discourse around the role of museums in the twenty-first century. Public value, with its focus on clearly articulated outcomes combined with appropriate measures and its inclusion of institutional, decision-making and public perspectives, provides a framework within which to address these issues.

Aims

Public value as a model for public sector management was the subject of Mark Moore's seminal 1995 book, *Creating Public Value: Strategic Management in Government*, published by Harvard University Press. Moore argued that, in the dynamic and changing world in which publically funded institutions operate, leaders need to be proactive and creative, constantly interrogating the environment in which they work, forging partnerships, managing assets strategically and creating and delivering programmes and services of value to the public and other stakeholders. That message resonates even more today as public benefit is emerging as central to securing funding. But for museum leadership, the literature on public value related to museums is fragmented and dispersed.

The aims of this book, therefore, are two-fold. Firstly, it seeks to empower museum leadership to confidently implement a public value approach in their management, planning, programming and relationship building. The benefits of adopting this approach are long-term public engagement and support which can be effectively used to demonstrate that valuable returns result from public investment in museums.

Secondly, it explores some of the unresolved issues of which museum leadership needs to be aware when adopting a public value approach. The book begins with the implications for institutional practice and goes on to explore examples of implementation. Models of working with the authorizing environment and issues surrounding this relationship are the subject of the final section.

Background to the Book

This book arose from an interest in the subject of museums and their value driven by my own experience of working in publically funded museums. My career in this sector began in the early 1990s as Manager of Evaluation and Audience Research at the Powerhouse Museum in Sydney, Australia, which, at the time, was the first position of its kind in Australasia. The work involved a type of 'strategic triangle'.

At one level, I was evaluating the museum's programmes and services with a view to continuous improvement. Another major facet of the work was audience research – identifying trends, patterns and relationships in visitor behaviour, motivations and satisfaction. A third dimension was our accountability to government and the provision of statistics for reporting against the performance criteria. Though these areas overlapped, there was no unifying model to link them in a cohesive way. In addition, change was occurring in each of these domains.

Government reform of the public sector at that time sought to tightly control and monitor publically funded institutions through performance agreements and outcome targets. Systems of accountability such as management by results and performance evaluation were being introduced and the value of museums was being judged by the degree to which they delivered on government policies.

At the same time, a quiet revolution was occurring in the relationship between museums and their audiences. Greater interest in the visitor and, particularly, how the visitor's knowledge and attitudes impacted on interpretation, was growing. Audiences were becoming more discerning consumers who exercised their rights to comment on service delivery and programmes. Technology was revolutionizing the way that people could engage with and comment on exhibitions and programmes. And, as leisure attractions proliferated offering many more options for an increasingly time-poor public, museums were required to research audience opinions, needs and values in order to maintain market share.

But though museums were looking upwards to governments and funders and outwards to audiences, we lacked a paradigm that would link all three components – the museum, the public and government – in a meaningful way. It was during this time that I began research for my PhD on identifying and measuring museum value. In the course of that research, I came across the work of John Holden and his model for conceptualizing cultural value based on the work of Mark Moore.

This was the first time that I had heard of 'public value'. It was a step change. It took the discourse beyond 'existence' value to value *creation*. Public value is dynamic. It makes the institution an active agent in the 'creation or destruction of what the public values' (Holden 2006, 18). It does this *with* the public and *with* policy-makers and funders.

Adapting Moore's model with its emphasis on conversations between the operational and authorizing environments in the creation of public value, Holden envisaged 'a new accord' between governments and the cultural sector and a move away from the deterministic and top-down agenda that had been a hallmark of the New Public Management throughout the late 1980s and 1990s.

In addition, Moore's contention that the public are the true legitmators of value, putting them central to any value creation, is synergistic with the more equal relationship evolving between museums, subject expertise and audiences. Within the public value framework audiences can become citizen co-producers.

The public realm can only be public if people take part in shaping and forming it, and so it not only comprises but is also based on the values that people hold. It is a foundational concept of democratic society, comprising the common set of assets to which people can relate and contribute. As a result, it is a space in which different values meet, merge and mingle and in which the development of society is negotiated. Culture is the expression of these values and so the forms in which it is manifest are the currency of the public realm and society itself. (Jones 2010, 33)

Why this Book Now?

Over the last five years, my interest in questions of museum value and the potential for the museum sector in adopting a public value approach have been the source of many publications and conference presentations. Through this, I have discovered a community of interest in arguing for, interrogating and exploring how public value can be implemented in museums.

One of the most productive forums for these conversations has been the American Association of Museums Annual Meeting at which I have organized sessions on public value since 2008. It is from the responses of museum professionals attending these sessions and to my co-presenters that I owe the inspiration for this book, the realization that there is a need to 'unpack' public value and the timeliness of exploring implications for implementation. We attempt to do this in the following chapters in relation to professional needs, practical application, unresolved issues meriting further conversations and a range of interpretations of public value within authorizing environments across the English-speaking world.

The book is organized into three sections broadly reflecting the three points of the strategic triangle. Following the introductory chapter and overview, the next three chapters examine implications for museum practice when the operational environment adopts a public value approach. Chapters 5 to 7 provide case studies of institutions who are engaging external stakeholders to create public value. The final section focuses on the authorizing environment and looks at the implications of policy, politics and changes for relationships in this area.

Acknowledgements

This book happened because every author to whom I extended a formal invitation agreed to write a chapter. They did so to demanding guidelines and for a demanding editor. Each one of them has been willing to redraft where necessary in a spirit of generosity and scholarship which is testament to their commitment and passion for this subject.

We have collectively enjoyed the very best type of support from our editors at Ashgate and we individually thank the spouses, children, friends and colleagues who have encouraged us to complete this important work.

C.A. Scott, London,
April 2013

References

Holden, J. 2006. *Cultural value and the crisis of legitimacy: Why culture needs a democratic mandate.* London: DEMOS.

Jones, S. 2010. *Culture Shock.* London: DEMOS.

Moore, M.H. 1995, *Creating public value: Strategic management in government.* Cambridge, MA: Harvard University Press.

1 *An Introduction to Museums and Public Value*

CAROL A. SCOTT

Abstract

We are living in times of accelerated economic, cultural, political and technological change.

Leaders of publically-funded museums simultaneously navigate the shoals of change on multiple fronts – addressing emerging social issues, responding to adjustments in government policy and adapting to new funding thresholds. Working with change, while maintaining institutional value and building a sustainable future for the institution is the work of today's museum leader.

Within this context, Mark Moore's vision for public management continues to resonate. He recognizes that leaders of public institutions operate within a dynamic environment. Instead of perceiving constant change as overwhelming, Moore envisages public managers as proactive stewards of public assets that can be directed purposefully to making 'a positive difference in the lives of individuals and communities' (Moore and Moore 2005, 17), and as leaders with influence to help governments 'discover what could be done with the assets entrusted to their offices, as well as ensuring responsive services to users and citizens' (Moore and Benington 2011, 3).

This vision is important at a time when a global economic crisis is affecting the amount of public funding available and notions of what kind of social return is expected on public investment. In Chapter 9, 'Museums and Public Value: A US Cultural Agency Example', Marsha Semmel refers to the 'shifting ecologies' of the funding landscape in that country. Shifts in the funding landscape are creating corresponding shifts in traditional notions of 'public good', in ideas of what constitutes 'essential' public benefits and to perceptions about which agencies deliver benefits worthy of funding support. In this climate, being able to demonstrate that museums create public value is ceasing to be an option.

Public value as a theory and model of management offers guidance, structure and purpose in these challenging times. It focuses us on the benefits that museums can create in the public sphere. It directs us to use scarce resources for maximum benefit. It offers an approach to building relationships with communities and governments that are long-lasting and sustainable.

It is now 17 years since Mark Moore published *Creating Public Value: Strategic Management in Government* (1995) but as a theory, model and practice it continues to be discussed, debated, received and adopted.

This introduction explores Moore's model and its place within a wider discourse on value in the cultural sector. It takes the pulse of public value today and examines the implications of adopting a public value approach for professional practice in museums.

Introduction

WHAT IS VALUE?

'Value' can refer to the moral principles of individuals and the ethical ideas that guide collective action such as beliefs in the principles of democracy and tolerance. 'Value' is associated with worth, importance, significance and usefulness. Outcomes of programmes and services that are 'valued' are those which have a beneficial impact for an end-user (Poll and Payne 2006).

WHAT IS PUBLIC VALUE?

Public value refers to planned outcomes which add benefit to the public sphere. Benington (in Moore and Benington 2011, 43) describes the public sphere as that 'web of values, places, organizations, rules, knowledge, and other cultural resources held in common by people through their everyday commitments and behaviours, and held in trust by government and public institutions'.

The focus on the *public sphere* situates public value in relation to decisions which are made in the general public interest. Benington (in Moore and Benington 2011, 45–6) argues that public value addresses 'unmet social needs'. Moore (2007) is more discursive, suggesting that public value can tackle social conditions which need to be ameliorated, substantive problems to be solved, rights to be vindicated and opportunities to be exploited.

HOW DO WE CREATE PUBLIC VALUE?

Moore (1995) developed his theory and model with governments and the publically-funded sector in mind. He envisaged governments and institutions working together with the shared purpose of creating value that would benefit the general public. Moore mapped this relationship through a 'strategic triangle', a framework for aligning three distinct, but interdependent, components (Moore 1995, 31).

The points of the triangle identify (a) the authorizing environment which provides legitimacy and support through approvals and funding, together with (b) the operational environment which applies its organizational capacity and assets to (c) the joint purpose of creating public value (see Figure 1.1).

The authorizing environment comprises those who have the power to grant or withdraw approval or place conditions on the allocation of resources. It includes policy-makers and legislators, bureaucrats and funders. In government, because many of these authorizers are elected 'representatives' who are tasked with making decisions on behalf of their constituents, the authorizing environment also includes all the individuals and interest groups who have a stake in decisions and who can influence those who are in

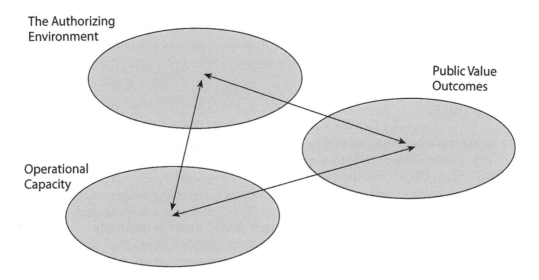

The Authorizing
Environment

Public Value
Outcomes

Operational
Capacity

Figure 1.1   Public value strategic triangle
Source: Moore, M. and Benington, J. (eds) 2011. *Public Value: Theory and Practice,* 31, reproduced
with permission of Palgrave Macmillan.

representative positions (Moore and Moore 2005, 37). This supplementary stakeholder
cohort is extensive and can include arts practitioners, representatives of arts and
cultural heritage organizations, special interest groups, professional associations, other
government departments, private agencies and the media.

The operational environment refers to the assets and capacity of publically-funded
organizations. These assets include the Acts under which organizations are established,
missions and purpose, history in pursuit of that purpose, leadership (Boards, CEOs
and management teams), human resources, available funds, collections and the depth,
breadth and efficacy of strategic partnerships. Public value focuses management on what
one *does* with the organization's assets. It offers '*a renewed emphasis on the important role
public managers can play in maintaining an organisation's legitimacy in the eyes of the public*'
(Blaug et al. 2006, 6) to achieve '*its politically mandated mission – roughly stated, to make a
positive difference in the individual and collective lives of citizens*' (Moore and Moore 2005, 17).

From the perspective of policy-makers and funders, public value is a way of framing
and accounting for governments' social return on investment (ABS 2008, 10) and
effectively targeting that investment in a time of rising demand within imitated budgets
for public spending. For museum leaders, it acknowledges the reality of the complex
and changing environment in which operations occur and the multiple stakeholders
with whom they must engage and to whom they owe accountability. It provides a focus
and direction for 'harnessing and mobilizing the operational resources ... both inside
and outside the organization, which are necessary to achieve the desired public value
outcomes' (Moore and Benington 2011, 4).

For Holden (2004), Moore's approach offered the possibility of a 'new accord' in
which governments and public institutions would work in a spirit of collaboration
and consensus, combining approval processes, funding and organizational assets to

create value in the public sphere. This was 'new' in relation to the structure of public administration that was in place when *Creating Public Value* was first published and is best understood within the context of that history.

Background

The model of public administration in place when Moore published in 1995 was called the New Public Management (NPM). It was part of a modernizing[1] agenda implemented by governments in OECD[2] countries from the late 1970s in response to both another world economic crisis in the early years of that decade, and the growing awareness that funding post-World War II welfare states to the degree current at the time was unsustainable.

Sweeping reforms were introduced to divest governments of the direct costs of what had previously been publically-provided services. Diversification and outsourcing of delivery were introduced. At the same time, cost savings were sought in a reduced public service which now had to be more efficient in its management of public funds and more accountable for their use. Governments looked to the private sector for models, adopting and adapting many features of commercial performance. Management by results, performance evaluation and budgetary control were introduced to monitor and regulate the public sector. Control was a major feature of the New Public Management. It was characterized by a top-down, regulatory environment which, though it initially focused on economic reform, eventually extended its remit to include social policy.

Under this regime, the 'arm's length' principle was diminished and funding for public institutions was more closely tied to delivering government policy. Policy was pragmatic, 'instrumental' and unashamedly interventionist. Its effectiveness was assessed through 'evidence-based policy' which formalized the need for performance data to provide proof of achievement against targets set by government.

THE NEW PUBLIC MANAGEMENT, MUSEUMS AND VALUE

The responses to the New Public Management from the museum sector can best be summarized as a combination of compliance, criticism and challenge. Though the regulatory environment required compliance as a condition of funding, the museum sector was not quiescent. It criticized governments for adopting a system originating in the profit-making, commercial world which measured success by a financial bottom line. It argued that the multi-dimensional briefs and wide range of stakeholders in the public sector make meaningful performance assessment a much more complex issue (Ames 1991; Bud et al. 1991; Walden 1991). The 'narrowness' of the instrumental agenda came under attack, with critics pointing out that it obscured other, equally important,

---

1   A programme to modernise the public sector with the common objectives of making the public sector more responsive, transparent, and efficient in meeting the needs of citizens.

2   Organisation for Economic Cooperation and Development (OECD) formed in 1961 comprises 30 countries including Australia, Austria, Belgium, Canada, Czech Republic, Denmark, Finland, France, Germany Greece, Hungary, Iceland, Ireland, Italy, Japan, Korea, Luxembourg, Mexico, Netherlands, New Zealand, Norway, Poland, Portugal, Slovak Republic, Spain, Sweden, Switzerland, Turkey, the United Kingdom and the United States. One if its prominent roles is fostering good governance in the public service of OECD countries.

outcomes which were not captured in systems of measurement favouring quantitative data at the expense of qualitative information.

An increasingly vociferous body of criticism argued for a more holistic view of the value produced by culture and more appropriate measurement systems to assess it. The result was a lively conversation about cultural value – what value, whose values and how that value should be measured. Holden (2004, 10) issued a call for an approach:

> capable of reflecting, recognising and capturing the full range of values expressed through culture, make explicit the range of values addressed in the funding process to encompass a much broader range of cultural, non-monetised values, view the whole cultural system and all its sub-systems, and understand how systemic health and resilience are maintained, recognise that professional judgement must extend beyond evidence-based decision-making, see the source of legitimacy for public funding as being the public itself, overturn the concept of centrally driven, top-down delivery and replace it with systemic, grass roots value creation.

WHAT VALUE?

Within this discourse, instrumentalism became associated with government policies that sought to achieve specific economic and social outcomes, 'going beyond function and having aspirations to contribute to a wider agenda of social change' (Davies 2008, 260). Though O'Neill (2008, 293) reminds us that the application of museum purposes and functions to wider social issues is not a new phenomenon, the concept of instrumentalism within the last decade of the twentieth century and the early part of this century became associated with increased demands for accountability and with funding allocations linked to delivering government policy.

Belfiore and Bennett (2006, 2), however, argue that the very predominance of the instrumental agenda and the vigour with which it was driven by governments created a tension which ultimately served a useful purpose; it focused the cultural sector on articulating its value, something which had been less necessary under traditional notions of funding culture as a 'public good'. In the search for a more holistic and nuanced paradigm, other value dimensions came to the fore. Initially, the debates coalesced around instrumentalism's opposite – intrinsic value.

'Intrinsic' describes 'the set of values that relate to the subjective experience of culture intellectually, emotionally and spiritually' (Holden 2006, 14). Intrinsic value was given prominence in publications by Holden (2004) and McCarthy et al. (2004) both of whom developed cultural value paradigms which included instrumental and intrinsic dimensions.

Holden's paradigm, however, included a third dimension which he termed 'institutional' value and which he described as 'the processes and techniques that organisations adopt in how they work to create value for the public … enhancing the public realm … as discussed in the work of Mark Moore' (Holden 2006, 17).

For Holden, one of the attractions of Moore's concept of public value was its vision of a relationship between governments and publically-funded institutions where the conflicts and contest which had characterized the New Public Management could be replaced with a more consensual approach to decision-making and where funders, policy-makers and cultural leaders could collaborate in decisions about what public value should be delivered and how it could be measured.

Public Value and Museums

Nearly two decades after it was first published, the theory of public value still resonates in terms of its outward-looking focus, its conceptual mapping of relationships with governments, stakeholders and the public and its emphasis on directing activity to creating benefit in the public sphere.

Moore (1995) aimed for a system of 'practical reasoning' (Horner and Hutton 2011, 122) which would guide managers to use state-owned assets to achieve public good. What constitutes that system of 'practical reasoning', the processes, procedures and issues involved and the issues that it raises for museums is explored in the following chapters which are organized under three general headings:

1. The operational environment: public value building blocks
    *   management: frameworks and processes
    *   intentional planning
    *   evaluation

2. Case studies: implementing public value
    *   planning for social impact
    *   co-production with the public: education and learning
    *   co-production with the public: exhibitions

3. Working with the authorizing environment
    *   measuring public value
    *   the United States: a federal agency and public value
    *   the UK: public value at national government level
    *   the UK: a professional association perspective
    *   the UK: a partnership in Scotland.

THE OPERATIONAL ENVIRONMENT: PUBLIC VALUE BUILDING BLOCKS

One of the first things required for a museum CEO considering whether to adopt a public value approach, is reassurance that theory and practice are congruent with current models of strategic management and standards of best practice.

Mark L. Weinberg and Kate Leeman address this topic in the next chapter. They begin by assessing public value against the outcomes of two recent research studies which identify factors necessary to achieve 'best practice' in strategic management and then outline a framework of five components that constitute a set of procedural guidelines for practical application.

They conclude that adopting a public value approach enables the leader of a non-profit organization to shift from 'ensuring continuity and consistency in executing mandates to one of a strategist, working to keep the organization relevant and improve performance over time' (Weinberg and Lewis 2009, 256). The resulting outcome empowers managers, enabling them to move from adaptive strategy to proactive leadership and to foster a culture that simultaneously focuses on value, operational assets and political issues.

In Chapter 3, Randi Korn drills deeper, offering insights on two fundamental principles underlying strategic planning to achieve public value- 'intention' and a focus on 'results'.

She applies these principles to the process of defining a value proposition, articulating a value chain and aligning systems. Korn suggests that a well-articulated value statement provides a basis for the meaningful selection of activities and programmes, enabling a museum to eliminate, or reduce to a lesser priority, activities which are not aligned with the public value it has set out to achieve. This may be a controversial notion, but in these challenging economic times, it provides a needed rationale to use scarce resources wisely and to maximum effect.

Public value planning is not complete without evaluation. In Moore and Moore's opinion:

> performance measures are so important in developing and executing a value-creating strategy that it would be fair to say that one does not really have a strategy until one has developed the performance measures that go along with it. (Moore and Moore 2005, 81)

In Chapter 4, Mary Ellen Munley locates evaluation within the broader ecology of systemic change occurring in museums. She argues that a public value approach is rapidly emerging as a logical extension of these wider systemic changes and that this has implications for the role of evaluation. 'Evaluating public value' is different from traditional programme evaluation. Munley explores these distinctions, demonstrating how the parameters change when evaluation is focused on social impact, when the process is embedded within organizational planning and when performance measures have to be adjusted to capture the quality, as well as the quantity, of the changes that result. She illustrates her arguments with three case studies which show how embedding evaluation within a public value paradigm can move museums from a position of potential to value-creating performance.

CASE STUDIES: IMPLEMENTING PUBLIC VALUE

This section begins with a chapter which demonstrates public value planning in action. Mike Houlihan, Director of Te Papa Tongarewa/the National Museum of New Zealand, explores how planning for public value has reconnected the museum with its own core values. In the process of revisiting these values, the museum has created a platform for reflection, analysis and organizational change which has resulted in a refocusing of institutional purpose for the next 10 to 15 years.

Activating each aspect of Moore's strategic triangle, the museum has integrated planned institutional impacts with both government views of social accountability and public engagement. Houlihan outlines three steps on the path to establish a strategic vision that will 'change hearts, change minds, change lives'. First, he explores the processes involved in *identifying public benefit* through clarifying what intended impact the museum seeks to have upon the nation; secondly, he explores *building capability and capacity* to achieve intentions; and finally, he discusses *seeking and sharing authority* across a variety of communities of interest. 'Sharing authority' segues into the theme of the next two chapters which both explore the role of the public in public value.

The Public in Public Value

In the public value model, the 'public' are active *citizens* with an interest in 'goals or aspirations' that are good 'for the society as a whole, rather than just individual consumers seeking personal satisfaction from services (Alford 2011 in Benington and Moore, 144).

Public preferences are at the heart of public value in a democracy where only the public can determine what is truly of value to them (Kelly et al. 2002, 6). Engaging the public in decision-making to decide what services are needed and what benefits those services should provide opens the path to a better understanding of established preferences and the capacity to predict emerging attitudes and expectations. Kelly et al. (2002) and Horner et al. (2006) claim that failures to create public value in the past by both the authorizing and operational environments have been due to the *under-representation* of the public in decision-making.

How and to what degree this engagement can and should occur is a 'live' issue. Though Moore (1995) insists on the centrality of the public, he claims that, in reality, taxpayers do not determine public value in some kind of referendum and that there is no process allowing them to earmark public funds. Rather, the question of what constitutes public value is subject to a complex political process in which individuals with formal power to provide funds make choices, based in part on the guidance of various stakeholders, about 'how much public money to spend' and 'for what particular purposes' (Moore and Moore 2005, 37). Moore and Benington (2011, 10) conclude that the public has to act 'as best as it can through the imperfect processes of representative government'.

Moore (2007) is the first to admit that is not an ideal state of affairs and, at worst, can involve 'incoherent, fickle mandates emerging from a chaotic authorizing environment'. He admits that policy and funding priorities can be affected by changes to governments, short-term political expediency, varying levels of interest in arts and cultural issues among policy-makers and funders and varying degrees of support, tension and differences of opinion amongst stakeholders about the best allocation of funds (Moore and Moore 2005, 17).

While direct engagement of citizens in decision-making at the authorizing level is patchy, at an organizational level public engagement is both necessary and possible. From the perspective of public sector managers, it makes sense to ensure that there is alignment between the values of an organization and those of the public. If the priorities and expectations of the public shift, and the culture of a public body does not, then satisfaction and trust in the service may be undermined, a point attested to by research indicating that service users are well attuned to the ethos of providers (Kelly et al. 2002, 24; Weil 2002 in Weinberg and Lewis 2009, 254).

Within a public value paradigm, managers of public institutions are charged with actively seeking input from the public to ensure an organization's legitimacy and engaging them as co-creators so that:

> value is being added to the public sphere, not through arm's-length market demand and supply, but through closer linking of users and producers in creative joint development of products and services tailor-made to meet unmet human need – co-creation of public value. (Benington in Moore and Benington 2011, 45)

One of the forms of authority-sharing gaining currency is co-production. Co-production recognizes that the museum public is active, autonomous co-creators of messages and meanings (Silverman 1993, 1995).

Both Ben Garcia and David Spence (with co-authors, Tom Wareham, Caroline Bressey, June Bam-Hutchison and Annette Day) address the issues of co-production within educational programmes and exhibition development in chapters 6 and 7 respectively.

Ben Garcia argues that museum educators, uniquely placed to serve as intermediaries between the museum's collections and the public, have a responsibility to advocate for, and help move, the museum towards embracing public value as a workable paradigm. He finds that public value is synergistic with many of the principles underlying the history and practice of museum education and that it offers a framework, especially with regard to co-production, within which museum educators can work with communities to create learning programmes that meet essential needs.

Engaging the public as co-producers of an exhibition that addresses challenging social issues is the theme of the chapter by David Spence, Tom Wareham, Caroline Bressey, June Bam-Hutchison and Annette Day. *London, Sugar and Slavery* is an exhibition which explores the history of London's involvement in the transatlantic slave trade and its legacies. The authors show that exhibitions can provide a meeting place between collections, the institution, audiences and unresolved social issues. Using the development of this gallery at the Museum of London as a starting point, the authors critically examine the many facets of co-production, each sharing their experiences and the challenges they encountered in the process.

WORKING WITH THE AUTHORIZING ENVIRONMENT

Moore's strategic triangle envisaged a collaborative relationship between governments and public institutions aligned around the shared purpose of creating public value. What form this relationship takes, what factors affect it and how issues are negotiated are the subjects of this final section.

One of the major sources of contention has been the way that governments measure public value. At the heart of these debates are different perspectives on what constitutes 'value', how it should be measured and what data should be captured.

The standard application of econometric measures by governments is seen by many in the cultural sectors to ignore other important outcomes while others (O'Brien 2010) contend that econometric measures offer a standard approach which can be applied with parity by governments across a competing range of calls on the public purse. Other critics claim that this argument is based on a simplistic interpretation of economics tied to market forces and financial bottom lines which ignores non-market values and obscures the deeper meaning of economics as the management of a society's resources. In Holden's opinion (2004, 31):

> *Economic value is determined by the extent to which something enhances or detracts from our well-being. Something has economic value if its benefits to the well-being of society (including future generations) are greater than or outweigh its costs. Though it encompasses commercial value – as expressed through monetary exchange within markets – economic value is not restricted to values that are revealed through markets. The full schema of economic value incorporates commercial (or market) value; use values not captured within markets; and non-use values.*

In Chapter 8, Lisa Conolly examines the kind of values that are being described by government within a public value paradigm, how policy is translated into measures and how measures are used. She raises questions about the audience for measurement data and draws comparisons between the public's concept of value and what the authorizing environment requires for purposes of accountability and decisions about public funding. She interrogates the use of numerical measures by the authorizing government and explains why, in the authorizing environment, numerical measures and 'size' count.

It is not only differences in measuring public value that have to be negotiated. The notion of public value sits within a wider context of political, economic and social ecologies. What is the impact on public value when there are shifts due to economic crises and political changes?

In the United States ...

While non-profit organizations such as museums can build public benefit, they are under threat in a funding climate where the severity of the economic crisis means that everything is on the table and long-standing assumptions about funding, public good and public value are being tested (AAM 2012, 8).

In the volatile world of global economics, decreases to public funding are becoming the norm in many Western democracies. Marsha Semmel scopes the situation in the United States where the full range of civic and cultural activities and expenditures is up for consideration. She argues that being able to demonstrate public value is more important than ever before for public agencies.

In an environment where the issue of 'public value' is under scrutiny and where what should be funded is no longer a given, Semmel describes how the Institute of Museum and Library Studies (IMLS) is building the capacity of museums to create public value. She illustrates how the IMLS contributes to public policy, fosters public value in the programmes that it funds and demonstrates the public value of the museum and library sectors to both the public and the authorizing environment.

In Great Britain ...

David O'Brien illustrates how public value has been affected by political changes.

The 2010 national election brought a new Coalition government to power in the UK. The resulting change has witnessed the divesting of many of the ideas, policies and programmes which enjoyed currency under the previous regime. One of those was public value.

David O'Brien considers the trajectory of public value as an idea, the reasons for its disappearance from the national agenda and its loss of currency in the English conversation about public policy. He points out that one of the weaknesses of public value is the lack of specificity in definition which has made it both susceptible to interpretation and vulnerable to shifts in political ideology, a view shared by Benington (in Moore and Benington 2011, 42), who notes that:

there is a danger in the UK, at least, of public value getting used loosely, as a broad portmanteau phrase expressing ideals and aspirations about public service, but also capable of meaning many different things to different people. There has been less rigorous development of the definition and of the theoretical assumptions behind the notion of public value, and less and less testing of the concept through the lens of different academic disciplines and policy contexts.

Lack of clarity around the concept of public value also emerges from the interviews with museum leaders in the UK which Sharon Heal conducted as part of her research for Chapter 11. Heal finds that confusion surrounding the debates about 'value', what kind of value and how to measure it have contributed to a degree of 'value fatigue' amongst the museum sector which has only served to weaken interest in the concept of public value.

Into the vacuum created by the absence of government policy on public value, the museum sector's professional association in England has independently chosen to adopt *creating social impact* as the cornerstone of its long-term strategic plan 2012–2020. This strategic decision seems to reflect Holden's (2004, 47) argument that one of the contributory ideas of public value is that 'organisations must determine, and be committed to, *their own* purposes rather than being given them by others' with 'the consequent radical conceptual shift away from a top-down, target-driven culture'. Though frustrated by the imposition of instrumentalist policies when handed down by previous governments, the English museum sector, through its professional association, is implementing its own agenda of social impact in a spirit of self-determination and self-definition.

A Scottish Partnership

The ideas developed by Mark Moore in *Creating Public Value* challenged the then orthodox thinking about the role of government in society. In Moore's view, governments' role was 'not just as a rule-setter, service-provider and social safety net, but potentially as a creator of public value and a pro-active shaper of the public sphere (politically, economically, socially and culturally)' (Moore and Benington 2011, 3).

Visionary though this is we may well ask whether there are any examples where the vision approaches reality. It may be that an answer is in Scotland, where a partnership between the Scottish government and Museums Galleries Scotland, the sector's professional association, has resulted in a national strategy with public value at its heart.

Initiated by the Scottish government, the National Strategy and Delivery Plan followed an intense period of discussion and consultation with the Scottish museums sector. The result is not only a strategic future for Scottish museums. It is also one of the few examples of the type of collaboration possible between authorizing and operational environments envisaged by Moore.

This collaboration is a fascinating case study. It has required a complex set of negotiations and compromises to achieve the wider goal of a unifying purpose and a common way forward. Joanne Orr's chapter provides an insight into the journey and how government and museums can work '*proactively to try to develop some kind of shared vision or common purpose out of the diversity of perspectives, and to negotiate and mobilize coalitions of interest to achieve communal aims*' (Benington, in Moore and Benington 2011, 36–7).

Conclusion

What are the benefits of adopting a public value approach for the contemporary museum leader? In discussing the theory underlying public value, Moore and Benington (2011, 13) point to the need for the public sector leader to be adaptable in a dynamic environment of constant change:

> *Whereas traditional public administration assumes a context of relative political economic and social stability, and whereas new public management trusts the logic of free market competition, public value recognizes the complexity, volatility and uncertainty in the environment. While the landscape and contours of government and public management are changing, and the maps are no longer as accurate or useful, public value may offer a compass to provide a sense of direction and destination.*

This dynamic environment includes managing scarce resources, dealing with public expectations and developing sustainable relationships.

As public sector spending comes under intense scrutiny over the next few years, museums may find that adopting a public value approach assists them to be selective, choosing what is sustainable to achieve maximum public benefit rather than always trying to 'do more with less'. Engaging the public in decision-making processes means that benefits do not just reflect the interests of the institution or the interests of one particular group. Rather, real issues based in real social needs become the focus of planning. Finally, as museums engage upwards to the authorizing environment and outwards to the public, the necessity of working and accounting to both groups is an opportunity to plan effective and valued outcomes that build the legitimacy of the institution and contribute to the public sphere. In the end, a public value framework encourages museums and their leadership to integrate the directions of elected governments with the needs of citizens-whom both governments and public institutions serve.

References

Alford, J. 2011. Public Value from Co-Production by Clients, in *Public Value: Theory and Practice*, edited by M. Moore and J. Benington. London: Palgrave Macmillan, 114–57.

American Association of Museums (AAM). 2012. *TrendsWatch 2012: Museums and the Pulse of the Future*. Washington, DC: American Association of Museums.

Ames, P. 1991. Measures of Merit? *Museum News*, Sept/Oct, 55–6.

Australian Bureau of Statistics (ABS). 2008. Cat. 4915.0.55.002. *Arts and Cultural Heritage: An Information Development Plan*. Canberra: Australian Bureau of Statistics.

Belfiore, E. and Bennett, O. 2006. *Rethinking the Social Impacts of the Arts: A Critical-Historical Review*. Centre for Cultural Policy Studies, University of Warwick.

Benington, J. 2011. From Private Choice to Public Value? in *Public Value: Theory and Practice*, edited by Moore, M. and Benington, J. 2011. London: Palgrave Macmillan, 31–51.

Blaug, R., Horner, L. and Lekhi, R. 2006. *Public Value, Politics and Public Management: A Literature Review*. London: The Work Foundation.

Bud, R., Cave, M. and Haney, S. 1991. Measuring a Museum's Output. *Museums Journal*, January, 29–31.

Davies, S. 2008. Intellectual and Political Landscape: The Instrumentalism Debate. *Cultural Trends*, 17, 4, 259–65.

Holden, J. 2004. *Capturing Cultural Value: How Culture has Become a Tool of Government Policy.* London: DEMOS.

Holden, J. 2006. *Cultural Value and the Crisis of Legitimacy: Why Culture Needs a Democratic Mandate.* London: DEMOS.

Horner, L. and Hutton, W. 2011. Public Value, Deliberative Democracy and the Role of Public Managers, in *Public Value: Theory and Practice*, edited by M. Moore and J. Benington. London: Palgrave Macmillan, 112–26.

Horner, L., Lekhi, R. and Blaug, R. 2006. *Deliberative Democracy and the Role of Public Managers: Final Report of The Work Foundation's Public Value Consortium.* London: The Work Foundation.

Kelly, G., Mulgan, G. and Muers, S. 2002. *Creating Public Value: An Analytical Framework for Public Service Reform.* London: Strategy Unit, Cabinet Office.

McCarthy, K., Ondaatje, E., Zakaras, L. and Brooks, A. 2004. *Gifts of the Muse: Reframing the Debate about the Benefits of the Arts.* Santa Monica: Rand Corporation.

Moore, M. 1995. *Creating Public Value: Strategic Management in Government.* Cambridge, MA: Harvard University Press.

Moore, M. 2007. *Creating Public Value: Strategic Management in Government.* Presentation at CIPFA Conference, Scotland, 12–14 June.

Moore, M. and Benington, J. (eds) 2011. *Public Value: Theory and Practice.* London: Palgrave Macmillan.

Moore, M. and Moore, G. 2005. *Creating Public Value Through State Arts Agencies.* Minneapolis: Arts Midwest.

O'Brien, D. 2010. *Measuring the Value of Culture: A Report to the Department for Culture, Media and Sport.* London: Department for Culture, Media and Sport.

O'Neill, M. 2008. Museums, Professionalism and Democracy. *Cultural Trends*, 17, 4, 289–307.

Poll, R. and Payne, P. 2006. *Impact Measures for Libraries and Information Services.* Available at: http://conference.ub.uni-bielefeld.de/2006/proceedings/payne_poll_final_web.pdf [accessed 7 October 2007 and 30 August 2012].

Silverman, L. 1993. Making Meaning Together: Lessons from the Field of American History. *Journal of Museum Education*, 18, 3, 7–11.

Silverman, L. 1995. Visitor Meaning Making in Museums for a New Age. *Curator: The Museum Journal*, 18, 3, 161–9.

Walden, I. 1991. Qualities and Quantities. *Museums Journal*, January, 27–8.

Weil, S. 2002. *Making Museums Matter.* Washington, DC: Smithsonian Institution Press.

Weinberg, M. and Lewis, M. 2009. The Public Value Approach to Strategic Management. *Museum Management and Curatorship*, 24, 3, 253–69.

The Operational Environment: Public Value Building Blocks

2 Creating Strategic Value: Thinking, Acting and Learning

MARK L. WEINBERG and KATE LEEMAN

A key point to be emphasized again and again: the important activities are strategic thinking, acting and learning.

John M. Bryson,
Strategic Planning for Public and Nonprofit Organizations, 2011

Introduction

Within the private sector, a manager's primary goal is to create value for customers and stakeholders, typically measured in financial terms such as increased sales volume, larger profit margin or higher stock price. At the most basic level, business strategy is simply the development of a plan for using available resources (such as equipment, skills or knowledge) to more effectively exploit opportunities (such as new technologies, emerging markets or changing customer preferences) to create this increased financial value. As Bryson states above, a critical role for public and nonprofit managers is also strategic thinking, acting and learning, leveraging resources to transform opportunities into value. At a minimum, these managers must demonstrate that the outcomes generated by their activities are worthwhile – that is, literally worth more than the resources invested in their production (Moore 1995; Spano 2009). As described by Mark Moore, Hauser Professor of Nonprofit Organizations at Harvard University and one of the originators of the public value approach, 'the aim of managerial work in the public sector is to create public value just as the aim of managerial work in the private sector is to create private value' (1995, 28).

However, despite this common goal, the challenge faced by public and nonprofit managers is considerably less straightforward. Unlike the universally agreed upon system of financial measurements utilized in the private sector, public value represents a diverse range of qualities that are notoriously difficult to quantify or measure. In addition, the relative worth of specific public values (such as safety or privacy) is not fixed, but varies over time and across communities. Finally, unlike goods and services provided in the private sector, many public values are the responsibility of multiple government and nonprofit agencies, resulting in complex coproduction environments that complicate both service delivery and performance measurement so that 'to really see impact, we have to ratchet it up a notch and talk about entire ecosystems – collections of organizations working on a common set of problems' (Hanna 2011, 5).

The public value approach facilitates strategic management within the public and nonprofit sector by acknowledging these differences and by providing a workable framework for evaluating opportunities, assessing strategy, prioritizing activities, managing change and guiding performance measurement efforts (Weinberg and Lewis 2009). Further, interest in the approach appears to be growing, as evidenced by the recent call for papers on public value by a leading public administration journal in the United States, related publications by the Work Foundation in Britain and implementation efforts conducted with arts agencies, museums and other institutions throughout the world.

Formulated by Mark Moore, the public value approach combines the public and nonprofit sectors' focus on mission and politics with the for-profit sector's emphasis on value creation, strategy, strategic alignment and entrepreneurship. The resulting 'strategic triangle model' calls upon managers to actively seek entrepreneurial solutions to balance the diverse demands of funders and other critical stakeholders (the authorizing environment) with the reality of the organization's available resources and distinctive competencies (operational capacity) and the institutional imperative to make a meaningful difference within the community (value creation). This results in a fundamental shift of managerial orientation and attention, 'from one of ensuring continuity and consistency in executing mandates to one of a strategist, working to keep the organization relevant and improve performance over time' (Weinberg and Lewis 2009, 256). The purpose of this chapter is to show that the public value approach is consistent with current strategic management literature. It will demonstrate that the model encompasses key elements that can guide efforts to operationalize public value and that these elements are consistent with findings on key aspects of 'best practice' in current strategic management theory and practice.

A Comparison of Public Value with Current Strategic Management Literature

Although research on strategic management in the public sector has increased in recent years, much of this work has focused primarily on describing what is occurring, rather than attempting to accurately assess the impact of specific practices on overall organizational processes or outcomes (Bryson et al. 2010; Poister et al. 2010; Stone et al. 1999). As such, the existing research 'can be characterized more as shallow pools of knowledge rather than as a deep reservoir of theory' (Poister et al. 2010, 540). However, despite these limitations, two literature reviews have recently been published, synthesizing information from over 100 studies of public sector strategic planning and management efforts.[1] Each of these 'mega-analyses' was spearheaded by a researcher at the forefront of public strategic management theory[2] and published in the leading public administration journal within the United

---

1   Bryson et al. (2010); Positer et al. (2010).

2   John M. Bryson is the McKnight Presidential Professor of Planning and Public Affairs at the University of Minnesota. His definitive manual on public and nonprofit strategic planning is currently on its fourth edition, and in 2011, he received the Dwight Waldo Award from the American Society for Public Administration for 'outstanding contributions to the professional literature of public administration over an extended scholarly career'. Theodore H. Poister is Professor of Public Administration at Georgia State University and been active in the fields of public planning, management and performance measurement for over 30 years.

States. Both reviews seek to summarize the current state of knowledge and practice in this area based on related studies published in leading public administration journals over the last 20–25 years.[3] In addition, a somewhat less recent literature review performs a similar analysis of over 65 studies of nonprofit strategic management.[4] Each of these analyses takes a different approach to the topic, resulting in varying recommendations for future strategic management efforts and research. However, all three literature reviews evidence support for key components of the public value approach including four interrelated areas of managerial attention seen to be associated with effective public and nonprofit strategic management efforts. These include directing attention to:

- organizational learning and responsiveness;
- mission and alignment;
- diverse stakeholder demands; and
- implementation.

ATTENTION TO LEARNING AND RESPONSIVENESS

The most basic requirement of effective strategic managers is to remain focused on learning and responsiveness. Further, cultivating this spirit of inquiry seems to be more important than utilizing any particular strategic planning tool or process. This is because all organizations operate in a unique, dynamic and nonlinear environment (Bryson et al. 2010; Poister et al. 2010; Stone et al. 1999). On any given day, museum directors are barraged with information related to collections, programming, personnel, technology, funding, stakeholder relationships and positioning as well as numerous other details that may or may not have a significant impact on the future management of their institution. Strategic planning efforts often fail to acknowledge this chaotic reality, suggesting 'the world is supposed to hold still while a plan is being developed and stay on the predicted course while that plan is being implemented' (Mitzberg as quoted by Stone et al. 1999, 410). Instead, research suggests that effective strategic managers continuously seek information, gauging its potential effect on organizational goals, and developing appropriate, timely responses. As such, rather than a static, mechanistic process, 'strategic planning or management should be understood as partially routinized strategic thinking, acting and learning behaviors ... based on context-specific, situated and local judgment and improvisation' (Bryson et al. 2010, 497–8). Alford and O'Flynn find that Moore's strategic triangle provides public sector managers with a model to 'diagnose the existing situation (e.g., the value currently being produced, where the authorizing environment stands, and the existing operational capabilities)' and to 'help structure thinking about what ought to be the case (e.g., what value do we want to produce, and how far will the authorizing environment and operational capabilities allow us to do that?)' (2009, 174).

---

3   Bryson et al. (2010) include research within the last 25 years while Poister et al. (2010) limit their analysis to the last 20 years. Both focus primarily, though not exclusively, on studies conducted within the United States.

4   Stone et al. (1999). Melissa M. Stone is currently the Gross Family Professor of Nonprofit Management and Professor of Public Affairs and Planning at the University of Minnesota. Her analysis includes articles published over 22 years, primarily, though not exclusively, on studies of nonprofit strategic management efforts within the United States.

ATTENTION TO MISSION AND ALIGNMENT

Effective strategic managers also focus on coordinating organizational resources and activity to pursue specific ends (Bryson et al. 2010; Poister et al. 2010; Stone et al. 1999). Although this may seem obvious, it is not necessarily easy. Particularly within the public and nonprofit sector, reaching agreement regarding mission can present a series of challenges. Museum mission statements and mandates are often vague and subject to diverse interpretations. This can result in differing ideas about the institution's priorities, ranging from preservation and education to economic development and community engagement. Further, although economic, technological and societal changes may challenge long-standing norms and activities, it may not be immediately clear how a museum's existing organizational competencies and established structures can be adapted to further a new, more relevant vision. Even when senior management succeeds in defining a shared goal, additional hurdles may be faced regarding its effective communication, implementation, and maintenance over time. As a result, research suggests that 'strategic management is in large measure about creating and sustaining a mission and goal-related alignment across organizational levels and functions, between inside and outside' (Bryson et al. 2010, 508).

Attention to both mission and alignment is one of the unique strengths of the public value approach. Unlike Kaplan and Norton's balanced scorecard and most other strategic management models, it was not developed for the financially-focused private sector and then modified to accommodate mission-driven outcomes within the public and nonprofit sectors. Instead, the public value approach starts with mission (or value creation) as its foundation, and insists that 'the manager's task ... is to seek to identify and press for the most valuable purposes' (Alford and O'Flynn 2009, 174).

Further, in addition to including value creation as a central component, Moore's strategic triangle serves as a visual reminder that efforts to create value must also always remain in alignment with the organization's authorizing environment and operational capacities (both of which are addressed in detail later in this chapter). As summarized by Moore, the strategic triangle 'focuses managerial attention on the three key questions managers must answer in testing the adequacy of their vision of organizational purpose: whether the purpose is publically valuable, whether it will be politically and legally supported, and whether it is administratively and operationally feasible' (1995, 22). On a practical level, this balanced approach provides museum leadership with a model for decision-making that simultaneously acknowledges the centrality of mission as well as the reality of political and operational limitations.

ATTENTION TO DIVERSE STAKEHOLDERS

In addition to focusing on learning, responsiveness, mission and alignment, effective strategic managers develop strategies for obtaining regular input from a wide variety of constituent groups (Bryson et al. 2010; Poister et al. 2010; Stone et al. 1999). Although limitations in available data restricted their ability to accurately measure the impact of most planning activities, Poister et al. assert that 'including multiple stakeholders in the process is one factor that has been shown to lead to improved outcomes' (2010, 539). Similarly, Bryson et al. describe 'paying careful attention to stakeholders' as one of three areas that 'strategic management theory now emphasizes' (2010, 496). To some extent, this concern with stakeholder preferences reflects the complex authorization and funding environment of the public and nonprofit sectors. However, even in the for-profit sector, consulting individuals with diverse roles both internal and external to the company is seen as useful 'to ensure the strategy is not a reflection of the biases (and possibly ignorance) of the management team' (Christensen 1997, 142).

As mentioned previously, the public value approach recognizes the centrality of mission but also explicitly acknowledges that 'within an increasingly complex authorization environment it is inevitable that processes of accountability will involve a whole host of actors and relationships' (Blaug et al. 2006, 33). Maintaining a museum's legitimacy and support requires ongoing attention to the shifting expectations of diverse constituents, including funders, board members, elected officials, and others. This necessitates actively seeking stakeholder input and, to the extent possible, incorporating this information into decisions regarding how the organization will pursue its mission. Put another way, Moore identifies political management as one of three areas of alignment that make up the strategic triangle, and Alford and O'Flynn reiterate this point by saying, 'If the most valuable thing to do is out of alignment with what the key players in the authorizing environment will find acceptable, the manager can either seek to persuade the key players to move their position, or revise the value-proposition so that it is more in line with their wishes, or some combination of the two' (2009, 174).

ATTENTION TO IMPLEMENTATION

Finally, effective strategic managers recognize that 'success ... ultimately depends on an organization's ability to implement the system it creates' (Poister et al. 2010). Although research suggests general agreement regarding the importance of implementation (Bryson et al. 2010; Poister et al. 2010; Stone et al. 1999), opinion differs somewhat regarding the specific organizational attributes most likely to contribute to successful implementation activities. Those most often referenced indicate that museum leaders need to focus particular attention on demonstrating consistent support for strategic initiatives, effectively communicating the strategy to both internal and external audiences, cultivating appropriate collaborative partnerships, and incorporating strategic goals into diverse management tasks, such as resource allocation, staffing, systems development and evaluation (Bryson et al. 2010; Poister et al. 2010; Stone et al. 1999).

The public value model also acknowledges the critical role of implementation. Moore identifies operational capacity as the third component of the strategic triangle, arguing that managers 'cannot simply command an organization to pursue new goals or invent new operational programs to achieve them' (Moore 1995, 239). Instead, he echoes the strategic management literature by stipulating that specific implementation actions must be taken, including 'some that communicate new purposes, some that build outside support, some that reengineer operations and some that restructure responsibility and accountability among their subordinates' (Moore 1995, 239). Further, Moore challenges managers to employ administrative imagination and innovation to expand the services provided, enhance the efficiency of their production, improve the fairness of their distribution, encourage those outside the organization to serve as co-producers and/or to effectively 'capture' the value created through measurement systems (Moore 1995, 211). The public value approach asserts that 'an organization has control over a set of assets and is responsible for using its assets most effectively in the light of existing conditions' (Scott 2010, 274).

To summarize, proponents of the public value model argue that strategic management of an organization dedicated to providing a public service, such as a public or nonprofit museum, requires balancing the commitment to achieve one's mission with maintaining political authorization and ensuring sufficient organizational capacity. Put another way, strength in any two of these areas cannot compensate for weakness in the last. A worthwhile and achievable goal will not be successful if opposed by key stakeholders. Similarly, a worthwhile goal with extensive community support cannot succeed if the organization lacks the resources to implement it. Finally, although it may be technically possible to achieve a meaningless goal with sufficient support and capacity, it would be difficult to deem this accomplishment a success.

Clearly, although public value provides an approach uniquely suited to the public sector, its central tenets are validated in mainstream public and nonprofit strategic management literature. Further, this approach has received some initial empirical support from a study conducted with over 500 Texas school superintendents that attempts to assess the impact of public value management characteristics on student and school performance. Specifically, participating superintendents were asked questions about their management style, objectives and habits to assess the frequency and nature of their contact with a network of actors within their immediate environment (to represent value creation or managing outward), with elected school board members (representing political management or managing upward), and with the school principals within their district (representing operational capacity or managing downward). This information was compared with five years' performance measures for each district, including attendance and dropout rates as well as student performance on state assessments and college entrance exams, with steps being taken to control for differences in district demographics and resources. The outcomes were mixed, but indicate a clear association between regular interaction with a network of environmental actors and positive performance. Although evidence of the impact of frequent communication within the public education hierarchy (either downward to school principals or upward to elected school board members) is more ambiguous, the researchers nonetheless conclude, 'managing upward, downward, and outward constitute different managerial patterns ... and all may offer partial keys to delivering performance and increasing public value' (O'Toole et al. 2003, 22). Although limited in scope, this tentative affirmation arms the public value approach with more empirical support than the vast majority of similar models.

Finally, it is worth noting that the components the public value approach urges managers to attend to – learning and responsiveness, mission and alignment, diverse stakeholder demands and implementation capacity – are also highlighted in the characteristics of museum mission and planning excellence as defined by one of the world's largest museum associations, the American Association of Museums (no date):

2. Mission and Planning
   2.1 The museum has a clear understanding of its mission and communicates why it exists and who benefits as a result of its efforts.
   2.2 All aspects of the museum's operations are integrated and focused on meeting its mission.

2.3 The museum's governing authority and staff think and act strategically to acquire, develop, and allocate resources to advance the mission of the museum.

2.4 The museum engages in ongoing and reflective institutional planning that includes involvement of its audiences and community.

2.5 The museum establishes measures of success and uses them to evaluate and adjust its activities.[5]

Using the Public Value Approach to Facilitate Strategic Management

We have shown that the primary components of the public value approach are supported by research as well as industry-identified best practices. But how can public value and the strategic triangle actually be used by museum leadership to help facilitate strategic management? To date, much of the writing on this topic has either avoided detailed application discussions or focused on specific, non-generalizable case studies. This lack of process information seems to reflect one of the inherent challenges of the public value model. Any guidance that is offered must be flexible enough to accommodate the ongoing, nonlinear and responsive nature of truly effective strategic management. Put another way, 'public agencies vary widely in terms of how they formulate strategic plans, and a "one-size-fits-all" approach is probably not beneficial' (Poister et al. 2010, 527).

That said, for the public value approach to be more widely adopted, some general suggestions must be offered regarding how to use it on a day-to-day basis. As a first step in this process, some critical overarching activities can be inferred based on a consideration of the public value approach. These include assessing the environment and institutional components, defining a value proposition, articulating a value chain, aligning systems to the value chain and evaluating results by analysing key data. As in the preceding section, current research supports these activities as critical to effective strategic management. Figure 2.1 illustrates a conceptual framework recently proposed to 'represent the logic underlying the principle elements of strategic management, their determinants, and their impact on an organization's capacity and performance' (Poister et al. 2010, 525). Each of the activities described below directly addresses one or more of the elements outlined in Poister et al.'s strategic planning and management framework.

ASSESSING THE ENVIRONMENT AND INSTITUTIONAL COMPONENTS

First, since effective strategies are necessarily context-specific, museum managers interested in practising the public value approach must assess their environment. The public value framework suggests that formulating effective strategy requires gathering information by directing attention upwards (to the authorizing environment), downwards (to the organization's existing resources, activities, capabilities and institutional constraints) and outward (to forces that may present new opportunities or threats) (Moore 1995). Christensen recommends 'nominating factors – technological, competitive, demographic, regulatory, economic, or organizational that might be driving forces' (1997, 144) such as mandates, community expectations, funding requirements and other stakeholder demands.

---

5   Excerpt from the American Association of Museums (no date).

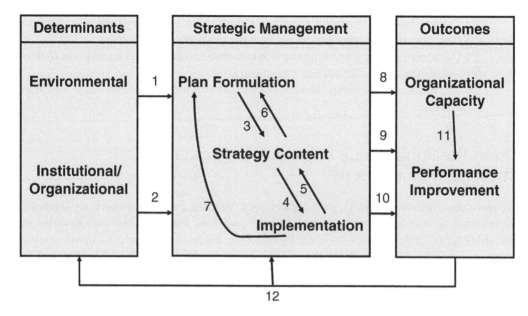

Figure 2.1   Strategic planning and management conceptual framework

In a previous section, attention was drawn to the importance of learning and responsiveness. Christensen takes this a step further by stressing the need for being selective about information enabling 'management to focus on and agree about what [is] going on at a conceptual level, and then to collect data only on those aspects of the analysis for which conclusions would hinge on more precise data' (1997, 146).

Finally, once there is agreement regarding the key problems or strategic issues to be addressed, Christensen recommends taking time to discuss this shared understanding with additional individuals who might offer further insight, altering the concept maps as needed based on new information and collecting or clarifying data where useful. For museums, those asked for feedback could include front-line employees, board members, volunteers, partner organizations or other stakeholders. In addition to encouraging shared understanding and focusing attention on strategically important data, this approach also effectively ensures that the strategic planning and management process is firmly grounded in organizational learning and responsiveness. Most importantly, 'when a management team is united in its understanding of the problems to be tackled, agreeing on and implementing solutions is much more straightforward' (Christensen 1997, 148).

DEFINE THE VALUE PROPOSITION

The second activity involved in strategic management is utilizing this shared understanding of strategic issues as the foundation for defining the organization's value proposition or, to put it another way, determining how the organization will position itself within its environment (see Plan Formulation in Figure 2.1). In the business sector, 'strategy is choosing to perform activities differently than rivals do' (Porter 1996, 64). For example, all automobile manufacturers sell cars, but BMW is pursuing a very different strategy than Volvo or Hyundai. A value proposition summarizes the manner in which a company is 'deliberately choosing a different set of activities to deliver a unique mix of value' (Porter 1996, 64), in these examples related to luxury, safety and economy, respectively.

Similarly, public and nonprofit organizations must tell 'citizens and their representatives ... a story contained in a policy' (Moore 1995, 54) that persuasively connects their work to the solution of a problem or the attainment of a social goal. Not simply public relations efforts, these stories must provide a coherent proposal for producing useful results based on the reality of the situation to be addressed, available resources and stakeholder expectations. These narratives are important because they can have a powerful impact on organizational outcomes. Because 'value is rooted in the desires and perceptions of individuals' (Moore 1995, 52), a compelling story can reframe how the public understands an issue, generating significant new external support and funding. Similarly, a well-articulated public value proposition can help to streamline decision-making, increase alignment between resource use and goals and reduce the need for micro-management. Finally, because the range and depth of relevant demands frequently exceeds organizational capacity, often 'creating public value requires a political decision about what needs should have priority' (Spano 2009, 335). Defining value propositions is a topic of further discussion and elaboration in Chapter 3 of this volume.

ARTICULATE A VALUE CHAIN

If the first two activities clarify the organization's current environmental context and the future value to be created, the value chain lays out the actual method that will be used to affect this change (described as 'strategy content' in Figure 2.1). All strategies are grounded in assumptions about how to solve a particular problem or, as Moore describes it, 'a casual theory that claims that if we engage in a particular set of activities we will, in fact, achieve the desired result' (Moore 2002, 11). Similar to a mathematical equation or logical proof, a value chain is a way to visually represent these assumptions, specifically how various resources invested in specific activities are expected to result in outcomes that contribute to the defined value proposition. Put another way, the value proposition clarifies the end to be achieved, and the value chain maps out what will be done to achieve it.

Although they share many features with the logic models used in planning public and nonprofit programmes, value chains were originally developed in the for-profit sector and differ in subtle but important ways. In part due to pressure from funders, logic models have been widely adopted as planning and communication tools designed to provide a visual representation of how specific investments and activities will result in defined outcomes. Although defining desired outcomes is a necessary component of the planning process, it is useful to keep in mind that an outcome represents a measure of value, not value itself. By making the value proposition (rather than outcomes that measure it) the end point, a value chain facilitates strategic management by simultaneously decreasing and increasing managerial latitude. When compared to logic models, value chains more effectively constrain activity within the proposed value creation strategy (or value proposition) and therefore decrease the opportunity for so-called 'mission drift'. However, by focusing directly on value, the value chain also holds open the possibility that, based on changes within the environment, specific outcomes may need to be altered or replaced. To put this another way, value chains encourage focusing directly on value creation, whereas logic models tend to be one step removed, prioritizing the fulfilment of outcomes that have been developed to achieve value. Although seemingly slight, this difference is critical because it furthers strategic alignment and introduces a level of flexibility necessary for managers to cultivate an entrepreneurial, opportunity-seeking approach.

ALIGNMENT OF SYSTEMS TO THE VALUE CHAIN

As described earlier in this chapter, both the public value approach and current strategic management theory recognize that, once a strategy has been developed, success is dependent upon the organization having the capacity to implement it effectively. Referring again to the conceptual framework in Figure 2.1, this is reflected in the inclusion of implementation as the final stage in the strategic management process. To state this another way, strategy is always 'a blend of what was intended with what emerges in practice' (Bryson et al. 2010, 509). As a result, strategic management necessarily involves ensuring that decisions made regarding the value proposition and value chain are accurately incorporated into how the organization actually functions.

To achieve mission-related alignment, museums are encouraged to incorporate their value creation goals and strategies into all aspects of the organization, including major components such as resource allocation and staffing decisions as well as day-to-day details, such as the structure of board meeting agendas and the tools provided to help children interact with exhibits primarily aimed at adults. For-profit businesses are increasingly enhancing strategic alignment through the use of management control systems. These tend to be integrated combinations of technology and process that are designed to ensure that a company's structure, systems, investments and culture all work together to reinforce key goals, track progress and identify areas in need of improvement. Public and nonprofit organizations have an additional responsibility to incorporate systems for engaging community members in an ongoing dialogue regarding the value to be created, both informing and soliciting their opinion about the institution's diverse roles (Moore 1995; Spano 2009) because 'the public value approach requires public organizations to seek out, listen to and guide public conceptions of value' (Blaug et al. 2006). Spano argues that this calls for the development of 'a new kind of management control system … which gives a different role to customers and citizens, putting them at the centre' (2009, 341). Although labour-intensive, achieving alignment of organizational capacity with value creation and stakeholder demands is the core managerial activity of public and nonprofit managers as well as critical to successful strategy since 'problems in strategic planning are largely technical and related to implementation' (Poister et al. 2010, 538).

ANALYSE KEY DATA TO ASSESS STRATEGY

Developing appropriate, accurate evaluation methods and strategic performance management systems 'is, probably, one of the most difficult aspects regarding public value' (Spano 2009, 338). The dynamic and creative nature of public value requires well designed performance measures that will provide the data needed to effectively measure value creation, foster a strong sense of internal accountability and identify areas in need of additional improvement. Perhaps even more importantly, managers must be able to weave together these 'established mechanisms of accountability' to tell a compelling story about 'the past and future performance of their organization' to ensure ongoing support

Figure 2.2   Key public value management activities

and authorization (Moore 1995, 53). Interestingly, these functions of data analysis mirror the four areas of managerial attention highlighted in the first half of this chapter (mission and alignment, implementation, learning and responsiveness, and diverse stakeholder demands).

Sifting through available data to isolate the most useful elements for evaluative purposes is a challenge that has been both mitigated and exacerbated by recent technological advances. Moore recommends using the strategic triangle to prioritize evaluation efforts, developing systems for measuring key elements of operational capacity, political support and value creation (2002). Other advocates of the public value model suggest examining the value chain to identify important relationships or interactions to be monitored, 'generally focused on less confident assumptions, and assumptions most critical to success' (Epstein 2001, 13). Alternatively, Kaplan and Norton's balanced scorecard approach recommends focusing on measurements of four perspectives – financial, customer, operational and learning/growth. Finally, a few organizations have combined computer technology with detailed metrics to create highly responsive data tracking and analysis systems, similar to the New York City Police Department's Compstat system. Since each of the approaches offers a variety of useful tools and strategies, selection is primarily a matter of finding those that seem best suited to an institution's needs, capacity and culture. These issues are further developed in Chapter 4 of this volume.

Conclusion

Although additional research is necessary, the public value approach appears to correspond well with existing knowledge regarding effective strategic management in public and nonprofit organizations as well as current thinking about museum management best practices. Specifically, all three encourage managers to pursue value creation and strategic management with a focus on learning and responsiveness, mission alignment, diverse stakeholder demands and implementation.

Efforts are being made to explore ways to utilize the public value approach and the strategic triangle as management tools (Benington and Moore 2011). Consideration of the public value model within the context of current management literature suggests that important overarching strategic management activities would include environmental assessment, definition of a value proposition, articulation of a value chain, alignment of systems to the value chain and analysis of key data to measure impact and effectiveness.

It may initially appear that these activities should be completed in a particular order (see Figure 2.2). For example, the value chain clearly needs to be developed before systems can be aligned to support it. However, it is crucial to note that in practice, the process is less linear and more organic. Environmental assessment should actually be ongoing, key stakeholders may need to be consulted about the value proposition before moving on to the development of the value chain, and at any point, an event within the community, a change in funding or a new collaboration opportunity may require plans and systems to be altered. Because the public value approach conceives of strategic management as a continuously evolving process, it is appropriate to revisit various stages as needed, tweaking and revising as the context shifts.

Regardless of the order in which the steps are taken or the tools that are employed, both the public value approach and strategic management research suggest that the most important component is the cultivation and maintenance of a learning and responsive organization. When approached from this orientation, the public value model provides leadership with a powerful tool for self-diagnosis, assessing the organization's current balance of value creation, operational capacity and responsiveness to the authorizing environment (Nutt 2004). Further, this model can help structure managerial thinking, guiding decisions about the nature of the value to be produced in the future and how best to harness resources, skills and expectations to pursue this strategic course. Finally, the public value model can also be employed as a guide for management behaviour, focusing attention on key information and activities to drive strategic leadership and change. In short, this model offers an expanded vision of museum leadership, involving the active confrontation of institutions' altered landscapes and the invocation of 'managerial imagination' (Moore 1995, 13) to strategically move towards a more valued, and valuable, future.

References

Alford, J. and O'Flynn, J. 2009. Making Sense of Public Value: Concepts, Critiques and Emergent Meanings. *International Journal of Public Administration*, 32: 171–91.

American Association of Museums. N.D. *Characteristics of Excellence for U.S. Museums.* Available at: http://aamus.org/aboutmuseums/standards/upload/Characteristics-of-Excellence-reg-and-pe.pdf [accessed 4 January 2012].

Benington, J. and Moore, M.H. 2011. *Public Value: Theory and Practice.* New York: Palgrave Macmillan.

Blaug, R., Horner, L. and Lekhi, R. 2006. *Public Value, Politics and Public Management: A Literature Review.* Available at: http://www.work foundation.com/assets/docs/publications/117_politics_lit_review.pdf [accessed 6 January 2012].

Bryson, J.M. 2011. *Strategic Planning for Public and Nonprofit Organizations.* San Francisco: Jossey Bass.

Bryson, J.M., Berry, F.S. and Yang, K. 2010. The State of Public Strategic Management Research: A Selective Literature Review and Set of Future Directions. *The American Review of Public Administration*, 40(5): 495–521.

Christensen, C.M. 1997. Making Strategy: Learning by Doing. *Harvard Business Review*, 75(6): 141–56.

Epstein, P.D. 2001. The Performance Value Chain: A Valuable Tool for Learning 'What Works'. *The Bottom Line*, 9–14.

Hanna, J. 2011. The New Measures for Improving Nonprofit Performance. *HBS Working Knowledge Faculty Newsletter* [online, 14 December], Harvard Business School, 1–12. Available at: http://hbswk.hbs.edu/cgi-bin/print/6825.html [accessed 2 February 2012].

Moore, M.H. 1995. *Creating Public Value: Strategic Management in Government.* Cambridge, MA: Harvard University Press.

Moore, M.H. 2002. The 'Public Value Scorecard': A Rejoinder and an Alternative to 'Strategic Performance Measurement and Management in Non-Profit Organizations' by Robert Kaplan. The Hauser Center for Nonprofit Organizations, Harvard University, Working Paper 18. Available at: http://www.cof.org/files/Documents/Emerging_Issues/EI%20for%20Philanthropy/Strategic%20Planning/Public_Value_Scorecard_-_Moore_0503_-_Hauser_no18.pdf [accessed 1 February 2012].

Nutt, P.C. 2004. Prompting the Transformation of Public Organizations. *Public Performance and Management Review*, 27(4): 9–33.

O'Toole, L.J., Meier, K.J. and Nicholson-Crotty, S. 2003. Managing Upward, Downward and Outward: Networks, Hierarchical Relationships and Performance. Paper to the 2003 Annual Meeting of the American Political Science Association, Philadelphia, PA, 28–31 August.

Poister, T.H., Pitts, D.W. and Edwards, L.H. 2010. Strategic Management Research in the Public Sector: A Review, Synthesis, and Future Directions. *The American Review of Public Administration*, 40(5): 522–45.

Porter, M.E. 1996. What is Strategy? *Harvard Business Review*, 74(6): 61–78.

Scott, C.A. 2010. Searching for the 'Public' in Public Value: Arts and Cultural Heritage in Australia. *Cultural Trends*, 19(4): 273–89.

Spano, A. 2009. Public Value Creation and Management Control Systems. *International Journal of Public Administration*, 32(3/4): 328–48.

Stone, M.M., Bigelow, B. and Crittenden, W. 1999. Research on Strategic Management in Nonprofit Organizations: Synthesis, Analysis and Future Directions. *Administration & Society*, 31(3): 378–423.

Weinberg, M.L. and Lewis, M.S. 2009. The Public Value Approach to Strategic Management. *Museum Management and Curatorship*, 24(3): 253–69.

3 Creating Public Value through Intentional Practice

RANDI KORN

Introduction

Intentional practice in museums, as a concept, belief and action, is fundamental to creating public value. The notion of thinking about museums in the context of public value is not necessarily new, as 100 years ago, in Newark, New Jersey, on the east coast of the United States, John Cotton Dana, who founded the Newark Museum, said 'a museum is good only insofar as it is of use' (Peniston 1999). While this quotation is often recited by many museum professionals, presently it is receiving considerable attention as museums are beginning to hear the wisdom of its meaning in a new way.

The museum world is under increasing stress. Public and private funds for museums are shrinking as the pool of museums continues to grow. Funders have raised the accountability bar and now want to see evidence that their support is delivering what museums intend and the public's expectations for a fulfilling museum experience have evolved with individuals looking to museums to broaden as well as deepen the human experience.

Creating public value is no longer an option. It is required by many who comprise the authorizing environment (Moore and Moore 2005) and many museums realize they must start paying attention and change how they think about and pursue their work. This chapter presents a theory of practice for creating public value called intentional practice.

Context

With challenges from the external environment mounting, intentional practice offers a sustainable path into the future because it negotiates with and accounts for everyone's requirements – those of the museum, the funders and the public. It is a unified, well-planned organizational strategy that aligns practices and resources to support intended results, evaluates achievement and reflects on results to learn what can be improved.

Intentional practice works best when it is an endeavour guided by a strong leader who can inspire and rally staff to work collaboratively towards a common purpose, meaning that all staff, from across and up and down the museum, work together to articulate their museum's purpose and the public value they hope to create (Korn 2007). When a museum director leads an entire organization to create public value using carefully deliberated strategies, s/he is operating with holistic[1] intentionality. While the latter describes an ideal scenario for implementing intentional practice, any staff member who is cognizant of the complex set of relationships amongst participants in the authorizing environment and between the museum, the public and the authorizing environment can take initiative and work within his or her sphere of influence and begin transforming how the institution approaches its work.

Intentional practice is a planning model similar to strategic planning, yet it differs significantly in a few important ways. Strategic planning is typically mission driven, focusing on what a museum does, while intentional planning is mission *and impact* driven, focusing on the *end result* of a museum's work. Strategic planning focuses on organizational performance and outputs such as completing projects and initiatives, while intentional practice focuses on creating public value outside the museum in the form of outcomes and impact. With input from the authorizing environment, the museum applies laser-focused attention on creating very specific results. The process begins with articulating a clear vision of the end result.

Introduction to Intentionality

Intentionality derives 'from the Latin word *intentio*, which in turn derives from the verb *intendere*, which means being directed towards some goal or thing' (Siewert 2011). Intentionality, or being intentional in one's work, is an essential concept because it highlights the importance of working towards a particular goal or being directed towards a particular goal. The result of such a goal is sometimes called an 'impact'.

'The very things that make a museum good are its intent to make a positive difference in people's lives', a phrase that museum scholar Stephen Weil introduced (2002, 73) to explain impact – is similar to the phrase that Harvard scholar Mark Moore uses to describe public value: 'to make a positive difference in the individual and collectives lives of citizens' (Moore and Moore 2005, 17). Intentional practice is an organizational process where everyone's efforts focus on delivering results using a deliberate, collaborative process where the entire museum pursues the goal of making a demonstrable difference in people's lives.

Intentionality presupposes an interest in pursuing a well-articulated end-result around which all work will be organized. Intentional practice requires that the museum negotiate a vision of public value between the organization's unique assets and capacity *and* what stakeholders and the public deem as valuable. Inside the museum, staff skills are considered, as are organizational resources (for example, time and money).

The museum, however, is not an island working in isolation. Outside the museum is the authorizing environment – all those who 'hold the formal power to supply or withhold public money and authority and/or to place conditions on the distributions of these resources' (Moore and Moore 2005, 37). All of these stakeholders have varying ideas about what constitutes public value and collectively wield considerable power. For example, in the United Kingdom, the National Museum Director's Conference commissioned a study to 'take stock of the UK's national museums and galleries ... to assess their place within

---

1   Holistic is used here to explain the belief that the parts of something, such as an organization, are interconnected and strongest when functioning as one entity with a common belief and purpose.

the wider social and economic framework of society' (Travers and Glaister 2004, 4). To that end, Travers and Glaister demonstrated how museums and galleries contribute to the economy, to civic engagement in communities and to creativity and innovation amongst individuals. The study suggests there is an opportunity for museums to refocus their efforts, explore their relationship with stakeholders and communities and rethink what they have the capacity to deliver and what public value they hope to create. Intentional practice is an organizational strategy for pursuing this public value-driven work.

The Cycle of Intentional Practice and Public Value

Intentionality is an approach and intentional practice is a strategic way of working. Together they provide a viable planning approach for creating public value. Given that public value is emerging as the necessary work of an organization, museums need a holistic organizational approach for doing this work. While museums can create public value through other kinds of organizational strategies, the chance of making a positive difference in the collective lives of a community is greater if an organization is intentional in its pursuit. The clarity with which an organization describes the public value it hopes to create is important, as a clear statement of its intentions suggests a roadmap for moving forward the organization's work. Clarity of intentions is a vital component of intentional planning.

There are distinct steps or actions that comprise intentional practice illustrated in the cycle shown in Figure 3.1 and explained in the rest of this chapter. The cycle is defined by four actions and corresponding questions. It offers a strategic approach to working by focusing on:

- clarity: museums need to clarify what public value they want to create;
- alignment: bringing practices and resources into line with planning intentions is essential;
- evaluation: deciding how to measure intended impact helps the organization focus on what public value will look like;
- reflection: evaluation results are not final; they are used to deepen learning about practice and achievement.

Fundamental to intentional practice is inquiry. It is the overarching method for facilitating organizational work. Inquiry is not a new idea to museums – many museums use it as a teaching strategy in their galleries (Villeneuve and Love 2007). Evaluations have shown that inquiry develops self- esteem, builds confidence to share personal ideas and ways of knowing, and models open-mindedness among visitors (Gutwill and Allen 2010). The same results emerge when inquiry is used as an organizational development strategy among professionals (Preskill and Torres 1999). When inquiry is used to investigate how staff members think, it fosters an understanding amongst all staff while building the collective mind of the museum. In fact, deep inquiry allows all staff to learn about their museum together and discover their shared passions and re-conceive their organizational drive.

A leader who supports and models systematic inquiry in the workplace creates a civil, collaborative environment where questions are freely asked and opinions are shared and

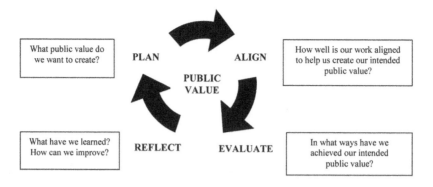

Figure 3.1   Cycle of intentional practice (Korn 2007)

respected (Korn 2007). Using inquiry while practising intentionality builds and reinforces a culture of professional and personal learning where everyone pursues the work of their museum together without fear of judgment or failure (Axelrod 2007; Hammond and Mayfield 2004; Preskill and Torres 1999; Hammond 1996). The ultimate benefit of a culture of inquiry is learning. A culture of inquiry challenges participants to investigate their own thinking and practice (Preskill and Torres 1999) when clarifying with their colleagues the public value they would like to create. Question-asking, whether during planning or evaluation, upholds a spirit of enduring inquiry – a benefit and characteristic of intentionality (Korn 2007).

Planning for Public Value

Public value is in the centre of the cycle because it is the driving force behind a museum's work. The planning aspect seeks clarity about the purpose of a museum's work so that all staff can focus to that end. The question in the 'Plan' quadrant of the cycle asks a bold question, 'What public value do we want to create?' The clarity with which a museum can describe its intention is paramount.

Conceptualizing the public value a museum strives to achieve is a relatively new idea. At the turn of this century, the notion of public value was hardly mentioned; now one hears and sees it frequently. A new awareness is emerging about museums' responsibilities beyond their walls (Gurian 2010; Goodale 2009; Koster 2006). Yet few museums can describe the positive difference that they want to make in the public sphere.

Similarly, museums are also realizing that a mission statement, by definition, may fall short in describing these emerging concepts. While in some countries, overarching results may be part of the mission statement, the United States has adopted a more functional approach, often using the mission statement to describe the collecting, preserving and educating work of a museum. In such cases, a public value statement complements the mission statement by describing the *results* of the museum's work. A public value statement can also be used to highlight the unique features of a museum and to address the vital 'To what end?' question. Most would agree that museums are educational organizations, but how might a museum describe the result of its education work among those who experience the museum?

Crafting a public value statement, like crafting a mission statement, takes time and thought. It is best done in a collaborative environment with a diverse group of stakeholders including staff from across the museum, board members and community representatives. Dialogue around the following three questions can provide the raw material for crafting a public value statement.

1. What are staff members' deepest passions for their work?
2. What are the unique characteristics of the museum, including its intrinsic value?
3. What is relevant to whom?

WHAT ARE STAFF MEMBERS' DEEPEST PASSIONS FOR THEIR WORK?

Personal passion and professional commitment are essential ingredients for intentional practice and planning. Most museum professionals exude passion for their work and their passion pushes them to do their best every day. Personal passion for one's work leads to and builds professional commitment and responsibility – not just to the museum but to the profession (Korn 2007). Personal passion and professional commitment, though to a degree intangible, are necessary ingredients to achieve public value and determining factors for success (Pink 2011; Collins 2001). Museum professionals know that passion plays a vital role in producing excellent exhibitions and programmes. Likewise, as noted by Scott, these intangible assets build organizational capacity to create value (Scott 2011, 2).

A museum can explore staff passions by asking 'five why' questions. This is a strategy that business author, Jim Collins, presents in his book *Built to Last* (1994). Collins used the 'five whys' to help companies 'frame their work in a more meaningful way' (1994, 227). The exercise drills down to underlying reasons for passion using a simple series of 'why' questions:

1. What about your work is most meaningful to you? And, after hearing the response;
2. And why is *that* important? And, upon hearing that response, asking again;
3. And why is *that* important?

Until the deepest layer of meaning is uncovered.

When museum staff talk about their passions, patterns emerges. Staff express their passion for personal learning and growth, teaching others, science, art or history – depending on the museum type – or in the case of administrators, a passion for organizational effectiveness and efficiency. Collectively, if all staff respond to the 'why' question a few times, a common, uniting passion or series of passions will likely surface.

WHAT ARE THE UNIQUE CHARACTERISTICS OF THE MUSEUM, INCLUDING ITS INTRINSIC VALUE?

Understanding a museum's unique characteristics, qualities and strengths are other important elements that can contribute to the content of a public values statement. What makes this museum different from other museums in its surrounding community, region, state or country?

If a museum concentrates on creating programmes that deliver and accentuate its distinct qualities, there is a greater chance that it will be able to create public value. For example, some museums are most known for their specific collections or exhibition programmes, others are most known for their educational programmes and some others are most known for their research. Identifying the single one area of work where the museum is most poised to make a difference can help staff determine the unique public value their museum can create.

This is a challenging exercise. A museum may have a very difficult time identifying only one area of work as its distinct quality or its primary strength. And while many museums may excel in multiple areas, prioritizing does not mean that other areas are ignored or negated. It simply means that all staff recognize the museum is *best* in this one area. Indeed, it is possible to infuse more than one distinct quality into the crafting of a public value statement, as will be evident in the examples that are provided below. However, reflecting on a museum's greatest and most unique asset is both clarifying and empowering.

These two ideas – passion and unique value – are similar to two of the three elements identified by Jim Collins in something he calls his Hedgehog Concept (2001). When working with businesses, Collins uses the Hedgehog Concept to explore three vital ideas:

1. what are you passionate about;
2. what are you the best at; and
3. what drives your economic engine.

The Hedgehog Concept's first two ideas are embodied in the first two guiding questions of intentional planning described above. The third idea in the Hedgehog Concept (what drives your economic engine?) is about resources and is vitally important to consider as museums carry out their work towards creating public value in a challenging economic climate.

In Collins' words, 'The essence of the Hedgehog Concept[2] is to attain piercing clarity about how to produce the best long-term results, and then exercise the relentless discipline to say, *No thank you* to opportunities that fail the hedgehog test' (2005, 17). While Collins' publications have focused on business in the private sector in *Good to Great* (2001) and on not-for-profits in *Good to Great for the Social Sectors* (2005), there are similarities between the elements of the Hedgehog Concept, intentional practice and crafting public value statements. Like Collins' requirement for 'piercing clarity', a public value statement must be clear about the value a museum wants to create for its constituents. Similarly, in the cycle of intentional practice, alignment requires a museum to determine how to effectively use the resources at its disposal to achieve the public value it would like to create.

---

2   A hedgehog is a nocturnal mammal with a spiny coat and short legs, which is able to roll itself into a ball for protection. The Hedgehog Concept was named from a story about a fox and a hedgehog. The fox was always trying to attack the hedgehog and he was consistently met with the hedgehog's simple defence of rolling into a ball of spikes. Collins compares thriving companies to the little hedgehog – they always focus on their most consistent method of success. The simplicity of the hedgehog's response to the fox relates to the three vital ideas (purpose, uniqueness and feasibility) that successful companies (and museums) should take into account when planning and undertaking their work.

Collins argues that an organization must have deep knowledge of all three of these ideas to be a great organization. Passion is not enough. The same is true for a museum – all three guiding questions are explored, understood and articulated so they can become part of a statement that describes the public value a museum intends to create. Like the Hedgehog Concept, a statement of public value can be a single organizing idea that powers the organization to move forward with focus. Without passion and focused attention on what an organization does best – playing to its strengths – the museum's impact risks being subdued and difficult to measure.

WHAT IS RELEVANT TO WHOM?

Relevance is a powerful idea – one that museums discuss but sometimes struggle to apply to their strategic and daily work. *The Oxford Dictionary* defines relevance (2012) as issues *connected to the matters at hand*. Relevance is a vital part of the public value equation and necessary to consider for any museum that desires to achieve measurable results (Korn 2010). It is also the most complex element of planning because there may be differences in perceptions of what is relevant and of value between two groups external to the museum – the public and the authorizing environment. If those who live in the surrounding community find the museum's work pertinent and meaningful, they will value the museum. However, if the authorizing environment of government, education and other funding stakeholders have different ideas of what is relevant, there is likely to be tension and conflict. Moore (1995) has recognized that leaders need to negotiate among and between these different constituencies in addition to determining what their staff have the capacity to deliver. Thus, there are four significant challenges facing museum leadership in the context of relevance:

1. Identifying and learning about all the 'actors' in the authorizing environment (Moore and Moore 2005) and how they perceive or describe public value.
2. Identifying specific target groups among the public to whom the museum might focus its work without disenfranchising other audiences.
3. Leveraging the museum's collections, research and programmes.
4. Balancing the three components of (a) the intended public value results; (b) the museum's operational capacity; and (c) the museum's unique qualities and distinct identity.

One of these issues is audience prioritization. Targeting public value to audiences where there is a real need is both applying the principle of relevance and enabling museums to make difficult decisions about resource allocation. As much as museums would like to be all things to all people *and* achieve discernible results for everyone, achieving value across all public sectors at any one time may not be a realistic result in terms of a museum's limited capacity and resources. When considering to whom the museum is relevant, staff could start by identifying an audience with the greatest chance of experiencing the public value of the museum and explore what is relevant for that audience (Korn 2010). Simultaneously, a museum might study existing demographic data from its community and realize that a segment of the population may be able to find value in the museum's assets and consider exploring relevance with that population as well. Several years later, after achieving some success with specific population segments, the museum could decide to identify additional audiences on which it would like to focus. Thus, a museum can focus on varying audience segments over the course of a decade and ultimately create public value amongst all of them. Just as the notion of relevance is not static, neither should be a museum's selection of publics on which it will focus its work.

While museums need to learn about and accommodate their audiences' needs, they also need to simultaneously maintain their sense of self, identity and unique value (Korn 2004). Balancing these two forces – the museum and the audience – requires staff knowing the museum's institutional self, being sensitive towards and curious about those who comprise the public, having a strong desire to create and achieve public value and letting go of ways of working that do not support this ultimate aim. Infusing knowledge about audiences and relevance into a museum's ideas can spur new thinking about the museum's work and what it can deliver.

Statements of Public Value

A statement of public value is a relatively new concept for museums. Its inclusive development process and the final product are distinguishing characteristics of intentional practice.

Mission and vision statements reflect what the museum does and what it aspires to do. A statement about the public value the museum would like to create and achieve describes the *result* of the museum on the audiences it serves. A statement of public value is written from the perspective of what a community may experience, think about, or do as a result of having an engaging relationship with the museum over time.

Preparing a public value statement requires participation among staff, key board members and community stakeholders. While a public value statement can be used alone as a declaration of the difference a museum hopes to make in people's lives, it is best understood when it is in the overall context of a mission statement. Knowing that a public value statement is a companion to a mission statement will help staff members see the distinction between the purpose of a museum (mission) and the results of the museum's work on those served (public value). Having to craft a public value statement challenges the museum to think beyond its walls to consider how its work can potentially affect people.

A statement of public value can also serve as a guidepost for evaluation planning and implementation. When a museum is preparing to evaluate the ways in which it has achieved public value, the statement can become the platform for articulating specific outcomes, writing rubrics based on the outcomes, identifying target populations for the evaluation, designing appropriate qualitative and quantitative data collection instruments and analysing results (RK&A 2011). Planning and evaluation are inextricably linked. Data are examined according to the intended results and its associated outcomes and measures to conclude the extent to which the museum has achieved its intentions. It is the lens through which decisions are made, the engine for driving work, and the gauge for success. Below are a few examples of public value statements that museums have articulated.[3]

---

3   These statements were initially crafted as impact statements; for this publication they are referred to as public value statements.

1. Natural history and culture museum: *people will value their connection to all life – and act accordingly.*[4]
2. Art museum: *inspired by meaningful encounters with the museum's collection and artistic programme, visitors will expand their creative thinking, deepen their understanding of human experiences, and value the museum as a place for personal learning and civic engagement.*
3. Science museum: *inspired by discovery, visitors are encouraged to investigate the world around them and realize science impacts everyone and everything.*
4. Natural history museum: *the museum inspires people to value our biologically and culturally diverse world and to make a difference in its future.*

Aligning Work and Resources to Support Public Value Intentions

Alignment is a second feature of intentional practice and one that is particularly relevant in these challenging economic times. To create public value, museums need to align practices, resources and programmes in sustainable and feasible ways if their intentions are to be achieved.

The notion of aligning practices and resources to achieve public value is similar to an idea that Stephen Weil wrote about in his article 'A Success/Failure Matrix for Museums'. He noted that, 'Once a purpose has been established, the museum is still unable to move forward either until (a) all of the necessary resources can be identified and secured, or (b) the purpose has been scaled back to match the available resources' (2005, 36). Alignment is a no-nonsense, disciplined approach to resource management, and it is the part of the cycle that museum leaders may need to apply in difficult *as well as* good economic times.

Aligning practices and resources is important if a museum wants to live within its means. Alignment requires decisions to be taken and priorities to be determined. A public value statement provides guidance for alignment because activities that do not reflect the intentions behind the public value statement may be eliminated or reduced to lesser priorities. Taking away what is no longer germane to the museum's pursuit of public value is an important management strategy for achieving results. It requires discipline to say 'no' to programmes or initiatives that do not contribute or are not relevant to the public value that the museum envisions. In the context of intentional practice, alignment is about a museum rethinking what it does, how much it costs in terms of staff time and other resources and for whom it is doing what it does – the recipients of the museum's work. The goal is to be more deliberate with decision-making, thereby increasing the museum's chances of achieving intended results.

This perspective is reflected by the UK Museums Association: 'Museums have to work within the resources available to them. The sustainable answer may be to do less, but do it better … Museums need to be clear about their purpose and ensure that their most important activities are sustained' (Davies and Wilkinson 2008, 7).

There are several ways to begin exploring the idea of alignment. For example, one might consider only doing work that is relevant to the museum's community and stop doing work that is not. A museum might need to re-examine its mission and its community to determine which programmes are no longer *relevant* and, likewise, which programmes

---

4   This statement is the museum's vision statement.

do not contribute to the museum's public value and its greatest strength. Though this may seem reductionist, doing away with some programmes can free up resources and time for programmes that *can add value.* By examining all the activities a museum engages in, staff might be able to identify activities that are more relevant to the museum's community in the twenty-first century. Such consideration involves knowing what the community and the authorizing environment will endorse. If relevance and public value become the lenses through which to explore alignment, decisions will become more deliberate and intentional, thereby strengthening the museum and readying it to create and achieve public value in its community.

This does not mean that other challenges do not remain. Even though prudent decision-making and resource management in pursuit of a clearly articulated purpose makes sense, governments often send another message. 'More is better' is not a position which supports strong fiscal and resource management but it is an expectation held by many policy-makers and funders (Holden 2004) and one which has to be negotiated with the authorizing environment. It is made easier when an organization has a clear sense of its own purpose, why it wants to make a particular difference and for whom.

Evaluating Results in Pursuit of Public Value[5]

The third part of the cycle focuses on evaluation. Evaluation, specifically summative evaluation, measures results and examines them against intentions. However, a public value statement is not an adequate evaluative platform from which to design a reliable and valid study. The evaluator and staff will need to work together to deconstruct the public value statement and develop concrete, measurable outcomes against audience segments. In intentional practice work, evaluating the public value of a museum also provides a great opportunity to begin thinking about measuring value in quantitative *and qualitative* terms.

Success in museums is often discussed quantitatively. Governments may note the economic benefit of museums and museums might fuel the quantitative perspective by celebrating high visitation. Neither 'measure' expresses museums' intrinsic social values (Lagendijk 2011). At some point, someone might ask a museum director or chairman of the board to discuss the difference the museum made in the quality of people's lives (Weil 2002). Conversations about dollars and attendance fail to describe a museum's public value, intrinsic value and distinctiveness.

From the perspective of intentional practice, achieving public value is associated with quality rather than quantity. That is not to say, however, that quantity is unimportant. Numerical measures are an indication of one type of value as when museums have created quality programmes that also attracted high numbers of people. Outputs and outcomes have a place and purpose, and undoubtedly the value of 'how many' is important when evidence indicates increased dollars raised, increased number of community partnerships, increased number of memberships (Chesebrough 2010). However, numbers become much more meaningful when museums also explore, describe and communicate to policy-makers at both the local and national levels the *qualitative* value of museums to people and communities.

---

5   Chapter 4 is about evaluation practice; this section discusses evaluation from an intentional practice perspective.

As noted earlier, public value statements are constructed from a museum's distinctive characteristics. Describing how these characteristics are experienced by the public is a powerful endorsement of their value. Though challenging, each museum owes it to itself and its publics to define its *uniqueness* and embed that uniqueness in its public value statement – this can begin the process of thinking about success qualitatively.

If a museum expresses its measurable outcomes qualitatively as well as quantitatively, then the evaluation design will need to respond accordingly and include instruments and investigative strategies that support collecting and analysing numerical data *and* descriptive data. Planning an evaluation that studies how public value has been experienced by audiences offers evaluators a chance to innovate and experiment with qualitative data collection tools to support the unique experiences that museums afford.

Reflecting on Intentional Practice and Public Value

The fourth and final reflect quadrant follows the evaluation in the cycle (even though one can engage in reflective practice at any time) because evaluative information is an important component when determining whether intentions have been achieved, to what degree and with what impact.

Reflective practice, a formal approach for learning through inquiry (Schön 1983), requires taking the time to learn from evaluation results and one's daily work. Reflective practice is a process of periodically thinking about the museum's work and questioning how it supports the mission and the public value the museum wants to create. For leaders who are pursuing intentional practice through deliberate inquiry, reflection becomes a means to fulfil professional and organizational learning (Korn 2007). Given that there is a strong relationship between *taking the time to think about* one's work and *learning from* one's work (Korn 2008), *making* time becomes a relevant issue.

Schön (1983) identifies two types of reflective practice – reflection-in-action, which is when people share gut reactions the moment they have them and reflection-on-action, which is when people look back on their work. Both have value in professional and organizational learning.

The placement of the reflect quadrant, after the evaluate quadrant, does not necessarily assume that staff are reflecting only on evaluation data; in the absence of data, staff can share insights about their practice and the work of their colleagues. Evaluation data, however, provides the extra benefit of learning about the public in the context of public value. The focus of reflective practice sessions can vary, and a museum can orchestrate them according to needs, questions and challenges. The question in the cycle of intentional practice accentuates reflection-on-action, yet reflection time can be used for either type of reflection. When museum staff critique a newly installed exhibition, they may be reflecting-in-action, and when they discuss data from a programme evaluation or public value study, they may be reflecting-on-action.

There are five skills associated with reflective practice: being, speaking, disclosing, testing and probing (Raelin 2002). 'Being' is the skill most vital to the theory of intentional practice. Being signifies 'presence' (for example, being wholly present) which assumes vulnerability, curiosity, honesty, defencelessness, deep listening to understand, and letting go of old identities and perceptions (Raelin 2002; Senge et al. 2004).

Just as inquiry is used to explore staff members' passions and the organization's unique qualities, it also supports reflective practice. Asking questions is one way to explore ideas and build meanings individually and collectively. And perhaps the most important benefit of reflective practice is the collective learning that takes place as all staff begin to understand the work of their museum in the context of the public value they aspire to create.

Conclusion

In intentional practice, staff engage in the four actions that constitute the cycle, and their central focus becomes creating public value. Intentional practice invites everyone in the organization to discuss, debate and ultimately identify and support the museum's core purpose. Working intentionally demonstrates the entire organization's enthusiasm for and belief in their museum's purpose, unique value and desire to make a difference in people's lives. Museums that continually clarify their public value in the context of what is relevant to both the authorizing environment and the museum's audiences and which realign practices and resources to create that value are also working in an organization that is evolving. Intentional practice requires continuous work but the reward is being valuable, being valued and being sustainable.

References

Axelrod, N. 2007. *Culture of Inquiry: Healthy Debate in the Boardroom*. Washington, DC: BoardSource.
Chesebrough, D. 2010. Putting Public Value to the Test. *ASTC Dimensions*, January/February, 7, 12.
Collins, J. 1994. *Built to Last: Successful Habits of Visionary Companies*. Tenth Anniversary Edition. New York: HarperCollins.
Collins, J. 2001. *Good to Great*. First Edition. New York: HarperCollins.
Collins, J. 2005. *Good to Great and the Social Sectors*. New York: HarperCollins.
Davies, M. and Wilkinson, H. 2008. *Sustainability and Museums: Your Chance to Make a Difference*. London: Museums Association.
Goodale, C. 2009. Museums' New Mantra: Connect with Community. *Christian Science Monitor*. Available at: http://www.csmonitor.com/The-Culture/Arts/2009/0721/p17s01-algn.html [accessed 14 May 2012].
Gurian, E. 2010. Museum as Soup Kitchen. *Curator: The Museum Journal*, 53(1), 71–85.
Gutwill, J.P. and Allen, S. 2010. *Group Inquiry at Science Museum Exhibits*. San Francisco: Exploratorium.
Hammond, S.A. 1996. *Appreciative Inquiry*. Second Edition. Bend: Thin Book Publishing Co.
Hammond, S.A. and Mayfield, A. 2004. *The Thin Book of Naming Elephants: How to Surface Undiscussables for Greater Organizational Success*. Bend: Thin Book Publishing Co.
Holden, J. 2004. Capturing Cultural Value: How Culture has Become a Tool of Government Policy. Available at: http://www.demos.co.uk/files/CapturingCulturalValue.pdf?1240939425 [accessed 29 May 2012].
Korn, R. 2004. Self-Portrait: First Know Thyself, Then Serve Your Public. *Museum News*, 83(1), 33–5, 50–52.
Korn, R. 2007. The Case for Holistic Intentionality. *Curator: The Museum Journal*, 50(2), 255–63.

Korn, R. 2008. To What End? Achieving Mission through Intentional Practice. *ASTC Dimensions*, May/June, 3–4.

Korn, R. 2010. When Less is More. *Museum*, September/October, 25–7.

Koster, E. 2006. The Relevant Museum: A Reflection on Sustainability. *Museum News*, May/June, 67–70, 85–90.

Lagendijk, E. 2011. The Social Value of Museums: More than Beautiful Collections Alone. *Newsletter of the Network of European Museum Organizations*. Available at: http://www.ne-mo.org/fileadmin/Dateien/public/NEMONews/nemoNews_1-11www.pdf [accessed 29 May 2012].

Moore, M. 1995. *Creating Public Value: Strategic Management in Government*. Cambridge, MA: Harvard University Press.

Moore, M. and Moore, G. 2005. *Creating Public Value Through State Arts Agencies*. New York: The Wallace Foundation.

Oxford Dictionary. Definition of Intentionality. Available at: http://oxforddictionaries.com/definition/relevant?q=relevancy#relevant__4 [accessed 23 February 2012].

Peniston, W. (ed.) 1999. *Increasing the Usefulness of Museums. The New Museum: Selected Writings by John Cotton Dana*. Washington, DC: American Association of Museums.

Pink, D. 2011. *Drive: The Surprising Truth About What Motivates Us*. New York: Penguin Group USA.

Preskill, H. and Torres, R. 1999. *Evaluative Inquiry for Learning in Organizations*. Thousand Oaks: Sage Publications.

Raelin, J. 2002. 'I Don't Have Time to Think!' Versus the Art of Reflective Practice. *Reflections*, 4(1), 66–79.

Randi Korn & Associates, Inc. 2011. *Audience Research: Study of Visitors to the Freer Gallery of Art and Arthur M. Sackler Gallery*. Unpublished manuscript. Washington, DC. Freer Gallery of Art and Arthur M. Sackler Gallery.

Schön, D. 1983. *The Reflective Practitioner*. New York: Basic Books.

Scott, C. 2011. Measuring the Immeasurable: Capturing Intangible Values. Marketing and Public Relations International Committee of ICOM (International Council of Museums) Brno, Czech Republic, 19 September. Available at: http://network.icom.museum/fileadmin/user_upload/minisites/mpr/papers/2011-Scott.pdf [accessed 14 May 2012].

Senge, P., Scharmer, C.O., Jaworski, J. and Flowers, B.S. 2004. *Presence: Exploring Profound Change in People, Organizations, and Society*. New York: Society for Organizational Learning.

Siewert, C. 2011. Consciousness and Intentionality, in *The Stanford Encyclopedia of Philosophy (Fall 2011 Edition)*, edited by E. Zalta. Available at: http://plato.stanford.edu/archives/fall2011/entries/consciousness-intentionality/ [accessed 10 March 2012].

Travers, T. and Glaister, S. 2004. Valuing Museums: Impact and Innovation among National Museums. Available at: http://www.nationalmuseums.org.uk/media/documents/publications/valuing_museums.pdf [accessed 14 May 2012].

Villeneuve, P. and Love, A.R. 2007. Rethinking the Gallery Learning Experience Through Inquiry, in *From Periphery to Center: Art Museum Education in the 21st Century*, edited by P. Villeneuve. Reston: National Art Education Association, 194–204.

Weil, S. 2002. *Making Museums Matter*. Washington, DC: Smithsonian Institution Press.

Weil, S. 2005. A Success/Failure Matrix for Museums. *Museum News*, January/February, 36–40.

4 *Evaluating Public Value: Strategy and Practice*

MARY ELLEN MUNLEY

Introduction

Many museums throughout the world state their intention to serve broad and diverse audiences. Yet, throughout history, museums have been criticized for being elitist, out of touch, and often not relevant to pressing social issues (Conn 2010). Recently they have come under fire for overemphasis on blockbuster exhibitions, merchandising, and other revenue-generating activities that make museums available only to those who can pay. Some worry that inordinate attention to earned revenue as an indicator of overall institutional health places too little emphasis on the larger social mission of museums.

In a comprehensive review of the literature about the effectiveness of public value theory when applied in public agencies, Williams and Shearer (2011) conclude that while there is little hard data, there are reported indications that the presence of a public value orientation is linked to increased levels of engagement and civic participation There is also emerging evidence that museums that stay laser-focused on their public value work are successful in garnering support in many forms – public testimonials, additional resources available through partnerships, and funding from a larger set of private foundations and public sources that share a common social goal.

Ken Berger, President and CEO of *Charity Navigator*, the United States' leading independent charity evaluator, recently announced that their ratings will no longer depend only on financial metrics, but will now also assess effectiveness in realizing stated social goals. This shift in focus is aptly called 'the battle for the soul of the nonprofit sector' (Berger et al. 2010), and industry leaders predict that museums that can show evidence of their public value will have an advantage over those who do not.

As Stephen Weil warned, '[i]f museums are not being operated with the ultimate goal of improving the quality of people's lives, on what basis might we possibly ask for public support?' (Weil 2003, 10).

A NEW EMPHASIS FOR MUSEUM EVALUATION

Providing evidence for the public value of today's museums rests upon acceptance of what needs to change about how the role of collections, exhibitions, programmes, money, approaches to education, and audiences are understood by museum trustees, museum staff, visitors, private and public supporters, and the general public.

Collections are central, but they are not the raison d'être for museums

In his astute history of the meaning of museums in society, Conn (2010) concludes that museums are no longer solely houses for collections. If the golden age of museum-building came a century ago, he observes, then it is fair to say that we are now witnessing a second golden age – and age of meaning. He concludes that 'In the end, simply bringing us together, whether to marvel at art or explore questions of science, may be more precious than anything we come to see' (Conn 2010, 232).

A critical mass of activity is important, but it is not enough

Most museum annual reports document attendance, the number of exhibitions mounted each year, the amount of public programming, and the number of community outreach programmes. Based on a review of 180 reports from science museums and science centres Garnett concluded that the museums put many programmes in place that benefit society, but 'on the whole, they have not developed the methodology to measure the impact that they have at a societal level' (Garnett 2001, 8).

Porter and Kramer (1999) identified a new agenda for philanthropy focused on value creation and the ultimate results of an organization's work. Yet museum assessments continue to focus heavily on *activities* rather than on *outcomes* even though it is believed that focus on the latter increases the likelihood of community support (Sherman et al. 2002). The Institute of Museum and Library Services now requires its grant recipients to engage in outcomes-based evaluation to document how much a museum does (activity), how well they do it (fidelity) and why their work matters (impact).

To meet the new standards set by funders and the public, museums need to: articulate the desired results of their work; specify targets that demonstrate that they are making reasonable progress towards providing those results; and document gains and demonstrate that they are achieving results (Berger et al. 2010).

Effective communication is a hallmark of museums, but it is not their main contribution

The publication of *Communicating with the Museum Visitor: Guidelines for Planning* (Communications Design Team of the Royal Ontario Museum 1976) marked an era in museum work that brought growing attention to the effective crafting of messages and strategies for delivering them. Evaluations focused on the percentage of people who understood museums' intended messages and exhibition teams honed their communication strategies. In 1992, a new gold standard in the much-acclaimed innovations in communications strategy was unveiled at the opening of the Monterey Bay Aquarium. There, scientists, exhibit developers and writers developed a reader-friendly 'storytelling' strategy and the idea of an aquarium persona, or 'voice' (Ramberg et al. 2002). Much is now known about effective communication strategies for engaging visitors. Evaluations of communication efforts indicate that museums can successfully hold attention, facilitate interaction with content and convey messages. They do not, however, demonstrate that the museum made progress towards realizing its mission.

Money is essential, but it is not the only bottom line

'In a world of changing demographics, globalism and rising technology, the crisis we face is not financial. The crisis we face is one of urgency and relevance' (Cameron 2009, 4). Collins argues that the key performance question is not 'How much money do we make per dollar of invested capital?' but 'How effectively do we deliver on our mission and make a distinctive impact relative to our resources?' (Collins 2005, 5). Despite pressures from their boards and others to focus more attention on the financial bottom line rather than on mission-related performance, there is evidence that the larger public agrees with Cameron and Collins. When asked what they value about a museum in their community, the majority of people surveyed gave their highest scores to the societal value of museums and lowest scores to the museum's economic contribution to the community (Yocco et al. 2009). Of course, good financial management is important, but increased revenues and balanced budgets are not the only measures of a museum's success.

In an effort to catalyse evaluation focused on public value, this chapter provides: discussion of differences between evaluating public value and evaluating other aspects of a museum's valued operations; a public value framework for evaluation that focuses on the distinctive characteristics of public value evaluation; and summaries of three museum evaluations that provide evidence of public value.

The Public Value Challenge

One of the first challenges for evaluating museums' public value is to distinguish public value from other aspects of a museum's work that also produce value. Porter (2006) asserts that defining value depends on choosing, specifying and weighting goals. For museums, he argues, the major goal areas of collections, education, visitation, visitor experience, and research and scholarship are all part of a museum's work, but none of them specifically addresses the ultimate purpose – the difference that the museum's work makes for society.

In Koster and Falk's (2007) conception of value, a museum has merit and will be held in high regard based on: the good that the organization provides its visitors; the assets of the organization, including particularly its intellectual capital and brand; the benefits provided by the organization to the community above and beyond the specific good generated for individual visitors or other stakeholders; the quality of the organization's workplace, including that each employee experiences continued growth and development; and the financial health of the organization.

Scott (2006) identifies three types of museum value: individual benefits; societal value provided to the community as a whole; and economic benefits to the community. Following this logic, one art museum conducted a study about how it was valued by interviewing people attending a large city festival. Responses provided empirical evidence supporting Scott's contention that the public at large attributes personal, social and economic value to museums (Yocco et al. 2009).

In Denver, the City Value Study looked at the value visitors attribute to museums. Information was gathered at 13 museums. The majority of respondents at the zoo, botanical garden and children's museums said they find the museum 'good for the kids' and a place for 'family activity'. The most frequent word used to describe the value of the city's museums across all of the 13 sites was 'education' (Trainer, 2012).

Historically, education is the most often claimed value museums provide for their visitors. Yet in today's information-saturated world that heightens the value of multiple perspectives, the singular, authoritative voice of the museum (through its curators) strikes some as arrogant and burdened by an assumption that only the museum specialist's interpretation has legitimacy.

Glasser (2008) argues that the overemphasis on education means that museums have succumbed to an overemphasis on words, giving primacy to language-based ways of knowing at the expense of visual literacy. She challenges museums to give precedence to stimulating questions over providing answers. Warnings that it is time to reconsider the work of museums have reached a critical mass over the last decade (Conn 2010; Garnett 2010 Glasser 2008; Janes and Conaty 2005; Korn 2007; Koster 2010; Munley 2010; Selwood 2002; Weil 2002, 2003). The chief feature of the recommended change is to move from an internal to an external focus, a shift that brings with it challenges to the status quo.

Koster (2010) could have been speaking about all museums when he said: 'rather than pursuing their greatest possible purpose, the science museum and science centre field became overly enamoured with its invention of interactivity in exhibits and gradually also with the box office allure of blockbuster exhibitions ... [and in so doing] the field limited its potential scale of impact' (Koster 2010, 77). He captures the essence of recent critiques of museum evaluation when he posits that the only dial on a museum's performance dashboard that ultimately matters is external usefulness. A major part of defining this new sense of external value is an 'embrace of new subjects that require public conversation for greater clarity around what is truly important' (Koster 2010, 79).

Arriving at an understanding and evaluation of museums' value is a developmental and additive process (Koster 2010; Weil 2002). Museums have not outgrown the need to acquire and care for collections, mount engaging exhibitions and programmes or manage themselves responsibly. However, it is simply that in a responsive, contemporary search for meaning and authentic approaches to evaluation, museums need to focus on their contributions to the public good, 'including questions of social responsibility, social equity, civic engagement, and the meaning the institution has for the [entire] community' (Janes and Conaty 2005, 11).

A Return to Home: Reclaiming the Museum's Position in the Social Sector

History shows that when the museum field focuses its attention on setting standards and monitoring performance, it improves practice. This has been true for collections care, communicating with visitors and financial management. Now, it is time to turn attention to the museum's ultimate contribution – public value.

DEFINING PUBLIC VALUE

In 2002, Stephen Weil observed that in little more than a generation museums had shifted their primary focus from being concerned above all with the growth, care and study of collections to being institutions that turned primarily outward. In characterizing the features of an outward orientation, he offered one of the early definitions of public value. He argued that the new responsibility for any museum is to be 'an institution striving above all, to *provide a range of educational and other public services*' (Weil 2002, 1, emphasis added).

Public value, as defined here, is not synonymous with – nor as straightforward as – giving visitors what they want. Measuring visitor (customer) satisfaction may provide valuable information, but it is not a way to evaluate public value. There is an essential distinction between public value and the public's values. Public value is a civic concept and the public's values is an empirical finding about peoples' preferences (Williams and Shearer 2011).

Nor is public value synonymous with attracting and serving large audiences. Often, as Korza et al. (2005) point out, continuous engagement in *small* groups lead to *more* civic dialogue and action. As Glasser (2008, 33) notes, 'While the numbers look impressive, if we scratch below the surface they hold little real meaning and are certainly a poor indicator of the essential nature of museums'.

When people talk about museums, they frequently mention great exhibitions, a favourite work of art or even the influence of early museum experiences on career choices. Providing personally meaningful experiences is an important component of what museums do, just as sharing personal stories was an important part of the Americans for the Arts Animating Democracy project. However, in examining their data, the project's planners concluded that sharing personal stories did not in and of itself result in the kind of civic dialogue they aimed to foster. There is no clear distinction between personal benefits, experienced by individuals, and public benefits that accrue to society as a whole (McCarthy et al. 2004). Some benefits are solely of benefit to the individual; others are of value to the individual *and* also accrue public benefits, and still others are largely of value to society as a whole.

EVALUATION FOCUSED ON PUBLIC VALUE QUESTIONS

Based on her comprehensive review of literature and practice, Silverman observes that there is a 'growing belief among practitioners, policymakers, and the public alike in the power of museums to inspire hope and healing, improve lives, and better the world ... Today, the world's museums are embracing starkly bolder roles as agents of well-being and as vehicles for social change' (Silverman 2010, 2–3).

As expectations for museums continue to expand beyond their long-standing stewardship obligations, museum administrators and evaluators must be prepared to define new responsibilities and measures of success (Frasier and Sadler 2008; Korn 2007; Koster 2010; Munley 2010. Public value evaluation is an assessment of the contributions the museum makes to addressing long-standing and pervasive social issues like race relations, class, cultural identity, freedom of expression, equality, definitions of progress, and the relationship between humans and the natural world. Building on the work of the Animating Democracy Project, and a review of the accumulating evidence about the social work of museums (Korza et al. 2005; Silverman 2010), evaluations assessing public value might ask questions such as: to what extent do the museum's activities ...

- Enhance public awareness and understanding of civic issues?
- Increase participants' sense of self-efficacy and collective efficacy to take action?
- Enhance quality of, and capacity for, civic dialogue?
- Contribute to understanding and appreciating multiple perspectives?

Public value perspectives and evaluations are also concerned with equity of access and if the museum operates in ways that reach and serve *all* prospective audiences (Clewell 2009; Weinberg and Lewis 2009).

A Public Value Framework for Museum Evaluation

Evaluation of a museum's public value focuses on the degree to which the museum contributes to making a positive difference in the world rather than on personally valued outcomes or the ability of the museum to communicate the messages it alone decides are important. Public value evaluation examines the intersection of the museum's work with goals that are shared by people outside the museum in the larger social arena. Such evaluations look at the performance of the museum from the perspective of citizens and examine the broad social outcomes of the museum's work, the manner in which the museum operates, and who it serves. Citizens could be said to want museums that are (1) efficient and effective in achieving desired social outcomes, (2) known to be just and fair in the way in which they operate, and (3) whose efforts lead to just and fair conditions in the society at large. These three elements collectively make up the concept of public value and provide the foundation of the framework for evaluating it (Moore 1995, 2003; Moore and Benington 2011). A public value perspective differs from other approaches to evaluation in its focus and purpose.

FOCUS AND PURPOSE

Public value evaluations focus on social impact   The evaluation process begins with a clear statement of the institution's purpose in terms that articulate its intended contributions to addressing long-standing social issues or emerging contemporary issues. If the mission statement does not *explicitly* include a statement about intended impact, the results the museum intends to achieve, then a companion statement of how the museum's work creates public value will be needed.

Public value evaluations have a strategic focus and give attention to learning and change   The goal is not just to demonstrate what was accomplished in the past. The goal is to learn what factors contribute most to creating results. Based on that information, evaluation results serve two purposes: to demonstrate current levels of success and to guide strategic decisions about how to maximize impact in the future.

Public value evaluations extend beyond the views of visitors and museum members and involve other stakeholders and citizens, including those who do not use the museum   To gain public support, museums cannot only be valued by those who work in them and visit them. The museum needs to be successful in demonstrating the importance of its mission and work to the overall quality of life of the community.

Public value evaluations view other institutions and organizations as civic partners rather than business competitors   If a museum is addressing important social issues, then the chances are very good that others are working towards the same goals. Sometimes a museum can only accomplish its mission in partnership with others. The focus for public value evaluations is not only to demonstrate that the museum does something that no one else does. The focus is to demonstrate the ways that the museum, as part of a community-wide, coordinated effort, contributes to making a difference related to long-standing and complex social needs and aspirations.

Public value evaluations, when most useful, examine the alignment among resources, achieved outcomes and social needs   No museum can single-handedly be held responsible for alleviating long-standing and emerging social needs. Public value evaluations do not set such unattainable goals. They define goals in terms that are aligned with large social needs, and they wisely identify the specific types of contributions and targets that it is reasonable for the museum to assume.

METHODS AND MEASURES

No one metric or powerful story is sufficient to characterize a museum's public value contributions. A complete, convincing evaluation requires an array of evidence that, when tied together, provides an authentic picture of the institution and its effects.

The same standards and methods used in most evaluations apply to public value evaluation. Information is gathered using surveys, interviews, focus groups and observations. Study designs need defensible sampling procedures; instruments must be valid and reliable; analysis must be accurate and replicable; and interpretation must be based on evidence. Hills and Sullivan (2006) point out that in addition to well established criteria for adequate study designs and measurement techniques, evaluations of public value should also be:

Appropriate   Measures need to fit the real purpose and the specific situation. Paper and pencil surveys, for instance, may not be an appropriate data collection technique to use with people who are not avid readers. Questions about recall of content are not reasonable ways to address changes in a person's perspective about a topic or an issue.

Holistic   Public value evaluations need to account for complexity and provide ways of understanding specific elements of programme design and implementation. They also need to uncover concrete examples of positive changes in more abstract areas such as well-being, social capital and quality of life.

Democratic   Studies need to include a variety of participants and allow for multiple perspectives to emerge, even if they are in conflict. What may look like a positive experience and outcome to a teacher, for example, may not be an accurate reflection of students' perspectives and outcomes.

Trustworthy   Public value is built on trust. Though all research is bound by standards that respect participants' rights to know what the study is about and to freely elect to participate or decline, the integrity of a study may be under extra scrutiny when the outcomes being investigated have deep personal and social meaning and implications. Particular attention needs to be given to how information is gathered and how it is used by the museum and shared with participants and the larger community.

The process of evaluating public value often creates value in and of itself. This happens when evaluators use participatory evaluation methods and engage programme participants in decisions about what to measure and how to interpret the results. It can happen when the evaluation methods – the creation of a meaning map, for example – reveals something new to the participant, or when a World Café designed to gather information about long-term effects of a programme results in people making new connections that will further their work.

Quantitative results are not the only evidence that have the authority to demonstrate public value. An authentic evaluation of public value will necessitate, including quantitative data __and__ qualitative data representing the actual words of participants. The type of data matters less than that the evaluation is *rigorous* in assembling *evidence* (Collins 2005). 'If the evidence is primarily qualitative, think like a trial lawyer assembling the combined body of evidence. If the evidence is primarily quantitative, then think of yourself as a laboratory scientist assembling and assessing the data' (Collins 2005, 7). It is the combination of evidence, storytelling and a worthy mission that wins the day. Data, facts and verbiage, on their own, are not adequately matched to the task of deeply communicating about the impact museums have on people and society (Strand 2012, 58). Crafting words into a story about impact – a story replete with combinations of quantitative and qualitative evidence – is the aim of public value evaluation.

Demonstrating Public Value

Above all, museums need to establish authority for their claims of creating public value through an authentic and credible portrayal of their work. A survey of legislators (Craig-Unkefer et al. 2010), confirms that a combination of factors, not just presentation of quantitative data, is needed to establish a convincing case. Data can be quantitative or qualitative, what matters most is: non-biased presentations from trustworthy and knowledgeable sources; using researchers and commentators who are familiar with the topic, setting and distinctive features of the museum; information and data that are current; presenting both generalizations and case studies; using comparison and control groups; replication of findings; and longitudinal studies.

Adherence to these criteria for effective demonstration of public value allows museums to avoid the potential pitfall of depending on metrics that are reductive and reduce ambition in deference to easy problems with quick and easy-to-measure outcomes (Spano 2009). They also provide hope for those who shy away from the task of rigorously demonstrating their public value because they assume attempts cannot possibly capture the breadth and depth of their efforts (Berger et al. 2010; Wilkinson 2008). Several museums are leading the way in addressing the technical and measurement challenges associated with demonstrating public value. In every case, the museum focuses its information gathering and reporting on its ultimate purpose, not on the specific goals of individual programmes and activities – and that purpose is framed in language that aligns the work of the museum with larger social goals.

MONTEREY BAY AQUARIUM (MBA)

Evaluations at Monterey Bay Aquarium (MBA) extend beyond results for on-site visitors. The aquarium uses an ongoing evaluation programme to monitor results and modify strategies. Guided by the Inspiring Ocean Conservation Initiative (IOC), evaluations capture reports about the variety of ways people are inspired at MBA (Ferguson 2012). An evaluation report about MBA's Seafood Watch Guide Programme (Quandra and Galiano 2004) gains its authority from the use of multiple methods for gathering information – surveys, focus groups – and follow-up interviews. The Seafood Watch Guide (see Figure 4.1a/b) is a printed pocket guide that lists sustainable seafood choices for consumers in a 'Best Choices' column, and non-sustainable choices in an 'Avoid' column. To examine the impact of the guide on consumers' behaviour, the evaluation gathered information from visitors, restaurant owners, caterers and seafood retailers. As evidence of the Guide's successful distribution, MBA reported that nearly 30 per cent of randomly selected visitors had the Guide *before* their visit. Eighty per cent of those who had a guide said it had significantly changed their seafood buying habits.

The evaluators grounded their analysis in social change theory and hypothesized that those who were using the Seafood Guide were earlier to adopt the new message about responsible seafood choices and that such early adopters often function as opinion leaders. Opinion leaders spread the word and are successful in getting others to follow. Demonstrating that it provides support to change agents is one way that it effectively demonstrates its public value.

Honesty and dead-centre focus on the end result of ocean conservation are hallmarks of MBA's work. Rather than accepting an internal indicator of success (wide distribution and MBA visitors' reported changes in seafood buying behaviour), MBA set a higher bar and examined their efforts in a broader and larger context. They noted that according to 2004 national data there was no overall decline in purchase of non-sustainable seafood. This recognition of the capacity of MBA to 'do its part' but not be expected, on its own, to quickly change well-established national trends, strengthens its case. The evaluation demonstrates success in meeting short-term goals and underscores the importance of continued, long-term commitment to social change.

NATIONAL MUSEUM OF NATURAL HISTORY (NMNH), SMITHSONIAN INSTITUTION

A society needs trustworthy institutions, especially when citizens are grappling with controversial and contentious issues. One finding from an evaluation of NMNH's Human Origins Initiative (HOI) showed that, even when addressing a topic as contentious as human origins, NMNH held the trust of people both before and after experiencing its *What Does It Mean To Be Human* exhibition, website or programmes (Munley 2011). The museum was consistently rated 4.3 and higher on a 5-point scale for the accuracy, fairness and quality of its presentation about human evolution. It was also given high marks for providing current information on the topic. Analysis of conversations in the exhibition illuminated ways the exhibition encouraged people to ask questions and engage in thoughtful, respectful conversations with trained museum volunteers and with each other, even when they disagreed.

Why Do Your Seafood Choices Matter?

Worldwide, the demand for seafood is increasing. Yet many populations of the large fish we enjoy eating are over-fished and, in the U.S., we import over 80% of our seafood to meet the demand. Destructive fishing and fish farming practices only add to the problem.

By purchasing fish caught or farmed using environmentally friendly practices, you're supporting healthy, abundant oceans.

You Can Make A Difference

Support ocean-friendly seafood in three easy steps:

1. Purchase seafood from the green list or, if unavailable, the yellow list. Or look for the Marine Stewardship Council blue eco-label in stores and restaurants.

2. When you buy seafood, ask where your seafood comes from and whether it was farmed or wild-caught.

3. Tell your friends about Seafood Watch. The more people that ask for ocean-friendly seafood, the better!

Learn More

In addition to the recommendations on this guide, we have hundreds more available from our scientists.

To see the complete and most up-to-date list visit us:
- Online at **seafoodwatch.org**
- On our free app
- On our mobile site
- Or join us on Facebook or Twitter

MONTEREY BAY
AQUARIUM®

MONTEREY BAY AQUARIUM

Seafood WATCH®

YELLOWFIN TUNA

National
Sustainable
Seafood Guide
January 2012

Figure 4.1a Seafood Watch Guide
Source: Monterey Bay Aquarium.

BEST CHOICES

Arctic Char (farmed)
Barramundi (US farmed)
Catfish (US farmed)
Clams (farmed)
Cobia (US farmed)
Cod: Pacific (US non-trawled)
Crab: Dungeness, Stone
Halibut: Pacific (US)
Lobster: California Spiny (US)
Mussels (farmed)
Oysters (farmed)
Sablefish/Black Cod (Alaska & Canada)
Salmon (Alaska wild)
Sardines: Pacific (US)
Scallops (farmed)
Shrimp: Pink (OR)
Striped Bass (farmed & wild*)
Tilapia (US farmed)
Trout: Rainbow (US farmed)
Tuna: Albacore (Canada & US Pacific, troll/pole)
Tuna: Skipjack, Yellowfin (US troll/pole)

GOOD ALTERNATIVES

Basa/Pangasius/Swai (farmed)
Caviar, Sturgeon (US farmed)
Clams (wild)
Cod: Atlantic (imported)
Cod: Pacific (US trawled)
Crab: Blue*, King (US), Snow
Flounders, Soles (Pacific)
Flounder: Summer (US Atlantic)*
Grouper: Black, Red (US Gulf of Mexico)*
Herring: Atlantic
Lobster: American/Maine
Mahi Mahi (US)
Oysters (wild)
Pollock: Alaska (US)
Sablefish/Black Cod (CA, OR, WA)
Salmon (CA, OR, WA*, wild)
Scallops (wild)
Shrimp (US, Canada)
Squid
Swordfish (US)*
Tilapia (Central & South America (farmed)
Tuna: Bigeye, Tongol, Yellowfin (troll/pole)

AVOID

Caviar, Sturgeon* (imported wild)
Chilean Seabass/Toothfish*
Cobia (imported farmed)
Cod: Atlantic (Canada & US)
Crab: King (imported)
Flounders, Halibut, Soles (US Atlantic, except Summer Flounder)
Groupers (US Atlantic)*
Lobster: Spiny (Brazil)
Mahi Mahi (imported longline)
Marlin: Blue, Striped (Pacific)*
Monkfish
Orange Roughy*
Salmon (farmed, including Atlantic)*
Sharks* & Skates
Shrimp (imported)
Snapper: Red (US Gulf of Mexico)
Swordfish (imported)*
Tilapia (Asia farmed)
Tuna: Albacore* Bigeye*, Skipjack, Tongol, Yellowfin* (except troll/pole)
Tuna: Bluefin*
Tuna: Canned (except troll/pole)

Support Ocean-Friendly Seafood

Best Choices are abundant, well-managed and caught or farmed in environmentally friendly ways.

Good Alternatives are an option, but there are concerns with how they're caught or farmed – or with the health of their habitat due to other human impacts.

Avoid for now as these items are overfished or caught or farmed in ways that harm other marine life or the environment.

Key
CA = California   OR = Oregon
WA = Washington
* Limit consumption due to concerns about mercury or other contaminants.
Visit www.edf.org/seafoodhealth
Contaminant information provided by:
ENVIRONMENTAL DEFENSE FUND

EDF

Seafood may appear in more than one column

Figure 4.1b Seafood Watch Guide
Source: Monterey Bay Aquarium.

Rather than testing changes in peoples' knowledge or beliefs about human evolution as an indicator of success, the evaluation used interviews, accounts of in-gallery conversations, and visitor-drawn meaning maps to allow people to freely and holistically represent their personal, complex understanding of what it means to be human and for the museum to more completely understand its audiences. Coding and analysis of the maps showed that when asked what it means to be human, a majority of people before they experience the exhibition identify psychological, cognitive and sociological features of humanness, such as the ability to have feelings, to learn, and to raise families. Those same features were prominent on maps drawn by a comparable sample of visitors who had spent time in the exhibition. However, people who had experienced the exhibition expanded their ideas about what it means to be human and added scientific concepts to their personal meaning maps. They included 67 per cent more concepts like the ability to walk upright, changes over time and brain size on their maps than did those who had not experienced the exhibition. The design of the evaluation provided evidence that NMNH engages millions of people in thoughtful consideration of what science has to offer to our understanding of what it means to be human. It provides a forum and a way of presenting information that facilitates dialogue about a contentious social issue.

UNITED STATES HOLOCAUST MEMORIAL MUSEUM (USHMM)

Bringing the Lessons Home (BTLH) is an intensive youth programme that enrols about 20 students each year. By focusing on impact, instead of numbers of students participating, an evaluation of the programme convinced internal and external decision-makers that the small-in-numbers programme had far-reaching impacts on society. USHMM's mission is to advance and disseminate knowledge about the Holocaust, to preserve the memory of those who suffered, and to encourage visitors to reflect upon the moral and spiritual questions raised by the events of the Holocaust as well as their own responsibilities as citizens of a democracy. A responsibility statement that is a companion piece to the mission states that the organization accepts its responsibility: 'To assure that the Museum truly is a *living* memorial, that the lessons of the Holocaust – lessons about moral responsibility, the fragility and importance of democracy, the dangers of anti-Semitism and racism, and the need to prevent genocide – not only are learned but also embraced by new generations' (United States Holocaust Memorial Museum 2002). Given the museum's stated social responsibility, the evaluation of *Bringing the Lessons Home* asked: (1) does BTLH increase young urban teens' capacity for recognizing injustice and seeing themselves as agents of change; and (2) do the young people then make a difference in their communities? The evaluation reported on the experiences of nearly 50 per cent of all the students who had participated in the programme over its 30 years. At the time of the evaluation they ranged in age from 18 to 31. Results indicated a link between programme participation and an inclination towards long-term civic engagement. Using a well-established measure of levels of civic engagement among teens (CIRCLE 2006), study results indicated that BTLH participants of all ages were more civically involved than the national average. Fifty-seven per cent of BTLH alumni were active in community groups, as compared to 20 per cent of youth nationally (Munley and Roberts 2008). Over

Figure 4.2   A student ambassador in the Bringing the Lessons Home programme waits in front of the United States Holocaust Memorial Museum in Washington, DC, for a bus to School Without Walls Senior High to participate in the Art and Memory Project

Source: United States Holocaust Memorial Museum.

half of the alumni (54 per cent) volunteered in their community, compared with 35 per cent nationally. These comparative data provide concrete evidence of the museum's public value because they document specific benefits to society.

In addition to using an online questionnaire, the study also included alumni interviews and a World Café. Interviews provided explicit examples of community work. The World Café is an innovative format (Brown and Isaacs 2005) that gathered alumni and people from their families, schools and work environments for a discussion that revealed the large number of community actions and programmes initiated by the youth as illustrated by Figure 4.2.

An unexpected outcome of the *Bringing the Lessons Home* evaluation was the emergence of a model that conveys the system of complex relationships between personal growth and individual outcomes and community actions and public value outcomes. The model (see Figure 4.3 on page 16) shows how the museum took on four different roles. Each role provided a bridge that eventually connected the learning of individual programme participants to changes in larger communities.

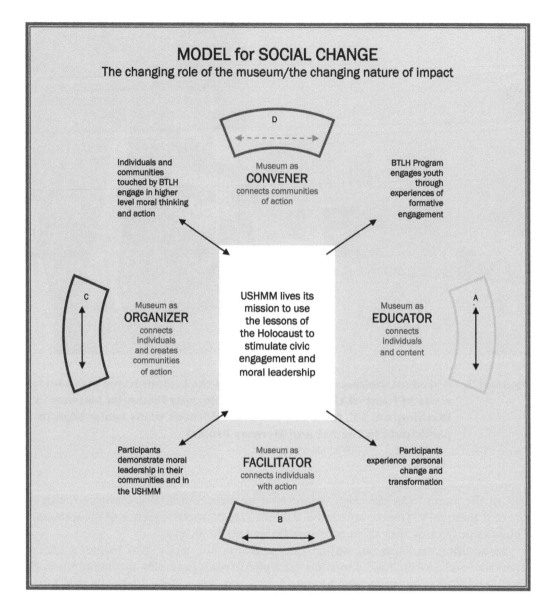

Figure 4.3   Social change model
Source: Munley and Roberts 2008.

Conclusion

As these examples indicate, museums can convincingly provide evidence of their public value. To do so they need to clearly and passionately articulate their contributions in terms that reflect their sense of social responsibility. They also need to understand the differences between personal benefits and social impact and create an institutional culture that involves a clear understanding of the importance of the relationships among financial health, effective operations, outcomes for individuals and maximizing public value. To paraphrase David Osborne and Ted Gaebler (1992):

> *If you don't measure results, you can't tell success from failure;*
> *If you can't see success you can't reward it;*
> *If you can't reward success, you're probably rewarding failure;*
> *If can't see success, you can't learn from it;*
> *If you can't recognize failure, you can't correct it;*
> *If you can demonstrate results, you can win public support;*
> *What gets attention gets done.*

All indications suggest that museums are evolving into their rightful position of being valued for their intended purpose. As e.e. cummings is reported to have said, '[i]t takes courage to grow up to become who you really are'. The dOedication of intellectual and financial resourcOes to public value evaluation is essential if museums are to take the bold step of presenting themselves to the world as essential contributors to realizing a better world.

References

Berger, K., Penna, R.M. and Goldberg, S.H. 2010. The Battle for the Soul of the Nonprofit Sector. *Philadelphia Social Innovations Journal*, 3. Available at: http://www.philasocialinnovations.org/site/index.php?option=com_content&view=article&id=163%3Athe-battle-for-the-soul-of-the-nonprofit-sector&catid=20%3Awhat-works-and-what-doesnt&Itemid=31 [accessed 14 March 2012].

Brown, J. and Isaacs, D. 2005. *The World Café: Shaping Our Futures Through Conversations That Matter*. San Francisco: Berrett-Koehler.

Cameron, B. 2009. *Prepared Remarks*. Illinois Arts Council members meeting and reception, 24 February. Chicago, Steppenwolf Theatre.

CIRCLE (Center for Information and Research on Civic Learning and Engagement). 2006. *The 2006 Civic and Political Health of the Nation: A Detailed Look at How Youth Participate in Politics and Communities*, October.

Clewell, B.C. 2009. Measuring Success and Effectiveness of NSF's Broadening Participation Programs: Suggested Monitoring Metrics and Evaluation Indicators, in *Framework for Evaluating Impacts of Broadening Participation Projects*, edited by B.C. Clewell and N. Fortenberry. Washington, DC: The Directorate for Education and Human Resources, The Division of Research on Learning in Formal and Informal Settings, National Science Foundation, 42–54.

Collins, J. 2005. *Good to Great and the Social Sectors: Why Business Thinking Is Not the Answer*. Boulder: Jim Collins.

Communications Design Team of the Royal Ontario Museum. 1976. *ROM: Communicating with the Museum Visitor: Guidelines for Planning*. Toronto: Royal Ontario Museum.

Conn, S. 2010. *Do Museums Still Need Objects?* Philadelphia: University of Pennsylvania Press.

Craig-Unkefer, L., Cardigan, K., Hottinger, J., McConnell, S. and Slawick, N. 2010. Using Dialogue to Bridge the Research-to-Policy Gap. A presentation to the Conference on Research Innovations in Early Interventions (CRIEI). San Diego, 25–27 February.

Ferguson, A. 2012. *Personal communication*, 9 March.

Fraser, J. and Sickler, J. 2008. *Why Zoos and Aquariums Matter: Handbook of Research Key Findings and Results from National Audience Survey*. Annapolis: Institute for Learning Innovation.

Gallant, M. and Kydd, G. 2005. Engaging Young Minds and Spirits: The Glenbow Museum School, in *Looking Reality in the Eye: Museums and Social Responsibility*, edited by R.P. Janes and G.T. Conaty. Calgary: University of Calgary Press, 71–84.

Garnett, R. 2001. *The impact of science centers/museums on their surrounding communities: Summary report*. Canberra, Australia: Questacon.

Glasser, S. 2008. Manifesto Destiny. *Museum*, 87(6), 31–3.

Janes, R.P. and Conaty, G.T. 2005. *Looking Reality in the Eye: Museums and Social Responsibility*. Calgary: University of Calgary Press.

Hills, D. and Sullivan F. 2006. *Measuring Public Value 2: Practical Approaches*. London: The Work Foundation.

Korn, R. 2007. The Case for Holistic Intentionality. *Curator*, 50(2), 255–64.

Korza, P., Bacon, B.S. and Assaf, A. 2005. *Civic Dialogue, Arts & Culture: Findings from Animating Democracy*. Washington, DC: Americans for the Arts.

Koster, E.H. 2010. Evolution of Purpose in Science Museums and Science Centres, in *Hot Topics, Public Culture, Museums*, edited by F. Cameron and L. Kelly. Newcastle: Cambridge Scholars Publishing, 76–94.

Koster, E. and Falk, J. 2007. Maximizing the External Value of Museums. *Curator*, 50(2), 191–6.

Lynch, R.L. 2005. Foreword. *Civic Dialogue, Arts & Culture: Findings from Animating Democracy*. Washington, DC: Americans for the Arts.

McCarthy, K.F., Ondaatje, E.H., Zakaras, L. and Brooks, A. 2004. *Gifts of the Muse: Reframing the Debate about the Benefits of the Arts*. Santa Monica, CA: RAND Corporation.

Moore, M.H. 1995. *Creating Public Value: Strategic Management in Government*. Cambridge, MA: Harvard University Press.

Moore, M.H. 2003. *The Public Value Scorecard: A Rejoinder and an Alternative to 'Strategic Performance Measurement and Management in Non-Profit Organizations' by Robert Kaplan*. Cambridge, MA: Hauser Center for Nonprofit Organizations, John F. Kennedy School of Government, Harvard University.

Moore, M. and Benington, J. 2011. Conclusions: Looking ahead, in Benington, J. and Moore, M. (eds), *Public Value: Theory & Practice*. London: Palgrave Macmillan, 256–74.

Munley, M.E. 2010. Raising the Bar: Aiming for Public Value. *Journal of Museum Education*, 35(1), 21–31.

Munley, M.E. 2011. *The Human Origins Initiative (HOI). What Does It Mean to Be Human? The Effectiveness and Impact of the HOI Education and Outreach Strategy. Evaluation Report #1*. Washington, DC: Smithsonian Institution, National Museum of Natural History.

Munley, M.E. and Roberts, R.K. 2008. *Knowing Better … Stepping up … Taking Action: Personal Transformation that Leads to Social Change. An Evaluation Report Based on a Longitudinal Study of Bringing the Lessons Home Program*. Washington, DC: United States Holocaust Museum.

Osborne, D. and Gaebler, T. 1992. *Reinventing Government: How the Entrepreneurial Spirit Is Transforming the Public Sector*. New York: Penguin.

Porter, M.E. 2006. Strategy for Museums. Presentation at the annual conference of the American Association of Museums, Boston, MA, 28 April 2006.

Porter, M.E. and Kramer, M. 1999. Philanthropy's new agenda: Creating value. *Harvard Business Review*, 77(6), 121–30.

Quandra Planning Consultants and Galiano Institute for Environmental and Social Research. 2004. *Monterey Bay Aquarium's Seafood Watch Program Evaluation*. Saltspring Island, British Columbia, Canada.

Ramberg, J.S., Rand, J. and Tomulonis, J. 2002. Mission, Message, and Visitors: How Exhibit Philosophy has Evolved at the Monterey Bay Aquarium. *Curator*, 45(4), 302–20.

Research Centre for Museums & Galleries. 2002. *A Catalyst for Change: The Social Impact of the Open Museum*. Leicester: Heritage Lottery Fund.

Scott, C. 2006. Museums: Impact and Value. *Cultural Trends*, 15(1), 45–75

Selwood, S. 2002. What Differences Do Museums Make? Producing Evidence On the Impact of Museums. *Critical Quarterly*, 44(4), 65–81.

Sherman, H., Weinberg, M. and Lewis, M. 2002. *Measuring Public Value Creation*. Athens, OH: Voinovich Center for Leadership and Public Affairs.

Silverman, L.H. 2010. *The Social Work of Museums*. New York: Routledge.

Spano, A. 2009. Public Value Creation and Management Control Systems. *International Journal of Public Administration*, 32(3–4), 328–48.

Strand, J. 2012. Telling Tales: A Conversation with Andy Goodman. *Museum*, 91(2), 55–8.

Trainer, L. 2012. Personal communication.

United States Holocaust Memorial Museum. 2002 [updated 2010]. *Securing the Living Legacy: A Strategy for the Second Decade*. Washington, DC: US Holocaust Memorial Council.

Weil, S.E. 2002. *Are You Really Worth What You Cost, or Just Merely Worthwhile? And Who Gets to Say? A Speech delivered to the Assembly 2002: Asking the Right Questions*. San Diego: Museum Trustee Association in collaboration with the Getty Leadership Institute.

Weil, S.E. 2003. Beyond Big and Awesome: Outcome Based Evaluation. *Museum News*, November/December, 40–45, 52–3.

Weinberg, M.L. and Lewis, M.S. 2009. The public value approach to strategic management. *Museum Management and Curatorship*, 24(3), 253–69.

Wilkinson, H. 2008. Conceptualizing Impact: Museums, Government and Value – Irreconcilable Differences? *Cultural Trends*, 17(4), 335–9.

Williams, I. and Shearer, H. 2011. Appraising Public Value: Past, Present and Future. *Public Administration*, 89(4), 1367–84.

Wittlin, A.S. 1970. *Museums: In Search of a Usable Future*. Cambridge, MA: MIT Press.

Yocco, V.S., Heimlich, J.E., Meyer, E. and Edwards, P. 2009. Measuring Public Value: An Instrument and an Art Museum Case Study. *Visitors Studies*, 12(2), 152–63.

B

Case Studies:
Implementing
Public Value

5 *Planning for Impact:*
A Case Study

MIKE HOULIHAN

Introduction

The Museum of New Zealand Te Papa Tongarewa[1] has been phenomenally successful since it opened in 1998. It redefined the visitor's experience of museums; has become an international benchmark for sharing authority and reconnecting cultures with their treasures; has enjoyed exceptionally high levels of visitation, with half of its annual visitors arriving from overseas; and run a successful international and domestic touring exhibitions programme. It also generates more than half of its annual income from commercial, fundraising and other business activities.

However, by 2009, the museum recognized that it needed to re-examine its direction. Accelerating changes in society, technology and the economic landscape created the risk of leaving Te Papa outpaced and outmoded. These demographic, lifestyle, museological and economic changes represented both a challenge and opportunity for the museum. To conduct its work effectively, it needed to understand fully the efficacy of its public value (Moore 1995). Equally, the economic imperatives obliged it to make choices around how it functioned, where it should focus its energies, staff and financial resources. Finally, its processes needed to recognize that authority for many of its activities rested amongst a diversity of stakeholders and that seeking out this endorsement underpinned the legitimacy of future actions.

This chapter explores, from an unashamedly managerial viewpoint, the steps that Te Papa's *Envisioning the Future* project has taken in planning for the total refocusing of the institution over its next 10–15 years. The three parallel and complementary streams of *Envisioning* work were, first, *identifying public benefit* through intended impact upon the nation; second, *building capability and capacity* to realize those ambitions; and finally in *seeking and sharing authority* across a variety of communities of interest.

---

1   Te Papa is New Zealand's national museum, being formed from the merging of the National Museum and the National Art Gallery in 1992. The collections span Art, History, Pacific, Māori and Natural Environment. Since Te Papa opened, 20 million people have visited. Its narrative-based, interdisciplinary and interactive approaches have enabled it to build an international reputation for being bicultural, scholarly, innovative and fun.

Identifying Public Benefit

GETTING THE VISION

Envisioning the Future began with two months of workshops designed to reflect upon Te Papa's institutional journey so far. Although this work was centred upon re-connection with the values and the organizational behaviours that had shaped that story (see below) it also tackled the articulation of a vision for the future. The product was to be a forum for change in Aotearoa New Zealand through *changing hearts; changing minds; changing lives*. In *changing hearts* we provide experiences and encounters that are relevant, satisfying, emotional and evoke a response. In *changing minds* we provide experiences that provoke thought, reflection and debate, and facilitate social interaction. In *changing lives* we provide experiences that improve the quality of life of individuals and communities, and extend the impact of a visit beyond the museum's doors.

This aspiration is not about social engineering, it is about public value. Through a combination of immersive approaches and different perspectives, the museum actively plans to enable people to form ideas about their world, so that they can make decisions from an informed position. All experiences at Te Papa would engage and inspire people, and help them to learn how they can have a positive impact.

On the face of it, this is a simple direction. But for Te Papa, it is a brave and difficult step. It meant that the *Envisioning the Future* process had to be a root and branch exercise that defined how we would impact upon the nation, as well as those changes needed in our own behaviour and systems to build the capability that would deliver our new direction. It has taught us that building programmes around issues of social engagement for impact requires a comprehensive assembly of the intellectual, cultural (both external and internal), financial and managerial.

ENVIRONMENTAL SCANNING

Constantly informing decision-making throughout the *Envisioning the Future* process was a flow of evidential data about the changing national and international environment; culturally, demographically, socially, technologically and economically.

First amongst these changes was a range of emerging demographic trends that would clearly influence the composition of Te Papa's audiences into the next generation. In summary, more New Zealanders were living in the north of the country; more were living overseas; and there was greater cultural and household diversity, with particular growth in Asian, Māori and Pacific populations.

Second, these significant demographic trends converged with a series of lifestyle changes that strongly affected the leisure behaviour and choices of New Zealanders. Some examples included the continued rise of the Internet as an information, entertainment and socializing device and the accompanying rise of mobile and personal technologies; the movement of environmental conservation from scientific idea to mainstream household behaviour; a surge of in-home entertainment technologies; and greater competition for leisure time, placing pressure on the cultural sector.

Third, at a museological level, it was recognized that museums, internationally, were at a pivotal moment in their own story. Ownership in terms of museum purpose, gallery spaces, presentations and, most importantly, collections had become one of the most contentious issues in museums. This debate focused not only on the ways in which museums re-connected communities, intellectually, spiritually and physically, to their collections, but also raised fundamental questions around where authority resided and how legitimacy was determined. Obvious examples of the latter were the Museum of the American Indian in Washington, Te Papa and the Australian Museum in Sydney. All places where it had been recognized that First Nations, Māori, aboriginal peoples and ethnic communities should exercise their authority and rights around the authoring and voicing of meanings about their own cultural artefacts and their pasts.

Te Papa, through its approach to biculturalism, had been, and continues to be, a catalyst for promoting this redefinition of the museum, by its users, as community property, a social space and a site for contemporary cultural development, dialogue and representation. However, the new demographic data told the museum that it needed a broader horizon, one that placed biculturalism within the context of an increasingly plural society.

Finally, the museum was by no means immune from the global recession and the severe pressure that this was placing on both public sector finances and personal pockets. For the foreseeable future, it was clear that in terms of government support it would be expected to do more with less. At the same time, there was an expectation that front-line public services would be maintained with a sharper focus on delivering better outcomes for the public through creative and innovative programmes. The winning formula was deceptively simple; reduce costs and overheads, increase revenues and, through greater efficiency, produce more.

The single, largest piece of environmental scanning work was the commissioning of a National Audience Segmentation Study (NASS). Te Papa's original audience segmentation model had been developed in the mid-1990s and provided the basis for an audience-led approach to the development of visitor engagement. The new piece of research moved wider than just leisure to explore other motivators for museum visitation. The NASS tried to 'capture' New Zealanders' needs, attitudes and behaviours in four broad areas; leisure, learning styles, domestic tourism, and culture and heritage. The findings would be a cornerstone for the development of strategy by informing content development, interpretative and communication strategies, collection development, research priorities and marketing.

MAPPING THE VISION PRIORITIES

In developing a statement of the museum's public value and capability aspirations for the next 10 years, Te Papa used the Vision Map process (Kaplan and Norton 1996). This model has the advantage of providing an approach that views the institution through differing lenses. As a classic Balanced Scorecard Model, the Vision Map usually considers four perspectives on performance. For a museum, these would include its obligations to its stakeholders as a first priority and the areas in which it needs to excel as a museum as the second. Third, it explores developing capability through investment in learning and growth and, finally, looks to where it is going to find the necessary financial and other resources to make that investment. The methodology has the advantage of taking an organization straight into the identification of its strategic priorities over a five-year period. It also confronts, early on, some of the classic, competing tensions within a museum, for example between curatorial, educational and the commercial. Finally, it

Table 5.1   Envisioning the future – strategic priorities

Perspectives	Impact on the nation – strategic priorities		
To reflect New Zealand's identities, past, present and future, both nationally and internationally, Te Papa will prioritize the following ...	**Accessing all areas** Te Papa will share its collections, skills and knowledge with the diverse communities across Aotearoa New Zealand and overseas.	**Being a forum for the future** As a cultural and intellectual leader, Te Papa will signpost pathways to the future by initiating, hosting and engaging in debates that explore a wide range of contemporary issues.	**Housing the treasures** Taonga (treasures) within the guardianship of Te Papa will be at the heart of the museum's activities.
To preserve taonga (treasures), and nurture exploration, curiosity and debate, Te Papa will prioritize the following ...	**Saving the planet** Te Papa will engage and excite by conducting leading edge research and by communicating and modelling environmentally responsible practices that are smart, accessible and inspiring.	**Connecting with people** Te Papa will make learning an engaging and entertaining experience. Te Papa will set the highest possible standards for an integrated and welcoming experience.	**Sharing authority** Te Papa will share decision-making with iwi (tribes), communities and individuals with respect to managing and understanding their taonga (treasures).
To invest, learn and empower, Te Papa will prioritize the following ...	**Going digital** Te Papa will use communication technologies to achieve its strategic priorities.	**Keeping fit** Te Papa will recognize that every experience is an opportunity for shared learning and that its future depends on the continuous development of its staff.	**Staying in touch** Te Papa will be aware that communication is two-way, and built on trust and transparency.
To be a successful business, Te Papa will prioritize the following ...	**Getting down to business** Te Papa will be commercially successful, entrepreneurial by nature, and disciplined with its business processes.	**Telling our story** Te Papa will be a persuasive and inspiring advocate on its own behalf and that of the museum, gallery and heritage sector.	**Building sustainable leadership** Te Papa will be proactive, flexible and nimble in its systems, processes and decision-making.

Source: Te Papa Tongarewa/The National Museum of New Zealand.

presents an easy-to-manage performance framework that, through indicators, measures and targets, can be developed alongside the establishment of strategies, programme objectives and initiatives.

It is important to ensure that the perspectives accurately reflect the institution's business model and direction. Normally, a museum will put the customer perspective at the top of the map and the financial perspective at the bottom. This reflects the logic that ultimate success is judged by the delivery of services to the people or the nation; and resources are raised to enable the organization to deliver to its stakeholders. The ordering of the perspectives should tell the strategic story of the institution. Reading the perspectives from top to bottom should explain *how* the museum will achieve its strategy in terms of describing its public benefits, the special way in which it delivers them, where it needs to invest and where the resources will be found. Going from bottom to top will explain *why* those strategic priorities have been chosen on the basis of developing resources to invest in improving delivery of the public benefit.

In developing the Vision Map, a number of workshops were held for staff with individual sessions for the executive leadership team and the Board. Even though the process is designed to provide the framework of a strategic plan, the 12 key headings that emerged (see Table 5.1) identified clear priorities for the future. They had both an external and internal focus. Whilst defining, at high level, how we planned to have an impact on the nation, they also identified areas of challenge around our own capability that would have to be addressed in order to deliver on our vision.

Strategic Priorities: Changing Hearts; Changing Minds; Changing Lives

Te Papa's vision for the future is *changing hearts; changing minds; changing lives*. The museum's role is to act as a forum for change in Aotearoa New Zealand. It is to help people form ideas about the world, through experiencing and sharing different perspectives, so that they can take action from an informed position.

At the heart of Te Papa's vision and long-term strategy is its philosophy of learning. The aim is that all experiences in Te Papa engage and inspire people, and help them to learn how they can have a positive impact on Aotearoa New Zealand and the world. The Vision Map sets out the museum's priorities, many of which are new. These priorities present the greatest opportunity for effecting change. The Vision Map also identifies how Te Papa itself will develop and change in order to achieve its vision.

In developing the vision and long-term strategy, Te Papa recognizes that it is operating in a dynamic and diverse country. All Te Papa's activities are informed by an awareness of the value and significance of Tangata Whenua (original people of the land) and all other peoples who have made Aotearoa New Zealand home.

DEVELOPING PROGRAMMES AND OBJECTIVES FOR PUBLIC GOOD

The next step was to develop a series of programmes and their associated objectives flowing from the strategic priorities of the Vision Map and the Key Performance Indicators (see below), which defined how success would look if the priorities were being achieved. Some 50 objectives, spanning public good and capability, were developed around the 12 strategic priorities. For the purposes of Public Good, these were then grouped into three Programmes of Activity, articulating Te Papa's new value propositions. The Programmes were:

1. *The Museum of Living Cultures*: reflecting and investigating our broadest cultural diversity and enabling communities, through the philosophy of Mana Taonga.
2. *Te Papa to Aotearoa New Zealand and the World*: taking New Zealand to the nation and the world; bringing the world to New Zealand.

3. *The Museum for the Future*: responding speedily, building the collections and developing the visitor experience to empower people to have a positive impact on the future.

A Director-level member of the Leadership Team provided governance to each Programme in the form of sponsorship, support and facilitation as we moved into the next level of iteration, the development of initiatives that would realize the Programmes.

DEVELOPING INITIATIVES

With the 55 Programme Objectives developed, the next step was to create performance measures for each objective as well as Initiatives that would form the activity plan for their implementation. Initiatives were defined as an activity or work task that is action oriented. It could be an activity that we were not currently doing; an adaptation of something that was already underway; it could be more of something that we were doing. Clearly, if a current activity didn't feature in the schedule of Initiatives the implication was that it should stop.

The exercise was another opportunity for distributing the leadership across the organization. Fifty-five Programme Objective Champions, reflecting Public Good and Capability development were drawn from amongst Tiers 3 & 4 staff (those with a middle-management responsibility) on the basis of their managerial skills, existing roles and individual expertise. The exercise was undertaken over an intensive period of four weeks from the initial briefing. Programme Objective Champions were tasked with creating and convening the teams that would enable them to develop their initiatives. It produced almost 150 initiatives that formed the basis for annual business plans and the museum's three-year strategic plan.

The statement of each initiative was worked into a standard template that called for 150–250 words of description and a clear cross-reference as to how it linked to the vision and the strategic priorities. Champions and their teams were also asked to describe how success would be measured. At a more mundane level, the template also explored timetabling, indicative costs, potential barriers to success and key personnel. For most staff, the Initiatives are the day-to-day level of engagement and activity where personal work plans and targets are articulated. The initiatives completed the final link in the chain that had begun with the Strategic Priorities of the Vision Map.

BUILDING CAPABILITY AND CAPACITY

Re-connecting with the values

Early interviews across the staff indicated that the clear values which had informed the early development of Te Papa had, over the last 14 years, become less visible in the organization and were, arguably, no longer a touchstone for 'how we do things around here'. On the one hand, individual team members were strongly supportive of one another but this did not always extend outside of that group to other crews. A common complaint was that getting things done outside of the team depended upon personal relationships rather than an integrated and interdisciplinary understanding of the job that needed to be done. As a result, silo working and patch protection was regarded as an acceptable, or certainly inevitable, way of working.

Staff were invited to take part in a series of workshops during October and November 2010. Each of the six workshops followed the same pattern in order to explore whether there was a convergence of underlying, shared beliefs and values within the museum that determined its organizational behaviour. Drawing upon Logan et al. (2008), the participants were guided through a series of questions specifically designed to unlock these underlying principles. At the end of the initial series of workshops, two more sessions sifted and refined the findings in order to encapsulate the core ideas. These showed a remarkable degree of convergence, with staff being invited to input further commentary on the intranet.

The agreed statement of values emerged in January 2011. Five values had been identified and articulated, bilingually, as:

- Hiranga | Excellence
- Mātauranga | Knowledge and learning
- Kaitiakitanga | Guardianship of the taonga or treasures
- Manaakitanga | Responsibility and caring towards our communities
- Whanaungatanga | Importance of relationships and caring for each other.

A set of behavioural principles were then developed, first, from an analysis of the inputs received from staff during the development of the values statement; second, core elements of the museum's existing Code of Professional Conduct; and third, the standards of integrity and conduct for the state sector. This was done for each of the values. The behavioural principles encompass the essence of the value statement, and provide a standard description of the behavioural expectations of each of the values. Also included is a quotation from a staff member on how living this value may contribute to Te Papa's future success. So, for example: Mātauranga | Knowledge and learning:

- We will actively promote Te Papa as a place of learning, for ourselves and our community, and strive to share our knowledge in open and engaging ways.
- We will encourage debate and acknowledge that we can learn from others.
- We will maintain strict integrity with regard to Te Papa's records, policies and information, neither withholding nor sharing information inappropriately.
- 'If we want to be sure that Te Papa Tongarewa is respected for its scholarship, we must look for opportunities to learn from others, and share what we know in a responsible, honest and open way.'

The next stage was to start a deeper process of bringing the values to life and integrating them into everyday work practice. The programme of *Embedding the Values* included a number of actions and initiatives such as Senior Leader Values Workshops and Senior Leader and Manager Facilitation Skills Workshops. The latter were specifically aimed at developing facilitation, coaching and leading-learning capabilities. These enabled managers, cascade style, to go on and facilitate staff sessions, working in groups of six with up to 50 staff. Other developments included Staff Values Workshops; awards; and the development of Senior Leader, Manager and Staff Behavioural Competencies; Action Learning Groups and Values Action Planning to explore how the values could be applied in day-to-day working situations.

This is not a time-limited piece of work. It continues today, driving further development around leadership, with values-based competencies forming a key component, alongside more conventional skills-linked criteria, in underpinning individual performance assessment.

DEVELOPING A PHILOSOPHICAL BASELINE

The work and discussion that had centred upon the development of the *values* highlighted the need to articulate three foundation philosophies as we moved into the development of the *vision*. These were identified as Mana Taonga; Te Papa's Museology; and Learning.

Mana Taonga

Mana Taonga captures the relationship between people, taonga (treasures) and ancestral narratives. It enables Te Papa to design and disseminate models of collaboration and co-creation that share authority and control with iwi (tribes), whilst embracing the changing demographics of Aotearoa New Zealand.

Since its inception, Te Papa has acknowledged the principle of Mana Taonga whereby individuals and communities that have a whakapapa (ancestral narrative line) relationship to taonga (treasures) in the museum's care have a right to determine how those taonga are presented, interpreted and managed. These rights of ownership are derived through a whakapapa or ancestral narrative that connects the taonga to their people through the original creator of specific taonga, the ancestors after whom the taonga may be named and the iwi (tribe) to whom the taonga is an heirloom. These are seen as rights of ownership; rights not always based on property law but rather of spiritual and cultural ownership. These rights confer on those communities the mana or pre-eminence in caring for their

Figure 5.1   The Marae

Source: Te Papa Tongarewa/National Museum of New Zealand.

taonga, to speak for them and to determine their use or uses by the museum. This right extends into Te Papa where the iwi (tribe) defines how their taonga should be cared for and managed in accordance with their own tikanga or customs.

However, in an increasingly plural society, it had become apparent that Te Papa needed to develop and disseminate new models for collaboration and co-creation that built on the achievements of the past. The Mana Taonga philosophy incorporates this approach at an institutional level.

Te Papa's museology

Closely allied to the task of expanding and redefining the philosophy of Mana Taonga was the implications of such work for Te Papa's museological approach. In particular, the increasing demand to share authority and re-connect with communities involved sharing decision-making with iwi (tribes), communities and individuals with respect to managing and understanding their taonga (treasures). This extended to working alongside communities to help both them and the museum in shaping and presenting their views and narratives around their collections. At the core of this process is the development and sustenance of relationships that recognize community ownership of collections. For any museum of the nation, its authority in the future will be founded upon the authority of its communities and the depth of its relationship with those authorities.

Issues of cultural entitlement, identity, social memory and cultural re-connection are posing some of the most important ethical and museological challenges to be faced by museums. If national museums, however the latter is defined, are really going to be about building identity, then a new museological approach is essential. Such a new museology places living culture at its core and the museum sees itself as part of that organism. Te Papa's philosophy seeks to de-colonize its museology from the Western constructs of preservation and authority by recognizing the contradictions in such an approach as well as the barriers it creates to building identity through the tasks of re-connecting with cultures and the sharing of authority, as described under Mana Taonga.

Both within the conventional museum building and in the new museum space of the community itself, there will be opportunities for dialogue between people and communities, as collections provide a gateway to understanding how other people live and uniquely view their world. The concept and reality of cultural re-connection, which can literally mean touching the taonga, may become a higher priority than preservation, because of the cultural benefits and powerful community reactions that it brings. For Te Papa the collection is perceived as a breathing part of a living culture. Museums cannot constrain living cultures in drawers; opening and closing their minds and our visibility to them as it suits.

The learning organization

Te Papa also recognized that as an organization it had a lot to learn. Most conceptualizations of the 'learning organization' seem to work on the assumption that 'learning is valuable, continuous, and most effective when shared and that every experience is an opportunity to learn' (Kerka 1995).

The development of a 'learning organization' can provide benefits at three levels. Organizationally, the benefits are in relation to being equipped to adapt to an ever-changing environment. For the staff, there are benefits in terms of Continuing Professional Development (CPD) and improved knowledge and skills. To the public, the 'learning organization' should provide greater responsiveness to needs and an improved ability to meet these needs. Overall, the outputs should include more effective identification of problems rather than symptoms, wasting less time on 'revolving door' problems that just keep coming back, increasing the choice of strategies available for meeting problems and shifting energy from individual and territorial struggles to agreed common objectives.

To provide a baseline assessment for future measurement, a *Te Papa Learning Survey* was undertaken to help determine how well it functioned as a learning organization and as a further feedback tool for the *Envisioning* project. The survey and questions contained within it were based on an assessment tool created by Harvard Business School (Garvin et al. 2008). The survey identified three components of a learning organization – a supportive learning environment, concrete learning processes and practices, and leadership that reinforces learning. There were 220 respondents giving a response percentage of 42.5 per cent. The results showed that whilst employees were given opportunities to pause and reflect, the environment did not support the development and implementation of the outcomes. In relation to concrete learning, there was evidence that essential information did not move efficiently enough to those who needed it. Finally, on leadership, the survey highlighted that dialogue and debate was not being used to encourage learning.

PERFORMANCE FRAMEWORK

An essential part of the *Envisioning* process was the development and incorporation of a Performance Management Framework as part of the detailed planning. The Performance Management Framework should give a balanced view of organizational performance ranging from the strategic headlines to the individual work plans of staff, allowing it to articulate and demonstrate success to funders, especially government, and other stakeholders. For the Board and managers, it is an essential tool to monitoring and intervening.

The 12 strategic priorities, from the Vision Map, each had a small number of *Key Performance Indicators (KPIs)* that focussed on the areas of Te Papa's performance that would be essential for future success. The time perspective was 3–5 years. These tended to be non-financial, but would have an important impact upon our work. At the Programme Objectives level *measures* were the next step in the performance chain, measuring success in key areas and processes that affect our visitors, our communities and other stakeholders as well as our business. At this level, ongoing financial performance and quantitative measures became more apparent, although staff were positively encouraged to develop qualitative measures of performance, especially in relation to education and learning. The last level in the Performance Framework was the *targets* linked to the initiatives; their time perspective was essentially the business year and would directly inform the individual work plans and outputs of staff (Figure 5.2).

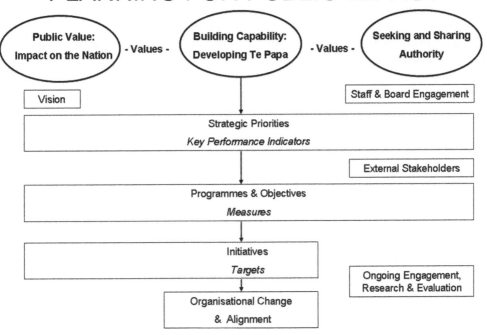

Figure 5.2   Planning for public impact
Source: Te Papa Tongarewa/The National Museum of New Zealand.

DEVELOPING PROGRAMMES, OBJECTIVES AND INITIATIVES FOR CAPABILITY

The Vision Map methodology, the development of Programmes and their associated Objectives and Initiatives, described above, also addressed the strategic approach to building capability and capacity. Six of the Vision Map priorities were concerned with the impact upon Te Papa as an organization. Three related and themed Programmes of activity were identified to deliver these six priorities:

- Learning: organizational transformation through learning.
- Building relationships: Te Papa takes its stakeholders, national and international relationships extremely seriously, and advocates its value confidently.
- Acting commercially: applying commercial thinking across the breadth of Te Papa's activities, but extending this to systems, processes and infrastructure in order to support effective delivery of the vision.

ORGANIZATIONAL CHANGE

The *Developing Te Papa* component of the Vision Map had indicated some key areas of focus. The development of the Programmes, their Objectives and the Initiatives, as well as the Performance Framework had created an action based approach to tackling the range of issues, which had emerged from staff, external consultation and the Learning

Survey. Second, it established clear criteria for organizational change that were based upon achieving public value and developing capability, rather than a redesign centred upon financial, functional or practice-based reconfiguration. Too often, organizational change is misunderstood as simply being about re-structuring. Instead it embraces a range of ways in which people work together and interact in an organizational context.

A range of issues emerged during the process, which the Programme Objectives, Initiatives and organizational change programme sought to address directly. For example:

Organizational culture

Relationships rather than roles emerged as a significant driver of personal and team-related engagement. Frequently, there was a lack of clear understanding of a team's key deliverables or core functions and its inter-relationship with and dependencies upon the work of others in different groups or professional practices. Establishing a physical working environment that was perceived as more creative and incorporating social spaces was recognized as important to developing these relationships. Having project team members located together was regarded as key to improving communication, as was an improved ability to work remotely.

We also knew that we needed to put systems in place to ensure that learning from previous projects was actively used to inform future work. But most significantly, it was recognized that there should be a recognition that a customer focus lay at the core of the Te Papa experience and all of its activities, be it front of house or back of house, commercial or non-commercial.

Processes

Awareness of working processes was regarded as undefined. Clarity of process was sometimes lacking in fostering clear goals, ownership, accountability and timely consultation with stakeholders. This was put down to two principal causes: communication and role definition. Communication and planning both needed to be addressed within teams and across the museum. This called for clearer steps as to who should be informed in the development of a concept/project, when they should be informed, and why they should be informed.

Decision-making

Clarity of decision-making sat alongside the issue of process in respect of who, why, where or when decisions were made. Decision-making processes also were regarded as overly bureaucratic with projects going through approval processes multiple times or with approved budgets frequently re-litigated. Ownership, authority and delegation in financial and operational decision-making was an issue for more junior staff. However, it was noted that worries around 'getting things wrong' sometimes prevented the appropriate staff from taking ownership of decisions.

Systems

Technology emerged as the single greatest capability gap. Operating systems and software were unable to integrate information. Consistency in capability and technical standards were identified as impeding the ability to deliver on ambitions.

Content

Content duplication was an unexpected theme that emerged; especially content that was being re-created across multiple projects and teams or not being re-used effectively. It was also apparent that there wasn't a system to share content efficiently across the organization.

Organizational structure

Any successful organizational structure allows the organization to achieve its goals efficiently and effectively. The product of effective alignment between strategy and structure can be enhanced performance. The *Envisioning* work at Te Papa had demonstrated the need to formalize boundaries across the organization, to delineate roles and accountability and to focus staff attention and activity on defined objectives.

Of course, it is a fundamental truism that no single structural model is more effective under all circumstances; and it will only be as effective as the people who inhabit it. However, the fit between organizational structure and strategy is critical and has to be organic, with structure evolving as the business and its operating environment change.

At the time of writing this chapter, Te Papa is engaged in developing a new structural approach, closer aligned to its strategies around delivering its public benefit over the next 10 years, whilst building the capability to do so. It will be based on a matrix that places three value propositions – Museum of Living Cultures, Museum for the Future, and Te Papa Enterprises – at the heart of its structural alignment. Thought leaders in Learning, Mana Taonga, Museology, Digital Futures and Leading Leaders will ensure innovative standards across the Value Propositions. The Offices of the Chief Executive and the Kaihautū (Māori Leader) will lead the ongoing task of planning and designing the future.

Seeking and Sharing Authority

Planning for public impact also requires a range of activities and understanding around the variety of 'authorities' who have a permissive role in ensuring the success of both a strategy and its implementation plan. These 'authorities' are wide and increasingly varied; they will include staff, governance members, government and/or funders, visitors and users, sponsors, and communities of interest (Figure 5.2).

During the *Envisioning the Future* development work, three consultation exercises were undertaken. This was in addition to ongoing relationship work with existing stakeholders, partners and, particularly, *iwi* (tribes). This work was built around presenting the proposed vision and long-term strategy to stakeholders and seeking their feedback. Stakeholders were selected on the basis of having corporate, strategic or governance relationships with Te Papa and the capacity to provide well-informed feedback. The selected stakeholders were invited to provide their views in a variety of ways including face-to-face meetings, email, post and online.

STAFF

Implicit in the methodology of the *Envisioning* process was a significant engagement with the views, ideas and creativity of staff. This work was seminal to the articulation of the values, the populating of the Vision Map and the creation of initiatives. Staff were also invited to share their ideas about how Te Papa could best organize itself for the future. Meetings and interviews were held with the Chief Executive and the Kaihautū (Māori Leader) over an intensive period of six weeks.

GOVERNMENT AND GOVERNANCE

The close financial links between national cultural institutions and government, as their principal funder, has led to a relationship of control based on a number of factors. These include accountability; compliance and measurement; and growing state influence over governance. Government, national or local, can therefore be a key determinant of an institutional plan.

National institutions, such as Te Papa, also carry statutory responsibilities which tend to channel them into certain obligatory and pragmatic solutions, for example centred upon the care, security and presentation of the nation's treasures. However, the wider a cultural institution reaches out to connect what it does to the people, the greater its role and impact within society. This can also present a channel of connectivity for government.

EXTERNAL STAKEHOLDERS

The engagement with external organizational and individuals stakeholders was conducted in two phases and focussed in particular upon the vision itself, the priorities emerging from the Vision Map and the proposed Programmes.

IWI (TRIBES)

Consultation with iwi focused upon the development of biculturalism in the future. There was both recognition of what had been achieved and a perception that momentum had been lost, with a concern that the building of Māori capability was no longer central to the museum's thinking. Organizationally, this meant that Te Papa must be prepared to take its external stakeholders with it to create advocates for Mana Taonga into the future. Second, the consultation identified an intellectual challenge to the vision in terms of developing a new English phraseology that would maintain Te Papa's bicultural intent and give centrality to Mana Taonga. The role of authority and how this is shared was closely linked to this debate.

OUTCOMES

The feedback was generally supportive of Te Papa's vision and long-term strategy. However, whilst stakeholders supported what was proposed, there were many comments which questioned whether Te Papa had the capacity to achieve the proposed vision and long-term strategies. Many of the suggestions provided by stakeholders therefore focused on *how* Te Papa could achieve the proposed vision and by noting *what* Te Papa needed to improve.

The key feedback issues which were raised around those priorities concerned with *Impact on the Nation* were primarily focused on Te Papa's purpose as a museum. Categories of commentary included the need for improved access and increased collaboration between stakeholders with Te Papa; whether Te Papa had the capacity to be an intellectual leader and how research could be developed; the need for improved understanding of taonga (treasures) and collection management and, finally, whether certain priorities such as Saving the Planet and Being a Forum for the Future were within Te Papa's mandate.

The consultation process around the priorities identified with *Developing Te Papa* highlighted issues such as the need for digital programmes to be integrated with the development of the programmes, the support for bilingualism, the requirement to be realistic around timetables and resources, the need for transparency in Te Papa's leadership and decision-making and the development of leadership skills at all levels within the organization.

All stakeholder comments and submissions across the consultation phases were assessed in order to assist the internal Vision Team in refining the proposed vision and programmes and to identify the aspects of the vision and programmes which required a response or clarification. Stakeholder responses also helped provide ideas for the development of more detailed initiatives.

Conclusion

Many museums are able to identify their undoubted strengths in offering public value. However, very few deliberately plan for capability and capacity around the delivery and impact of these value propositions. Instead, they falter around the need for a holistic and bringing together of the intellectual, financial and managerial. You can have all the principles absolutely right but a lack of recognition around capacity building and a plan for appropriate resource deployment too often leaves the strategic plan sitting on the shelf. So, planning for public impact is not just an exercise or an event, it is as much about taking your institution on a journey. A journey that will create a thinking organization; one that reflects, imagines, reasons, learns, narrates and, in so doing, does.

References

Garvin, D.A., Edmondson, A.C. and Gino, F. 2008. Is Yours a Learning Organization? *Harvard Business Review*, 86(3): 109–16, 134.

Kaplan, R.S. and Norton, D.P. 1996. *The Balanced Scorecard: Translating Strategy into Action*. Cambridge, MA: Harvard Business School Press.

Kerka, S. 1995. *The Learning Organisation: Myths and Realities*. Available at: http://www.cete.org/acve/docgen.asp?tbl=archive&ID=A028 [accessed April 2006].

Logan, D., King, J. and Fischer-Wright, H. 2008. *Tribal Leadership: Leveraging Natural Groups to Build a Thriving Organization*. New York: HarperCollins.

Moore, M. 1995. *Creating Public Value: Strategic Management in Government*. Cambridge, MA: Harvard University Press.

Moore, M. and Khagram, S. 2004. On Creating Public Value: What Business Might Learn from Government about Strategic Management. *Corporate Social Responsibility Initiative Working Paper No. 3*. Cambridge, MA: John F. Kennedy School of Government, Harvard University.

6 *Creating Public Value through Museum Education*

BEN GARCIA

Introduction

Mark Moore's public value model is closely aligned to the vision for the museum's role in society as promoted by museum educators since the early twentieth century.[1] For the last 40 years, museum educators have been among those at the forefront of advocacy for accessibility and shared authority in the museum. Many have applied the tenets of progressive education from the turn of the last century and of the co-intentional pedagogies of the 1960s to the realm of museum learning and as a result have created a discipline that is fundamentally interactive, transactional and therefore nuanced in its relationship to the question of authority. The degree to which museums have become creators of public value, 'pro-active shapers of the public sphere' (Benington and Moore 2011, 2), is in no small part due to the work of their educators. Because museum educators serve as intermediaries between the museum's collections and the public, they have a particular perspective on the societal impact of museums, the place of authority and the quality of relationships (or, to use the language of public value theory: 'interrelationships') that predicate museum experiences of value. Given this, museum educators are perfectly placed to work within a public value paradigm and have a particular responsibility to advocate for, and help move the museum towards, embracing public value as the primary product.

That Moore's theory of public value would be of particular relevance to educators makes perfect sense given that public value is created, according to John Benington (Benington and Moore 2011, 47), at the places 'where there is the most direct interaction between public service workers [in this case, museum staff] and users, citizens and communities'. Museum education has emerged, since the 1970s, as a discipline with a strong theoretical foundation, a growing literature and a plethora of scholarly training programmes in the United States and Britain (Schwarzer 2012; Ebitz 2007). For the

---

1 Early twentieth-century museum founders were committed to the democratization of culture such as former librarian John Cotton Dana (1856–1929) at the Newark Museum who encouraged museum leaders to reach out to a broader public and bring the museum from the 'splendid isolation of a distant park' to the communities that possess it both figuratively (through accessible interpretation) and literally (Dana 2004: 13–29), and former school teacher Phoebe Apperson Hearst (1842–1919) at the University of California's anthropology museum in San Francisco (now the Phoebe A. Hearst Museum of Anthropology in Berkeley) who wrote that her objective in founding the museum was 'the dissemination of knowledge among the many, not the pride of possession by the few' (Jacknis 2000: 62).

most part, however, scholars and practitioners in this field have addressed questions of pedagogy, visitor studies and socio-political context rather than advocacy. As this book seeks to illustrate, the public value model is powerful when applied to the museum sector broadly. Museum educators who seek to move their institutions towards engagement with the true needs of their community (however that may be defined) have in this public sector paradigm a model that shares the values of progressive, co-intentional and informal education. Embracing a public value framework will also serve educators when advocating for the value of museum learning with colleagues in the museum, members of the authorizing environment (such as departments of education, school systems and funding entities both public and private) and with the public.

    What Moore and the subsequent generation of public value theorists have provided to museum educators is the latest iteration of the argument for including the consumers of museum content in the process of producing that content. According to Moore and Benington (2011, 15), 'public value thinking and action includes the capacity to analyse and understand the interconnections, interdependencies and interactions ... between producers and users of service ... in new patterns of co-creation'. Moore's model advocates shared authority and access in education and culture (including museums) and was born of the spheres of governance and management in the context of the neo-liberalism of the early 1990s (Benington and Moore 2011, 3). It has some affinity with the social change movements of the 1960s and 1970s in its vision of a responsive system of governance that seeks to serve the true needs of its citizens by including them in programme design and decision-making. However the rhetoric is less charged than that of those earlier movements, and therefore more useful for museum educators who need to make a compelling case for the power of museum learning to benefit communities.

Museums, Public Value and Learning

Public value can draw upon the roles and responsibilities of governments to promote social justice, fairness and equity, access for all, and opportunities for participation in the public sphere; promoting community development and active engagement in public and political life through a wide range of community organizations; orchestrating the work of a wide group of partner organizations and stakeholders in the public, private, voluntary and informal community sector; acting as a catalyst for innovation and creative forms of engagement with political, civic and community networks; [and] protecting and promoting diversities of culture.

By replacing 'governments' with 'museums' in the quote above and 'public and political life' with 'cultural life', John Benington's (Benington and Moore 2011, 51) vision for the potential of Moore's public value model becomes a clear articulation of the role of museums at their most transformational. This public value model has been applied directly to the work of museums by a number of interested scholars including Lynn Dierking, Mary Ellen Munley and Carol Ann Scott who see in it a means to ensuring sustainability over time. Dierking (2010, 10–13) frames the issue as museums striving 'to achieve strategic impact *for and with* their communities rather than operational impact solely *for the institution*' and writes that at the baseline, public value is about museums connecting to 'the fabric and true needs of the communities in which they reside'. She suggests that rather than focus on how the museum will benefit or change from an undertaking, the most important question a museum needs to answer when 'planning strategically for public value' is: 'How will my community be different in positive and recognized ways because the museum exists and undertook this effort?'. Munley (2010, 30) argues that measuring and aggregating individual, positive visitor outcomes does not add up to public value, but rather that museums need to add 'attention to the public good defined broadly to the already established attention to outcomes for individuals'. Scott (2010, 36) writes about the roles that the public can occupy in the public value model, those of recipient (end-users of value created on their behalf), informant (providers of needed intelligence to the museum that enables it to better provide value) and producer (partners with the museum in identifying value and identifying common goals). While acknowledging that public value can be generated by institutions that relate to their public in any of the three roles, Scott (2010, 41) suggests that those institutions that engage with the public as producers will be best equipped to embody public value.

Museums have traditionally treated the public as recipients and often as respondents – through evaluation and interactive exhibitions and programmes. The producer (or co-producer) role for the public is the least comfortable for museums to embrace across their administrative, operational and public functions as it requires the museum to cede authority and to bring in another entity with the ability to weigh in on (and alter) decisions. However in the educational realm of museums, co-production has been around at least since 1916 in Boston when visitors were asked at the beginning of a gallery tour to choose the works that would be included (Kai-Kee 2011, 21) and then more regularly after the 1960s and 1970s when museum education was influenced by the co-intentional pedagogies of education theorists such as Paulo Freire and Loris Malaguzzi who proposed models of classroom teaching based upon shared decision-making between teachers and students (Garcia 2012).

What a public value framework for museum education offers now that is different from what theorists in the past have offered is 'sensitivity to the many dimensions of learning, including its informal, non-formal and tacit aspects' (Fryer 2011, 243). A public value approach in education is powerful in part because it ensures that individuals in communities most likely to be excluded from the social benefits of success will have a voice through a framework that provides multiple opportunities for recognizing and addressing systemic imbalances or inequalities (Benington and Moore 2011, 14–16).

Public value concepts like the strategic triangle, the authorizing environment and the public value chain (described elsewhere in this book) were developed to address the polycentric and multidimensional nature of governance (Benington and Moore 2011, 15). The place of the museum in society is, albeit on a significantly smaller scale, similarly complex. Museum educators, in their position as intermediaries between the public and the museum, navigate horizontally between multiple museum departments (such as curatorial, marketing, development, visitor services); vertically from funders of educational programmes (administration, boards of trustees, foundations and private donors) to implementers and participants in those programmes (front-line staff, visitors, communities); and diagonally across these networks. The characteristic of leadership in the public value model as articulated by Benington and Moore (2011, 6) is one of influence and persuasion rather than of formal authority. Thanks to decades of negotiating authority in precisely this manner with school systems, teachers, community-based entities, families and individual museum visitors, museum educators can find in the public value model (and particularly on the co-production relationship with the public) ways to reframe problems in their work more clearly so that they can act more effectively, transparently and intentionally (Benington and Moore 2011, 16).

The Challenge for Museum Educators

Over the past 40 years, educators have advocated for a place at the table within the museum and, despite occasional setbacks, museum directors and boards have largely been convinced that museum educators provide enough value to include them among senior staff and at the beginning of decision-making processes (albeit to different degrees in different countries and in different museum genres). The field of museum education is now facing a far greater challenge: how to secure a seat at the table of education policy-makers at the local, regional and national level for museums. Benington (Benington and Moore 2011, 47) writes about public education that:

> *The concept of public value highlights the importance of focusing on processes and outcomes ("what value is being added to the public sphere, by whom and how?") not just the inputs and outputs … Public value outcomes in education will take into account the cultivation of a life-long thirst for learning, questioning and reflection as well as … achievement.*

Museums and other institutions of informal learning play a role in cultivating a thirst for learning and in modelling educational experiences. Elliot Eisner wrote in 2002 that the culture of public schools in the United States is industrial, the values brittle, and the conception of what's important narrow. 'We pay practically no attention to the idea that engagement in school can and should provide intrinsic satisfactions, and we exacerbate the importance of extrinsic rewards by creating policies that encourage children to become point collectors'. 'Achievement', Eisner concluded, 'has triumphed over inquiry'. Despite many successful efforts on the part of formal educators and administrators to champion inquiry over point collecting, Eisner's assessment remains largely true a decade later. One of the most powerful arguments for the value of museums (and museum education) is that they are not tied to mandated educational outcomes as are institutions of formal learning. Museums (along with parks, libraries and other sites of informal learning) are places where intrinsically-motivated, self-directed and open-ended learning happens. Convincing the larger educational establishment of this is among the most crucial challenges facing museum educators today, and success in making this case can contribute greatly to the sustainability of museums as institutions of learning (and of value).

Benington (Benington and Moore 2011, 31) argues that public value can best be understood and achieved when two questions are addressed simultaneously: 'What does the public most value?' and 'What adds value to the public sphere?'. The first emphasizes 'dialogue and engagement with current users' while the second is focused on 'longer-term public interest and future generations'.

WHAT DOES THE PUBLIC MOST VALUE?

Museum educators engage with the public regularly through programmes and gallery interpretation and are often the advocates for a collaborative or co-productive relationship with the public (Scott 2010; Simon 2010). Although museum educators are well placed to answer Benington's question above, too often the evidence for their answer is not documented. Too much excellent work is still being done without being measured. In the United States, evaluation is required for museums seeking support from some governmental funding entities such as the National Science Foundation, but not from others such as the National Endowments for the Arts or Humanities. In the UK evaluation of museum education programmes is happening in part due to funding agencies such as the Museums, Libraries and Archives Council and the Department for Culture, Media and Sport. In both cases there are institutions taking advantage of the opportunity to better understand their value and evaluators doing significant work. However evaluation is too often motivated by a funding opportunity and not by a strategic desire to test the value of museum programmes against the public need (Pontin 2006).

Answering the question of what the public values in a manner that is credible with the authorizing environment (those public and private entities that determine the level of support afforded museums), operating environment (the museum's leadership and staff) and with the public requires a more rigorous approach to evaluation than currently is the norm. Evaluation can also help museum educators keep in alignment with the museum's overall public value approach. Nina Simon (2010, 274) describes a situation that occurs within 'some larger, more traditional institutions' where education staff members, 'hired in part for their ability to be responsive to and collaborate with community partners', become isolated in 'participatory ghettos'. Museum educators have in the public value model a useful framework for discussing the question of the museum's sustainability tied to value with their colleagues. Rigorous evaluation as an ongoing practice will provide museum education departments with a defensible answer to the question of what the public values.

WHAT ADDS VALUE TO THE PUBLIC SPHERE?

There are many kinds of value that museums add to the public sphere including social value, contemplative and connective value, spiritual value and civic value. One particularly productive way that museum education can contribute value to the long-term public interest, however, is in alignment with initiatives for developing twenty-first century skills. These initiatives, geared towards equipping youth to find professional success in the current century, have taken hold in governmental entities such as the Department for Education and Skills in Britain and the departments of Commerce, Labor and Education in the United States. It is a concept that has been championed in the private sector as well – notably by Cisco and by the Partnership for 21st Century Skills, a public/private consortium formed in 2002. Generally defined, these skills include: basic skills (literacy and numeracy), technical skills, critical thinking skills, communication skills, creative thinking skills, and the ability to self-manage (US Dept. of Commerce et al. 1999; Partnership for 21st Century Skills 2009; Fryer 2011). The Institute for Library and Museum Services (IMLS) has created a national initiative titled *Museums, Libraries and 21st Century Skills* and has been providing support to grantees in this category since 2009 (IMLS 2009a). Marsha Semmel (2010), Director of Strategic Partnerships at IMLS, suggests that museums will need to work in collaboration with a broader swath of 'learning institutions that can range from the school system to the university system to the chamber of commerce to social service organizations and to various types of businesses' and will need to focus on those twenty-first century skills that best fit with the museum's ability to make an impact: creativity, collaboration, communication and critical thinking (IMLS 2009b). In the twenty-first century skills paradigm proposed by IMLS, the education model in society is shifting from being institution-centred with formal degree attainment as the primary goal to being learner-centred, setting a premium on self-directed and lifelong knowledge with skills acquisition as the primary goal (IMLS 2009b). Museums, as places of informal, self-directed and lifelong learning, already fit the new paradigm better than many institutions of formal learning. Museum educators, framing and gearing their work towards concepts of public value and twenty-first century skills acquisition will find a new role for museum education beyond the currently accepted role of simply supporting formal educational outcomes. The twenty-first century skills framework provides a compelling rationale for museum educators who seek to shift the relationship with schools so that museum learning outcomes can co-exist with formal learning outcomes rather than be subsumed by them as has been the case since the advent of museum school and teacher programmes (Garcia 2012).

By regularly incorporating qualitative and quantitative evaluation and documentation of programming and by addressing the larger questions in national education policy, museum educators will be able to answer Benington's two questions authoritatively. The sustainability of any public entity rests on these questions and one advocacy challenge that faces museum educators is to make the case with museum leadership and with educational policy-makers for their own centrality to the museum's ability to effectively answer them.

Recipient, Informant, Producer: A Framework for Considering Public Value

One way of thinking about the relationship between the public and the museum that is of particular use to museum educators is through the roles assigned to members of the public in public value creation by Carol Scott (2010, 36–7). These roles: recipient (beneficiary), informant (respondent), and producer (creator) describe the visitor's agency, or, the relationship of the visitor (public) to the operating environment (museum). In Scott's model, all three roles are valid as long as the outcome of the engagement with the museum is the creation of public value, or in the case of museum learning, a beneficial educative experience.

The idea that visitors to a museum engage in different ways and have varied motivations is long-standing in the field of museum studies. Museum visitor motivation has been examined by experts such as Molly Hood (1983) and Bonnie Sachatello-Sawyer et al. (2002) among many others. More recently, audience research specialists Morris Hargreaves McIntyre identified eight audience types in a study for Tate: aficionados, actualizers, sensualists, researchers, self-improvers, social spacers, site seers and families (Meijer and Scott 2009); while John Falk (2009) proposed five visitor identities (addressing a more innate quality of the individual than motivation) that cover most museum visitors: explorer, facilitator, experience seeker, professional/hobbyist, recharger.

Additionally, multifaceted constructions of learning style, preference and ability like Howard Gardner's ubiquitous theory of multiple intelligences are widely accepted in museum education (Davis 1996). As a result of working in environments that have been constructed to elicit intellectual and affective responses and employing approaches to teaching and learning that are often imaginative, experiential or kinaesthetic (and based in tangible material or objects), museum educators have become some of the strongest advocates for a multiple intelligence model. Museum educators are already synthesizing and incorporating the public's multiple identities, motivations and intelligences as they deliver programmes and other educative experiences, Scott's model adds a needed dimension to their work because it looks not at the intrinsic qualities of the visitor (identity and motivation) but rather at the visitor's agency: the relationship of the visitor (public) to the operating environment (museum). It is this paradigm that enables the educator to construct (or co-construct) experiences of true value. By tuning visitors' intrinsic qualities to their agency, educators can create experiences of genuine value.

For the purposes of this chapter, I have adapted Scott's (2010) summary of the roles for the public in public value in Table 6.1 in order to focus on those roles in museums.

Table 6.1   Three roles for the public in public value-based museum learning

	Recipient	Informant	Producer
Definition	Recipient of museum's information/experience	Provider of information in response to museum prompt	Contributor to creation of shared experience
Role	Beneficiary	Respondent	Creator
Control of decisions	Museum	Museum	Museum and public

Source: Scott 2010.

RECIPIENT

Public value is created in some instances where members of the public are simply recipients of the museum's output: in the case of free museums, for example, or in a much larger subset of museums where some or all of the educational programming is offered free of charge. Generally, however, when public value is generated for the visitor-recipient, it will be in areas other than education such as exhibitions, performance programmes, or through the design of buildings or grounds. Providing a space for the consumption and contemplation of culture with no financial barrier to access is of value as cultural institutions are effective containers for social transformations of all kinds – and places where the kind of casual social interaction between strangers that are required for healthy communities occurs (Goldbard 2006; Putnam 2000). In educational programming, there is an entire category of content that is most effective (or valuable) when created by a single (or limited) vision and shared with visitors as recipients. This includes presentations by scientists, historians, authors or visiting artists. Engagement with the singular vision (of a visiting expert or artist) is essential for the education of the whole person. It can challenge and push a person's thinking about a particular issue, expand notions of intellectual and creative possibilities and model generative or reflective practices (Greene 2001). Educational programmes that present these kinds of perspectives to visitors are unquestionably of value.

However as Munley (2010) reminds us, public value creation is about an intentional process that the museum engages in with the community and not simply about individual experiences of value. In museums where the authorizing environment (museum leadership and funders) and the operational environment (in this case, educators) create programmes in a process that bypasses collaboration or co-creation with the public, public value as defined by Moore (1995) will rarely be created. In museum education particularly, the recipient model for the visitor, or learner, will not generally lead to educative experiences as described by John Dewey, Paulo Freire, Maxine Greene or any progressive educators of the past century. Freire, in *Pedagogy of the Oppressed* (2005, 72), called this the 'banking concept of education', describing a dynamic 'in which the students are the depositaries and the teacher is the depositor'. The visitor-recipient model is limited in museum education (and anathema to the development of twenty-first century skills) for the same reasons it was viewed by Freire as oppressive in formal education: it can reduce meaning to just one facet and minimize a learner's creative power.

INFORMANT

In the governmental sphere that gave birth to the public value paradigm, the informant or respondent role provides the authorizing and operational environments with information that allows them to better understand public needs and to predict future 'attitudes and expectations' (Scott 2010, 36). In museums, inviting visitors to participate in a respondent role, or creating generative experiences where visitors determine the outcome of an educational programme or exhibition element through participation, is probably the most common kind of public value work being done. Nina Simon, author of *The Participatory Museum*, cites many such examples and describes collaborative projects as 'institutionally driven' suggesting four main reasons that museums engage in them: 'to ensure the accuracy and authenticity of new exhibitions [or] programs', to test new programmes with intended users in order to improve the likelihood of their success, to provide opportunities for visitors to create their own content and to help visitors feel a sense of ownership for the museum's collections and programmes (Simon 2010, 231–2).

Public value is generated in the visitor-informant model of programme delivery over time as the museum learns from visitors what ideas, approaches or experiences meet their needs (and the needs of their community). At the Skirball Cultural Center in Los Angeles, for example, educational programmes for families and students are rooted in the notion of 'building a better world'. The centre offers visitors at the end of the gallery experience an opportunity to make a statement about how they will contribute in some concrete way to this goal. It then uses those statements to inform the choice of partner organizations that are incorporated into ongoing educational programmes for adults and children (Bernstein and Gittleman 2010). As the public responds to experiences like those at the Skirball and returns for more, the museum learns through a dialogical, if not co-productive, process how to create programmes of value.

Educators in traditional museums with histories of strong curatorial expertise can use the visitor-informant model to shift the institutional culture towards including community or visitor priorities across its functions as happened at the Dallas Museum of Art (DMA). A decade ago, the DMA found itself faced with a 'growing disconnect' with its surrounding communities (NEA 2011). The education department worked with the museum's leadership to launch an eight-year audience research project that changed the DMA's approach in all areas from being prescriptive to being collaborative. The museum embraced values of creativity and collaboration when engaging the public and their own staff through a *Framework for Engaging with Art* that became the guiding force for all the ways the museum works with the public (Pitman and Hirzy 2011). The research found that there were four categories that could be applied broadly to visitors (and potential visitors) in order to describe ways that they approached the museum's content. These categories were rooted in education theory and addressed the preferred learning modalities of the public when at the museum, dividing them up as observers, participants, independents and enthusiasts. By gearing all the efforts of the museum towards the documented learning needs of the public, the museum was able to garner the support of other community-based cultural entities (Pitman and Hirzy 2011, 128) and saw visitation double, according to its own website, with more than half participating in educational programmes (DMA 2011).

The problem of disconnection faced by Dallas a decade ago faces many traditional museums, large and small, today. One key to addressing it seems to lie in viewing visitors as members of categories that expand upon those that were applied in the 1960s–1990s (race, gender, sexual orientation and the like). As museums begin treating the public as observers (Dallas), social spacers (Tate) and rechargers (John Falk), they will begin to demonstrate the 'more sophisticated understanding of the complex relationships between culture, communication, learning and identity' that is required for connecting with the public in the current day (Hooper-Greenhill 2007, 189).

PRODUCER

Scott (2010, 37–9) writes that co-production 'is value-driven and built on the principal that those who are affected by a service are best placed to help design it'. The producer role is 'active and on-going' and 'based on principles of equity, a belief in the expertise of the public and a commitment to community involvement' on the part of the museum. Simon (2010, 263) uses the term 'co-creative' to describe this kind of role for the public and describes such projects as those that are not based solely on institutional goals but originated in partnership and take into account community and museum needs. John Alford (2011, 155) cites three reasons that recipients of government services would engage in co-production with government organizations. These are: intrinsic motivation (a 'sense of self-determination and competence'); a sense of confidence and autonomy; and sociality ('the inherent benefits of associating with others'). In museum education these same three motivators are known to play a role in successful, constructivist or co-intentional educational experiences (Csikszentmihalyi and Hermanson 1995; Falk and Dierking 2000). This may account in part for why co-productive approaches to developing content are happening in museum education departments even when it is not the case across the museum's other functions (Simon 2010, 274).

Scott (2010, 39) makes the point that the co-production approach is 'more likely to occur in museums where there is a limit to curatorial expertise and the ... perspectives or experiences of the public are required to complete the narrative' including social history and culturally specific museums. Indeed this bears out at museums like the National Museum of Mexican Art (NMMA) and the 'Imiloa Astronomy Center of Hawaii ('Imiloa).

The NMMA was founded by a small group of educators in 1987 and is now the largest museum of Latino arts in the United States. The museum employs a co-production model in determining where to put its resources through ongoing outreach to formal educators and administrators and the hosting of local school events at the museum. Programmes include parental education in English language and field trips for families to other Chicago cultural organizations in order to assist 'the integration of immigrant or first generation families into the larger society' (Villafranca-Guzmán and Tortolero 2010, 86). The museum's embracing of community-generated priorities has resulted in educational programmes related to issues of health (such as childhood obesity, blood pressure, diabetes, HIV and asthma), and political issues of concern to the community including immigration law. While these kinds of programmes might represent mission drift for some art museums, at the NMMA the mission is predicated upon the notion that 'the Museum serves its community because it IS the community' (Villafranca-Guzmán and Tortolero 2010, 91).

'Imiloa was developed in the 1990s by educators, scientists and community leaders who sought to create a science centre focused on the connections between traditional Hawaiian culture and the astronomical research conducted at the observatories on the sacred summit of Maunakea, Hawaii's highest peak ('Imiloa 2009a). The centre addresses historic exploration and settlement of the Pacific Ocean by seafaring navigators from the Pacific Islands and contemporary explorations of the same. 'Imiloa works alongside other Hawaiian organizations dedicated to reviving traditional voyaging and language including the use of Hawaiian star names and the four star families of traditional Hawaiian astronomy ('Imiloa 2009b). The number of native speakers in the state has risen from about 1,500 in the 1980s to about 10,000 today thanks to the work of several Hawaiian educational and cultural entities including 'Imiloa where bilingual exhibits, staff and educational programmes make it 'a place where the Hawaiian language can live and be spoken' ('Imiloa 2009c). One of the reasons cited by Simon (2010, 263) for museums to engage in co-creation is 'to give voice and be responsive to the needs and interests of local community members'. At 'Imiloa (and at the NMMA) what that means, in part, is giving voice to a bilingual community.

The visitor-producer role as enacted by the NMMA and 'Imiloa is most closely aligned with the co-creational aspects of public value creation central to Moore's (1995) premise. A co-productive approach to developing the museum is time-consuming and requires considerable social skills on the part of all museum staff (not just those that traditionally work with the public). It has been successful at the NMMA and 'Imiloa in part because both entities were started by educators who were working to redress cultural deficits in their communities and developed structures that allowed for the necessary processes and time.

Conclusion

What museums gain by embracing a public value paradigm is a clear understanding of their reason for being; one that is shared by the public and therefore easily articulated (in terms of public good) to the cultural and educational establishments and the museum's supporters both public and private. Museum educators are charged with a dual responsibility: to contribute to the well-being of the museum and of the public. They serve as advocates for the museum's collections, ideas and approaches with the public and for the public's interests and agency with the museum. Museum education occurs at the meeting places of museum and public and therefore has a positional role in public value generation. Because these meeting places are often at the edges of the museum, museum educators risk becoming peripheral unless they also regularly advocate for the value of museum education with their museum colleagues and leadership and with the larger authorizing environment.

As educators look to their role in advocating for a vision of the future of museums, they would do well to heed Eilean Hooper-Greenhill's counsel that 'new ways of articulating the educational values of museums are needed that acknowledge the shifts and continuities that characterize post-modernity' (2007, 201). A public value framework can be one of these 'new ways' in part because it is so closely related to a long-held view of value related to public access in museum education. Mark Moore's model combined with an approach to education that is multifaceted, holistic and ongoing (such as that offered by the twenty-first century skills paradigm) provides a clear and defensible platform for such advocacy.

References

Alford, J. 2011. Public Value from Co-production by Clients, in *Public Value Theory & Practice*, edited by J. Benington and M.H. Moore. Houndmills: Palgrave Macmillan, 144–57.

Benington, J. and Moore, M.H. 2011. Public Value in Complex and Changing Times, in *Public Value Theory & Practice*, edited by J. Benington and M.H. Moore. Houndmills: Palgrave Macmillan, 1–30.

Bernstein, S. and Gittleman, M. 2010. The Value of Risk: Noah's Ark at the Skirball. *Journal of Museum Education*, 35(1), 43–58.

Csikszentmihalyi, M. and Hermanson, K. 1995. Intrinsic Motivation in Museums: Why Does One Want to Learn?, in *Public Institutions for Personal Learning: Establishing a Research Agenda*, edited by J.H. Falk and L.D. Dierking. Washington, DC: American Association of Museums, 66–77.

Dallas Museum of Art (DMA). 2011. [Online]. Available at: http://www.dm-art.org/PressRoom/dma_384057 [accessed 20 May 2012].

Dana, J.C. 2004. The Gloom of the Museum, in *Reinventing the Museum, Historical and Contemporary Perspectives on the Paradigm Shift*, edited by G. Anderson. Lanham: Alta Mira Press, 13–29.

Davis, J. 1996. *The MUSE Book*. Cambridge: Project Zero Publications.

Dierking, L. 2010. Being of Value: Intentionally Fostering and Documenting Public Value. *Journal of Museum Education*, 35(1), 9–20.

Ebitz, D. 2007. Transacting Theories for Art Museum Education, in *From Periphery to Center*, edited by P. Villeneuve. Reston: National Art Education Association, 21–30.

Eisner, E. 2002. *What Can Education Learn from the Arts about the Practice of Education?* [Online]. Available at: http://www.infed.org/biblio/eisner_arts_and_the_practice_of_education.htm [accessed 12 March 2012].

Falk, J.H. 2009. *Identity and the Museum Visitor Experience*. Walnut Creek: Left Coast Press.

Falk, J.H. and Dierking, L. 2000. *Learning from Museums*. Walnut Creek: Alta Mira Press.

Freire, P. 2005. *Pedagogy of the Oppressed*. New York: Continuum.

Fryer, B. 2011. Learning, Social Inequality and Risk: A Suitable Case for Public Value?, in *Public Value Theory & Practice*, edited by J. Benington and M.H. Moore. Houndmills: Palgrave Macmillan, 225–43.

Garcia, B. 2012. What We Do Best: Making the Case for Museum Learning in its Own Right. *Journal of Museum Education*, 37(2), 47–55.

Greene, M. 2001. *Variation on a Blue Guitar: The Lincoln Center Institute Lectures on Aesthetic Education*. New York: Teachers College Press, 5–6.

Goldbard, A. 2006. *New Creative Community: The Art of Cultural Development*. Oakland: New Village Press.

Hood, M. 1983. Staying Away: Why People Choose not to Visit Museums. *Museum News*, 61(4), 50–57.

Hooper-Greenhill, E. 2007. *Museums and Education: Purpose, Pedagogy, Performance*. Abingdon: Routledge.

'Imiloa. 2009a. *About Us: Mission and History*. [Online]. Available at: http://www.imiloahawaii.org/105/our-history [accessed 12 March 2012].

'Imiloa. 2009b. *'Imi Na'auao*. [Online]. Available at: http://www.imiloahawaii.org/134/-imi-na-auao [accessed 12 March 2012].

'Imiloa. 2009c. *Explore: Hawai'i's Language Today*. [Online]. Available at: http://www.imiloahawaii.org/82/hawaii-s-language-today [accessed 12 March 2012].

Institute for Museum and Library Services (IMLS). 2009a. *21st Century Skills*. [Online]. Available at: http://www.imls.gov/about/21stcskills.aspx [accessed 12 March 2012].

Institute for Museum and Library Services (IMLS). 2009b. *Museums, Libraries and 21st Century Skills*. [Online]. Available at: http://www.imls.gov/assets/1/AssetManager/21stCenturySkills.pdf [accessed 12 March 2012].

Jacknis, I. 2000. A Museum Prehistory: Phoebe Hearst and the Founding of the Museum of Anthropology, 1891–1901. *Chronicle of the University of California*, 4, 47–78.

Kai-Kee, E. 2011. A Brief History of Teaching in the Art Museum, in *Teaching in the Art Museum*, edited by R. Burnham and E. Kai-Kee. Los Angeles: Getty Publications, 19–58.

Meijer, R. and Scott, M. 2009. *Tools to Understand: An Evaluation of the Interpretation Material used in Tate Modern's Rothko Exhibition*. [Online]. Available at: http://www.tate.org.uk/research/tateresearch/tatepapers/09spring/meijer-scott.shtm [accessed 12 March 2012].

Moore, M.H. 1995. *Creating Public Value*. Cambridge, MA: Harvard University Press.

Munley, M.E. 2010. Raising the Bar: Aiming for Public Value. *Journal of Museum Education*, 35(1), 21–32.

National Endowment for the Arts (NEA). 2011. *In Dallas, Igniting the Power of Art*. [Online]. Available at: http://www.arts.gov/artworks/?p=5333 [accessed 20 May 2012].

Partnership for 21st Century Skills. 2009. *Framework for 21st Century Learning*. [Online]. Available at: http://www.p21.org/storage/documents/P21_Framework.pdf [accessed 12 March 2012].

Pitman, B. and Hirzy, E. 2011. *Ignite the Power of Art: Advancing Visitor Engagement in Museums*. Dallas: Dallas Museum of Art.

Pontin, K. 2006. Understanding Museum Evaluation, in *The Responsive Museum*, edited by C. Lang, J. Reeve and V. Woolard. Aldershot: Ashgate Publishing Limited, 117–27.

Putnam, R.D. 2000. *Bowling Alone: The Collapse and Revival of American Community*. New York: Simon & Schuster.

Sachatello-Sawyer, B., Fellenz, R., Burton, H., Gittings-Carlson, L., Lewis-Mahony, J. and Woolbaught, W. 2002. *Adult Museum Programmes: Designing Meaningful Experiences*. Lanham: AltaMira Press.

Schwarzer, M. 2012. Museums Studies at a Crossroads. *Museum*, 91(1), 23–5, 53, 55.

Scott, C. 2010. Museums, the Public and Public Value. *Journal of Museum Education*, 35(1), 33–42.

Semmel, M.L. 2010. *Transcript of 21st Century Skills Podcast Episode*. [Online]. Available at: http://www.imls.gov/assets/1/PodCast/21C.pdf [accessed 12 March 2012].

Simon, N. 2010. *The Participatory Museum*. Santa Cruz: Museum 2.0.

US Department of Commerce, US Department of Education, US Department of Labor, National Institute for Literacy, Small Business Administration. 1999. *21st Century Skills for 21st Century Jobs*. Washington, DC: US Government Printing Office.

Villafranca-Guzmán, N. and Tortolero, C. 2010. The National Museum of Mexican Art: A New Model for Museums. *Journal of Museum Education*, 35(1), 83–92.

7

The Public as Co-producers: Making the London, Sugar and Slavery Gallery, *Museum of London Docklands*

DAVID SPENCE, TOM WAREHAM, CAROLINE BRESSEY, JUNE BAM-HUTCHISON and ANNETTE DAY

Abstract

This chapter demonstrates how exhibitions can provide a meeting place between collections, the institution, its audiences and unresolved public issues. The public value that museums create as forums for civic engagement is the subject of this chapter, illustrated through a case study exploring the engagement of Londoners with African-Caribbean heritage in the development of a permanent gallery, *London, Sugar and Slavery*, which explores the history of London's involvement in the transatlantic slave trade and its legacies. The introduction is by David Spence, Director of Programmes at the Museum of London and Managing Director of Museum of London Docklands when *London, Sugar and Slavery* was created. There are further contributions from Dr Tom Wareham and Dr Caroline Bressey, both curators who worked with the Consultative Group on the gallery and Dr June Bam-Hutchison, who was the Museum's Diversity Manager and a key facilitator between the museum, the Consultative Group and local London communities. Annette Day, the museum's Head of Programmes, concludes by describing how the work continues today.

Introduction

> *Black is not a binary opposite to white. It is pluralistic.*
> *(Burt Caesar, Consultative Group member)*

In 2005 it was clear that a number of cultural institutions were considering commemorating the forthcoming bicentenary of the British Parliament's 1807 abolition of the slave trade bill. Should the Museum of London and Museum of London Docklands (then Museum in Docklands) do anything to mark the bicentenary? Government organizations such as the Department of Culture, Media and Sport (DCMS) that funds national museums and galleries in the UK did not give direction on the matter but made it clear that additional funds would be available through a major government funding source, the Heritage Lottery Fund (HLF)[1] for activities that commemorated the bicentenary, were 'socially responsible' and in line with their aims and objectives.[2] As an institution we decided that the question should be addressed by our audiences, particularly those with a personal connection, such as black Londoners of African-Caribbean heritage. We did this by asking a friend of the museum, Baroness Young,[3] who had been key to addressing sensitive cultural issues as Head of Culture at the Greater London Authority, to bring together a group of Londoners whom she thought would want to engage with the museum on this subject. As a consequence of the discussions that followed, it was recommended that the museum should be active, not by just marking the bicentenary, but by setting an agenda that challenged what many feared would be an historical 'whitewash' – the word denoting, in this instance, both a bland covering up of unpalatable historical truths and a continuation of the white British interpretation of history that has dominated the discourse around Britain's involvement in the slave trade. The museum's response would be made manifest through the creation of a new permanent gallery at Museum of London Docklands, *London, Sugar and Slavery* (hereafter *LSS*), that explained London's involvement in the slave trade. Such a gallery was overdue given the associations with the location of the museum on West India Quay,[4] and the nature of the museum building, being a former sugar warehouse built to store produce grown by enslaved African labour on plantations in the West Indies owned, in many instances, by London-based absentee plantation landlords (see Figure 7.1).

During the run-up to the bicentenary, the voices of those descended from the enslaved – everyday Londoners who formed part of the African-Caribbean Diaspora – could find little opportunity for mainstream expression and yet the value of integrating their voices into the wider public discourse, manifested through outlets such as museums and galleries, commemorative events and print and broadcast media was evident to the museum. Here was an opportunity to address some of the deepest fractures in our society caused by the legacies of British colonialism – but only if members of the Diaspora could play a leading part in the process.

---

1   The Heritage Lottery Fund (HLF) is the largest dedicated funder of the UK's heritage. It is is administered by the National Heritage Memorial Fund which was given the responsibility of distributing a share of money raised through the National Lottery. It is accountable to Parliament via the Department of Culture, Media and Sport (DCMS). In 2005 it encouraged heritage and community organizations to apply for funds for activities related to the bicentenary of the abolition of the slave trade. The DCMS however did not specifically direct the heritage organizations that it funded to commemorate the abolition.

2   The Heritage Lottery Fund's Strategic Plan for 2002–2007 set out four aims as a guide its grant-making:

- to encourage more people to be involved in and make decisions about their heritage;
- to conserve and enhance the UK's diverse heritage;
- to ensure that everyone can learn about, have access to, and enjoy their heritage;
- to bring about a more equitable spread of grants across the UK.

3   Baroness Young of Hornsey was appointed life peer in the House of Lords in 2004. She is well known for promoting black arts and culture and is black British. She has advised the BBC on diversity and representation on and off screen. Her book, *Fear of the Dark: Race, Gender and Sexuality in Cinema*, was published in 1995. She was Head of Culture at the Greater London Authority from 2001 to 2004.

4   West India Quay can be seen to be one corner of the so-called 'triangular slave trade', the other two corners being West Africa and the Caribbean.

Figure 7.1   Former sugar warehouse at West India Quay, now home to Museum of London Docklands

WORKING WITH THE COMMUNITY

To set the agenda effectively it was agreed that the museum should set up a Consultative Group, crucially including black Londoners of African-Caribbean heritage, who would work with the museum to develop an historical narrative that challenged existing historiographies around the slave trade and, through a combination of their association with the museum and personal life experiences, provide an authentic and authoritative voice amongst the many that would be heard in 2007. The Consultative Group comprised individuals who were engaged in relevant work in London and most were already known to the museum through earlier encounters. These included, for example, Harrington Cumberbatch,[5] who worked locally with black Londoners with mental health problems, Burt Caesar, a Kittitian who located his surname in the museum's slave papers from the Mills plantation on St Kitts, and Hakim Adi, a founder member of the Black and Asian Studies Association.[6] The most important term of reference for the Group was that it was an equitable partnership. It had an equal voice with the museum on steering all aspects of the gallery development. One example of the work of the Group was to challenge the

---

5   Harrington Cumberbatch MBE was born in Barbados and emigrated to London in the 1950s. His work with Tower Hamlets African & Caribbean Mental Health Organisation (THACMHO) is based on the belief that one of the reasons why black Caribbeans suffer from higher levels of mental illness is because of the dislocation of identity caused by enslavement and the associated destruction of familial, cultural and spiritual references.

6   Dr Hakim Adi is a founder member of the Black and Asian Studies Association which was set up in London in 1991 to foster research and to provide information on the history of black people in Britain.

simplistic notion of abolition that was being repeatedly played out by many at the time. For example, the Wilberforce Museum in Hull was planning to re-open in 2007 following a multi-million pound refurbishment with a focus on the work of William Wilberforce[7] who was portrayed as a hero of the abolition movement and the bicentenary. Hull is in the constituency of John Prescott who was Deputy Prime Minister at that time and who was therefore able to foreground the Wilberforce story within political and media circles. The Museum of London Docklands could challenge this interpretation, presenting the more nuanced story of abolition. It could demonstrate that Wilberforce was not the most important agency behind the abolition of the slave trade in the views of many, and that this concept was offensive to many black Londoners. Attention should be drawn, for example, to the actions of enslaved Africans in resisting slavery which eventually made the slave system untenable and to the role of women in eighteenth-century London who formed a pressure group by boycotting the purchase of sugar grown on slave plantations.

The validity of the museum's approach to create the *LSS* gallery with its Consultative Group was recognized by the Heritage Lottery Fund, who awarded one of its largest grants at that time. The challenge the museum now faced was how to translate the goodwill, expertise, life experiences and passion of the Consultative Group into a gallery that would be valuable to all visitors, regardless of age, creed or colour. The question was how to create an historical narrative that challenged preconceptions that largely perpetuated the notion of the enslaved as passive 'chattels' who were subjugated, and subsequently liberated, by their white oppressors turned emancipators. As important, perhaps, was the aim to create an emotionally affecting experience and a 'safe space' that enabled visitors to engage with slavery legacy issues such as racism that continue to affect our lives today. The gallery asks visitors to think about the power of words. What is the difference, for example, between describing a person as a 'slave' as opposed to an 'enslaved African'? How has the imagery deployed by eighteenth-century abolitionists shaped the public perception of black people in the twentieth century? The gallery encourages visitors to leave a comment about their visit. Five years after the opening of the gallery, the museum has collected more than 2,000 comment cards. From these cards we learn that visitors actively engage with the issues presented in the gallery and consider the wider implications for society today. It is possible to say that this engagement is evidence of the wider public value of the gallery, particularly the 'core' values of 'democracy (involving the public), transparency, equity, authorisation (negotiating with different stakeholders) and trust' as set out by Blaug et al. in 2006. Examples of public responses to and subsequently incorporated in the gallery are included later in this chapter. These voices demonstrate what the exhibition has meant to the public. In the next sections of this chapter we hear from other voices – those who were directly involved in developing the exhibition. In their own words, they tell a story of co-production that is more than an exhibition – it is also the story of changing organizational culture and practice.

7   William Wilberforce was a politician and member of Parliament for Yorkshire. He opposed slavery and introduced the Abolition of Slavery Bill in the House of Commons. However he was in favour of gradual abolition and opposed the involvement of women in the campaign, and is seen today by some as having overshadowed the many other agents of abolition, not least Thomas Clarkson and Granville Sharp. His home in Hull is now a museum.

The Museum Curator – Dr Tom Wareham

A sensitivity to the nature of the subject to be addressed had motivated a team of Museum of London group curators to begin preparing for the *London, Sugar and Slavery* project well in advance of the procurement of funding. An internal lead curator was appointed to the project with part-time support from two colleagues, and Dr Caroline Bressey, University College London, was appointed as an external co-lead curator.

This team, together with colleagues from what was then the museum's Access and Learning Department, attended a number of public forums arranged by African-Caribbean organizations to discuss the bicentenary in 2007 and the events being proposed for that year. Attendance at these forums proved crucial, as the debates that took place within them heightened the museum curators' awareness of the complexity of opinion within the African-Caribbean community and of the huge reservoir of anger that lay just below the surface. It became very clear to the project's curators that, far from being an occasion for commemorating the abolition of the slave trade, 2007 might just become another betrayal of the voice of the descendants of the victims of slavery. Indeed, many of the public debates that took place within the forums began with the presumption by black participants that the state or its cultural institutions would merely use the occasion to underline the paternalistic parliamentary triumph of the abolition legislation, identify British fairness in the persona of William Wilberforce, while offering some safe, but patronizing, crumbs, as gestures towards a recognition of the black contribution to the struggle against slavery and the slave trade.

For the museum's curators listening to these debates it was clear that many members of the African-Caribbean community were already angrily anticipating something akin to a whitewash. Considering that this community also constituted the key critical audience to the new gallery, the curatorial team became acutely aware that the gallery would have to do more than simply reiterate the conventional abolition story. Furthermore, achieving something radically different would require a departure from the orthodox methods of gallery creation.

THE ROLE OF THE CURATOR

While the need for a genuinely participative Consultative Group was agreed, curators and learning staff set about devising key messages for what would be not just a gallery about the abolition of the slave trade, but a space in which London would be identified as a major slave trading port, a recipient of the financial benefits of slave labour in the Caribbean and the inheritor of the living legacy of slavery. While all galleries and exhibitions have key messages, those for *LSS* also constituted a manifesto, which could be offered to members of the African-Caribbean community. It stated, in a sense, the narrative which the museum could acknowledge and which could be offered to potential members of the Consultative Group as a starting point for negotiation. The key messages drawn up by the Museum of London's Curatorial and Learning Team for the creation of the *London, Sugar and Slavery Gallery* included a number of important statements which helped direct both the content and its treatment within the gallery:

- London played a central, largely unacknowledged, role in the transatlantic slave trade;
- London's wealth and Britain's industrial revolution were partly founded on the profits from the slave plantations of the Caribbean;
- the slave trade was the first manifestation of global capitalism, driven by the nascent consumer demand for sugar, fed by the application of 'factory' principles to sugar production, powered by enslaved Africans, and engineered by a rising entrepreneurial class in Britain;
- the slave trade and European intervention contributed to the destruction of complex and sophisticated societies which existed in Africa;
- the struggle to end slavery and the slave trade united the interest of people on both sides of the Atlantic, and saw the first mass mobilization in Britain of a diverse alliance of men and women from different social classes and racial backgrounds;
- the British defenders of slavery created an ideology of racism which still haunts us today;
- the later history of West Africa and the Caribbean are an integral part of British Imperial history; and
- West Africa, the Caribbean and London are irrevocably connected by the slave trade. This interconnection is still evident today and affects our understanding of both past and present.

Perhaps the most critical aspect of this process lay in the requirement upon the museum's curators to adopt a new role. Traditionally it is the curator's role to act as both the expert and guardian of a gallery or exhibition's content. He or she structures both narrative and interpretation, and identifies and selects objects and images that fulfil those, to deliver the completed product. Gallery and exhibition creation is, as many curators will admit, a theatrical trick which is dependent on expert knowledge, whether it be of history, art, science, etc. However, underpinning the process is the authority of the curator him/herself.

In order to deliver a gallery about slavery which might even begin to acknowledge the perspective and concerns of Britain's African-Caribbean community, the project's curators knew that this authority had to be relinquished to a substantial degree. As a team, the curators could still fulfil many aspects of their role and apply many of their skills to the project. For example, they alone had knowledge of the museum's collections and could undertake searches for material which might be useful in illustrating the narrative of the gallery. They could help refine the search, and could also look beyond the museum's own walls for objects which might be borrowed.

Working closely with Caroline Bressey, items within the museum's collections were assessed for possible alternative interpretations. It was realized, for example, that the museum's extensive collection of eighteenth-century fine china coffee cups represented not just the East India import trade and the social mores of the period, but also a London-centred culture of coffee houses and sugar consumption, where merchants, planters and sugar refiners met to discuss business relating to production in the Caribbean. Potentially useful objects and images were then offered to the Consultative Group for discussion, analysis and selection or rejection.

The selection and interpretation of objects and images were not the only aspects of the curator's role which were shared or surrendered. The whole narrative structure of the gallery was submitted to the Consultative Group as a proposal for discussion at an early stage. Having agreed an outline for the gallery, which involved a tightly constructed narrative which would focus on London and not be drawn into broader issues,[8] detailed elements were then discussed, analysed and considered for inclusion. The curators and the Consultative Group between them eventually negotiated all of the gallery content. Inevitably there had to be compromises on both parts. The dictates of space determined that some elements could not be included. For example, the curators and some of the Consultative Group wanted to include the story of the Sierra Leone colony, while some of the Consultative Group were keen to include details of Codrington's Plantation in Barbados because it highlighted the role of the church as a slave owner. Both elements were weighed and eventually had to be ruled out.[9]

The curatorial 'voice'

Having agreed upon structure, objects and images, actual writing of the text could begin with the curatorial team drafting text and submitting it to the regular meetings of the Consultative Group. Here, again, the curators had to adapt their role to enable the Consultative Group to insert their own interpretation of objects and events. In what was perhaps the pivotal moment of the collaboration, the curators had to suspend their own interpretation and listen to what was being said by members of the Consultative Group. Ultimately this would mean accepting substantial correction or change to the text, and even a complete change of meaning. It was at this point in the process that curators had to surrender the most valued part of their authority: their interpretation of history. One can understand why many curators are reluctant, and may even fear, to do this. However, allowing an alternative interpretation is not tantamount to abandoning historical accuracy. On the contrary, even allowing for an alternative view of history, it is still the role of the curator to ensure historical accuracy because, without this, the gallery would lose all credibility. But in a genuinely collaborative partnership, the voice of the other partner has to be allowed. At the heart of the process is trust. The curators must not lose a critical perspective; they must continue to challenge the views put forward by consultative group members in the search for accuracy, but the consultative group must understand that the challenge is a valid part of the process and not intended to undermine their co-authority. In the case of the *LSS* project this ultimately involved the joint re-writing of every piece of text in the gallery to ensure the voice of the curatorial narrative included an interpretive voice from the African-Caribbean community.

From the museum's point of view there were considerable benefits from this partnership and these were quickly appreciated by the curatorial team. Working with the Consultative Group brought new insights into the interpretation of objects and images, enabling curators to 'see' differently. It introduced nuances to the gallery which would have been missed by the internal curators because of their own cultural background,

---

8   For example, it was agreed after discussion that an introduction involving slavery in the classical period would make it more difficult later to narrow the focus to London and the slave trade. Similarly, a discussion of the Arab slave trade, or modern sex trade, would open up too many strands to be satisfactorily discussed within the physical space allocated for the gallery.

9   It is worth noting that the designers of the gallery can also have a significant influence on the selection of content. In the case of the *LSS* gallery some material upon which both curators and Consultative Group were agreed had to be ruled out at a late stage because it did not fit the design.

but which might have been noticed by visitors from an African-Caribbean background. Perhaps more advantageously from the curators' point of view, elements in the gallery were tested, changed and approved by the Consultative Group – thus providing some reassurance against possible future criticisms from visitors.

On another level, the Consultative Group were invaluable in assisting the museum to produce a gallery that not only hoped to reach an African-Caribbean community, but which could also reach out to an equally wary white community. Indeed, from the outset, the Consultative Group had asserted that while the gallery had to be challenging to all visitors, it also had to be accessible to all, regardless of their ethnic background. The primary target, after all, were Londoners of whatever origin. This required a balancing act that would have been impossible to achieve without mutual trust between the collaborating partners.

The External Co-curator and Academic – Dr Caroline Bressey

PUTTING REAL PEOPLE AT THE HEART OF THE GALLERY

The history of black men and women in Britain, particularly before the arrival of the *Empire Windrush*[10] in 1948, a moment which has come to mark the so-called beginning of multicultural Britain, is under-researched and the histories that are known still largely ignored within academic research, spaces of public history and heritage institutions such as museums and art galleries. *LSS*'s commitment to exploring the black presence in London during the period of the slave trade provided opportunities to locate existing research on black history within a larger narrative, challenging perceptions of black British homogeneity and reaching a wider audience than would usually engage with black history.

My academic research seeks to recover the lives of black men and women in Victorian Britain, particularly London. At first, it may appear that 'black Victorians' have little to do with the abolition story, but during discussions on how the 1807/2007 commemorations might be realized, many voices emphasized the need to ensure that the story did not begin and end with slavery. The historical narrative needed to arch over the history of enslavement including histories of Africa before Atlantic slavery and the legacy of that history for London life. The importance of black Victorians lies in the need for an understanding of the black presence as a continuous part of the history of London. As an academic researcher of the black presence I was able to bring knowledge of the dearth of records and the complexity of existing records to the exhibition's narrative.

For methodological reasons, my work has focused upon on institutions with photographic archives – asylums, prisons and children's homes. The men and women whose stories are in these archives offer a snapshot of the experiences of black women and men, their children and their extended family and friends. These people were members of multi-ethnic communities and their presence demonstrates that black people formed an integral part of London's communities during the nineteenth century. These histories are not always obvious and often come from the margins of the historical narrative.

---

10   The *Empire Windrush* arrived at the Port of Tilbury, Essex, on 22 June 1948, carrying 493 passengers from Jamaica. The passengers were the first large group of West Indian immigrants to the UK after the Second World War.

Those whose stories can be found in institutional archives are often only captured for a short period of their lives. In common with their working-class friends and families, the biographies of black Londoners are hard to pull out of the archives and put back together. Within these communities they had experiences that were both ordinary and extraordinary.

In recovering these biographies I have faced difficult methodological questions raised by the empirical hunt for their presence in the archives. The absence of 'colour' as a consistent identifier in nineteenth-century archives reveals that numerous archives have to be combined in order to research black Victorians effectively. By using only written sources, researchers have failed to recognize the diversity of archives. For example, some black women admitted to Victorian asylums have no record of 'ethnicity' or the colour of their skin recorded in their surviving records and it is only through using additional sources such as asylum photographic albums that the colour of their skin can be 'seen'. An example of one of these women, Caroline Maisley,[11] is featured in *London, Sugar and Slavery*. Such findings illustrate that a multicultural London has a far longer history than has been imagined. This argument underpins my contribution to the *LSS* gallery.

The *LSS* gallery provided an exciting opportunity for me to place aspects of my research into a larger narrative of London's history rather than a 'Black History Month' focus that is temporary and siphons off the black presence from its broader historical context. As such, it was important to illustrate to visitors that the black presence did not consist of a homogeneous black community of the marginalized. In *LSS*, alongside the portrait of Caroline Maisley is a portrait of Ina Sarah Forbes Bonetta taken in London following her marriage in Brighton to Pinson Lublo Davies. Although orphaned as a child in Africa, she became a god-daughter of Queen Victoria. Her association with the queen provided Sarah with financial security and social privilege. Appearing in the gallery together, Maisley and Davies complicate the relationship between blackness, empire and power.

It was a struggle to fit large, complex and inconclusive arguments suggested by the relationship between these two women into 75- or 35-word panels and captions. In the end there was a great amount of detail and some major themes we could not include, mostly because of space, and it was frustrating to have to leave them out. There was always more to add and it was very difficult to know what and how to take parts of the narrative away. It took much redrafting from us as curators and critical input from Consultative Group members to get a narrative that was suitably and acceptably pithy. Later on in the process I was surprised to realize that the narrative to be told would be constrained by the design of the gallery not the scope of our ambition. As a result, curatorial discussions with the designers were not only about how the story would be told, but what would be told. Our ability to persuade them of the importance of certain arguments rather than others became very important.

The gallery as a focus for public debate

The collaborative process was based upon continual debate, criticism and change. Working within a team of curators, consultants and museum workers was challenging for

---

11   Caroline Maisley was admitted to Colney Hatch asylum in November 1898. See Prescod (2007). Notable 19th century Londoners of African descent, in *Reading the London Sugar & Slavery Gallery*, Museum of London Docklands, 56.

someone used to being 'a lone researcher'. Discussions were at times tense and tiring for all involved. Building successful and equitable partnerships takes time and the museum began its discussions on 1807/2007 early on, although the time for the realization of the gallery was relatively short given its scope and aspirations. Still, the museum managed to create an atmosphere of trust between the different groups working on the gallery including the Consultative Group, the Learning Department and the curators. This meant difficult and confrontational arguments could be thrashed out, even if their conclusions did not always satisfy all those around the table. The gallery is far stronger for those discussions and the huge amount of input and effort from so many people with very different perspectives on 'the story' and the role of the museum in telling that story.

In creating gallery text there are some aspects of academic writing that are lost completely, most obviously the footnoting and referencing of sources. Although it makes for clean captions and easier reading, the loss of footnotes and references does open the narrative up to criticism. Visitors (who leave their comments) can assume that you've ignored certain sources they want to see referenced more directly and assume you don't have the evidence to back-up arguments they don't like or find particularly challenging. I've read comments that refuse to accept the extent of Britain's role in the slave trade because the visitor does not see the sources to back-up the narratives' claims.

As such, LSS is part of an ongoing public debate. Like a piece of academic research it is commented upon, critiqued and occasionally referenced to illustrate a number of sometimes conflicting arguments. One of the principal aims of those working on LSS was to generate debate, so here the gallery has been successful. There is however a danger that the gallery's narrative will become fixed as a new status quo. As Tom Wareham has outlined, a reassessment of the museum's collection provided a way to reinterpret many items and to illustrate a new narrative. However, we need to be mindful that this process is not only undertaken once, thus fixing LSS in 2007. This can be avoided by adding newly recovered research material onto an electronic interactive via computer screens in the galleries and this work is undertaken regularly by Tom Wareham who continues to work on LSS. Still, the written narrative on the panels of the gallery is curiously fixed. How to fully envelop the dynamic debate LSS can generate into the core gallery narrative is still being considered.

Although challenging, I greatly enjoyed the process of collaborative working and it has resulted on an ongoing working relationship with the museum, particularly with my co-curator, Tom Wareham. For my research, the experience developed my interest and strengthened my knowledge of the representations of history in museums that now forms an important aspect of my research work. For my own research on black Victorians there is no doubt that many more people know about Caroline Maisley and Sarah Forbes Bonetta from their visit to LSS than have read about them in my academic papers. Visitors have also seen their photographs that are not usually reproduced in academic papers. Although their stories are very different, in LSS they come together to form part of a narrative that does tell a part of the complex story of the African Diaspora in Britain. My contribution is not citable, nor the papers in which the research appeared referenced, but the story-boards in LSS effectively and engagingly help to illustrate that a multicultural London has a far longer history than has been imagined by many.

Managing Diversity and Community Mediation – Dr June Bam-Hutchison

THE WORK OF THE MUSEUM AS PART OF THE WIDER PUBLIC DISCOURSE ABOUT DIFFICULT HISTORIES

I arrived in London on 1 December 2004, on the anniversary of the Day of Emancipation of slaves at the Cape.[12] I came with the personal experience of slavery. My family and their community had been enslaved through the Dutch East India Company at the Cape in the 1600s and 1700s. Our history also encompassed the settlement of freed slaves from the Caribbean who settled in Cape Town in the District Six community, known later for the forced removals under Apartheid in the 1960s and 1970s.

I brought to the Museum of London's Docklands Diversity Programme my previous experience of working in post-apartheid heritage in South Africa on the transformation of museums and of heading South Africa's History Project to oversee the national rewriting of South Africa's official history. Shortly after joining the museum, I became part of the team working on *LSS*.

At the outset, the task seemed complex and difficult. Though the Museum of London Docklands is based in the wealthy Canary Wharf financial district of London, it includes a very diverse and poor local black community. It serves a wide range of visitors of various backgrounds, so the challenge was to demonstrate the relevance of *LSS* to all visitors, rather than appearing to be tokenistic and aimed at one particular community. Moreover, this objective needed to be understood not just by visitors, but by the museum's own workforce as well.

The challenge, therefore, was partly about internal organizational communication and transformation and involved convincing staff of the public value of the *LSS* gallery for all Londoners regardless of race, class or gender.

While working on the gallery with the consultative group, participating in the community discussion groups at the Museum of London Docklands and through the 2007 commemoration dialogues with other museum practitioners, it became apparent that unspoken racism and class prejudice within institutions was an issue which had to be tackled. Part of the *LSS* project, therefore, was diversity awareness training for all staff in order that the public offer, the *LSS* gallery, was also fully understood by employees of the museum.

The museum contracted a diversity training company led by an African-Caribbean man, Tony Warner, of 'Black History Walks',[13] to run programmes with all staff, including the directors. The diversity managers participated in each training programme (comprising mixed groups of staff from all parts of the organization).

This proved to be an emotionally demanding and intense programme. Reactions amongst staff differed. There was resentment amongst some staff, while others became emotionally engaged (especially those in Human Resources who received more intense training). Others were sceptical of being trained and 'educated' by a black professional.

---

12   1 December is the anniversary commemorated in South Africa for Emancipation Day, when slavery was finally ended on this day in 1838.

13   Tony Warner is an historian and the founding director of Black History Walks (BHW), guided tours that highlight influences and contributions that people of African descent have made over the centuries to some of the most popular places in London.

However, the life story methodology employed in the training programme showed our interconnectedness in terms of race. There was value for us all to hear the human story of suffering and exploitation and its contemporary relevance. At a personal level, this methodology gave profound meaning to my own life story of coming from an enslaved background, living under apartheid for over 30 years and having been an anti-apartheid activist. It helped me facilitate strategic meetings and engage in discussion of race sensitive issues with David Spence and colleagues on the steering group. Not only was I bringing expertise on the topics of dealing with racism, discrimination, use of terminology, working with the people directly affected and traumatized by colonialism and exploitation, but I was also learning about my own new place of belonging in the world and in London.

I felt that, at one level, there were resonances of 'home' as explosive discussions in the community forums, Consultative Group and diversity training took me back to the dark days of the killing of Steve Biko[14] as we confronted the anger expressed about the Stephen Lawrence[15] murder in London. Issues I had encountered in South Africa, such as contested notions of beauty and stereotypical representations connected to race, were being played out in London through discussions around slavery and its legacy of racism.

The gallery and public value

But the gallery had to convey a narrative that was of public value to all visitors, as reflected in the introductory film to the gallery commissioned from Stephen Rudder,[16] *This is Your History*.

How were we going to do this? As the project progressed, the visitor hosts[17] expressed anxiety. They were being confronted by angry black community activists and other visitors who viewed the museum building itself as a site of shame because of its history in the exploitative sugar trade. Anxious white visitors were also expressing fears about being identified as 'the guilty parties'. It was the opinion of some staff that Britain needed a truth and reconciliation commission around this history.

The staff wanted to know what the museum was planning to do to address these issues. A special training programme was facilitated with the visitor hosts run by myself in close collaboration with a white visitor host team leader who shared his own challenges in dealing with racism. These sessions were run on site at the Museum of London Docklands. The life story methodology again provided an in-depth approach to dealing with prejudice and the trauma of either feeling 'guilty' or 'victimized'.

Without fail, the key question that came up in every consultation session was 'What is the value of this gallery for the wider community'?

---

14   Stephen Bantu Biko (18 December 1946 – 12 September 1977) was South Africa's most influential and radical student leader in the 1970s, founder of the Black Consciousness Movement (BCM), and a law student at the time of his death following arrest at a police roadblock and interrogation by officers.

15   Stephen Lawrence (13 September 1974 – 22 April 1993) was a black British teenager from Eltham, south-east London, who was murdered while waiting for a bus in a racist attack by a gang of white youths.

16   Stephen Rudder is a Londoner of African Barbadian heritage. His company, Quiet Voice, was commissioned by the museum to make the introductory film. This included an ethnically diverse range of actors speaking the words written by the eighteenth-century African abolitionist Olaudah Equiano.

17   Visitor hosts are the staff that work with the public on the gallery floor, and are known in some museums as stewards or docents.

It was answered for me (and hopefully for many) in this way: 'We would have succeeded in giving value to the people of London, if they leave with questions about their own lives, identities and roles in society for which they'll be encouraged, through the narrative of the gallery, to find answers.' The gallery was created, not to provoke anger through the 'pornography of violence' in the words of the Consultative Group's Burt Caesar, but through the value of the narrative to facilitate an intelligent sense of belonging and inclusivity and draw our attention to the unfinished business of today's global issues of economic and cultural reparations, peace and justice.

As a postscript, the University of York's 2007 *Commemorated*[18] project included a research element where visitors to LSS were interviewed in the gallery shortly after the opening. The exhibition attracted a high number of visitors who had not visited the museum before (73 per cent, i.e. 128 out of 179). Half of those visitors were 'white' (60 out of 128) and another half belonged to BME[19] groups (61 out of 128). The second main reason, after education, for visiting the exhibition for those respondents who defined themselves as white or white British was to find out about Britain's role in slavery. For BME visitors, the second main reason after education was to think about the lives of enslaved Africans, what they endured and what they achieved.

Table 7.1   Comparison of reasons for visiting the *London, Sugar and Slavery* exhibition between BME groups and those who defined themselves as 'white' or 'white British'

Reasons for visiting the *London, Sugar and Slavery* exhibition	Ethnicity			Total
	White	BME	Other	
Recreation/leisure	20	3	0	23
Education generally	29	24	1	54
Taking the children	5	1	2	8
To find out about Britain's role in slavery	17	15	3	35
To mark the abolition of Britain's role in the slave trade	3	6	0	9
Think about abolitionists and their movement	1	2	1	4

Source: Smith 2008b.

In addition, a significant proportion (16 per cent) of BME respondents stated that they came for other reasons such as to evaluate the museum's position, to see how the museum defines ethnic migrant identity, to learn about a hidden history, to teach their children and to see whether the exhibition shows how Britain 're-invented' slavery back to India.

---

18   *1807 Commemorated* was a project coordinated within the Institute for the Public Understanding of the Past (IPUP), a research centre in the University of York. The central aim of the *1807 Commemorated* project was to both map and analyse public debate and activity regarding the bicentenary, identifying and understanding how 1807 is being marked by different agencies and communities in Britain. See www.history.ac.uk/1807commemorated/about.html.

19   A term used in the UK to describe people from black, minority and ethnic groups.

Further visitor responses came from comment cards in the gallery and revealed the range of reactions that the exhibition provoked:

Growing up in Walthamstow [London], there were no coloured people. When I was about 10, I was at the front of Lloyds Park and I saw my first African, smartly dressed with a blazer with a City of London badge. I just stared at him. Today I feel bad about this. My feeling is that if people live here they must understand our ways, but we must understand theirs. There are good and bad in all nationalities.

We cannot change the horrible things we have done in the past but we can make up for it in the future.

This Museum up until now has been very interesting and informing. It is wrong that we should apologise for something that happened in a previous life. It is also wrong that we should have 'political correct' thrust upon us in this way. Whoever compiled this Museum should keep politics out of it. Just show it how it was!!!

I would like to say that we have come from France (Paris) to study in this museum. We are impressed by the courage shown in the description of what will stay as a dark period of our European history. I would like, and my pupils, to thank the museum for such a brilliant experience.

Conclusion: The Legacy of *LSS* at the Museum of London Docklands – Annette Day

The Museum of London Docklands is now working on its next major gallery development. *Many East Ends* is a programme of activity intended to create a new kind of imaginative and responsive contemporary history gallery. Across the museum and community heritage sectors, a distinct paradigm has emerged for capturing and relating 'community histories'. Though museums have been working with community-based partners for some time, in recent years there is increasing emphasis upon 'equitable partnerships' and much debate about what this means and how it can be achieved (Crook 2007; Newman and Selwood 2008; The Mayor's Commission on African and Asian Heritage 2009; Lynch 2011; Sandell and Nightingale 2012).

Over the past 15 years, significantly enabled by the Heritage Lottery Fund, community-based groups have themselves increasingly been the drivers of partnership-led community history projects. Whoever the initiator is such projects often focus on single internally diverse communities, foreground oral history and photography and rely on films and displays.

Many East Ends aims to further this practice, underpinned by three fundamental principles. The first is bringing together diverse community-based partners, academics, artists and creative agencies to weave multiple strands of narratives anchored by place. As with *LSS*, this includes a core consultative group, involved from the earliest concept development phase. Much of the content will be created through collaboration, working with East Londoners in imaginative ways, often through the agency of artists. The emphasis here is on bringing together people from different backgrounds to reflect upon specific, mutually significant places – a street, a building, an open space. Although a very different subject-matter, the imperative is not dissimilar to that for *LSS*: the need to create a gallery that is authentic, complex and nuanced – reflecting a place, the East End, which has most often been interpreted by outsiders.

The second key principle is the connection of inside and outside, encouraging visitors to walk unfamiliar parts of the East End or to walk familiar streets and see them differently, rooting the museum more firmly in its locality. And the third principle is the commitment to creating a gallery that can be challenged and refreshed through an ongoing collaborative programme.

The intention for *Many East Ends* is to create an array of opportunities for refreshment, so the gallery becomes the focus and platform for the museum's ongoing community collaboration programme and a dynamic space able to respond to the East End itself.

One of the characteristics shared by *LSS* and *Many East Ends*, along with other key initiatives at the museum, including *Belonging: Voices of London's Refugees* (2004–7) and *Stories of the World*, a major youth engagement programme (2009–12), is the scale of their ambition, visibility and impact. *LSS* was transformational for the museum, and *Many East Ends* should continue this trajectory.

References

Blaug, R., Horner, L. and Lekhi, R. 2006. *Public Value, Politics and Public Management: A Literature Review*. London: The Work Foundation.

Crook, E. 2007. *Museums and Community: Ideas, Issues and Challenges*. London: Taylor & Francis.

Day, A. 2009. They Listened to My Voice, *Oral History*, 37(1), 95–106.

Day, A., Harding, J. and Mullen, J. 2010. Refugee Stories, in *Changes in Museum Practice: New Media, Refugees and Participation*, edited by H.-L. Skarveit and K. Goodnow. New York and Oxford: Berghahn Books, 35–47.

Lynch, B. 2011. *Whose Cake is it Anyway?* London: Paul Hamlyn Foundation (PHF).

Mayor's Commission on African and Asian Heritage, The. 2009. *Embedding Shared Heritage: The Heritage Diversity Task Force Report*. London: Greater London Authority.

Newman, A. and Selwood, S. (eds) 2008. *Cultural Trends*, 17(4). London: Taylor & Francis, reporting on the findings of *Cultural Capital and Social Exclusion: A Critical Investigation, 2003–2004*.

Prescod, C. (ed.) 2007. Notable 19th Century Londoners of African Descent, in *Reading the London Sugar & Slavery Gallery*, Museum of London Docklands, 56.

Sandell, R. and Nightingale, E. (eds) 2012. *Museums, Equality and Social Justice*. London: Taylor & Francis.

Smith, L. 2008a. *1807 Commemorated*. University of York [Online]. Available at: http://www.history.ac.uk/1807commemorated/about.html [accessed 6 July 2012].

Smith, L. 2008b. Museum of Docklands – London, Sugar and Slavery audience report, *1807 Commemorated*. University of York [Online], 13. Available at: http://www.history.ac.uk/1807commemorated/audiences/reports/docklands.pdf [accessed 6 July 2012].

Young, Baroness L., of Hornsey. 1995. *Fear of the Dark: Race, Gender and Sexuality in Cinema*. London: Taylor & Francis.

C
Working with the Authorizing Environment

8 Measuring Public Value: Reflections from Australia

LISA CONOLLY[1]

Abstract

In this chapter, the author looks at the role of measurement in public discourse about the work of museums, which underpins judgments about public value. She examines the kind of policy expectations that are being described by government, and how policy is translated into measures and how measures are used. Questions about the audience for measurement data are discussed, including the public's need to understand what museums do for them and the need for accountability of public funding to museums.

Introduction

'Measurement' implies precision yet all measures have some element of error, and they only measure the defined construct for which they were designed. At the Australian Bureau of Statistics (ABS), the production of statistics begins with understanding the needs for data, and ends with evaluating the use of data. In between these end points there is the design, collection, processing, analysis and dissemination of data. This chapter will open with a discussion of the common uses of museum statistical data – with examples from public discourse about the value of museums.

Once we know what data may be most useful, then it is simply a matter of designing the research process to produce that data (assuming you have resources to do so). Here we can hit a snag. The concepts we want to measure are often complex and multi-faceted – such as culture; economy; social cohesion; creativity and learning. Part of the design process is to define concepts for the purposes of undertaking research or producing data. For museums, a key issue to be tackled is producing data relevant to understanding the value of the 'cultural' work of museums, which requires definition. The second part of this chapter explores the *research design* issues that face museums in providing evidence to support public discussion about the contribution of museums to the citizenry.

---

1   All comments within are those of the author and not necessarily those of the Australian Bureau of Statistics (ABS).

Scope and Terminology

For this chapter, the core cultural work of museums is defined as the 'preservation of culture through the collection and management of objects and ideas that represent ways of life of particular groups of people' (ABS 2008a, 3), using culture in the anthropological sense. Museums make cultural information or knowledge accessible to people through a range of museum services.

Throughout this chapter, I am using the concept of public value as originally outlined by Mark Moore (1995) and as explained more recently by Alford and O'Flynn (2008). Most museums in Australia receive a majority of their funding from one of the three tiers of government (Australian federal government; state/territory government; or local government). These museums are part of the 'public service' – but this does not equate with the concept of public good or public value. In the private sector, public goods[2] may be produced which also have public value, as is the case with privately funded museums. In defining public value, 'it is not who produces it that makes value public. Rather, it is a matter of who consumes it' (Alford and O'Flynn 2008, 9). Many public service museums also rely on private investment to deliver their services (e.g. through donations from sponsors), but must demonstrate public accountability, and present evidence of public value since they rely on the public purse for their survival.

In discussing 'museums', I focus on publically funded museums, which both provide public goods and which are accountable for their expenditure of public funds. Museums include art museums and other museums, as defined within the ABS industry classification. Museums belong to a wider 'cultural heritage' sector which includes libraries and archives (ABS 2008c). In ABS museum statistical reports, the 'museums' being reported on may be either private or publically funded or both, but note that commercial art galleries are not included as they are not art museums.

In writing this chapter, I am drawing on my experience as Director, Culture and Recreation Statistics at the Australian Bureau of Statistics, from 2003 to 2008. The ABS works with government arts and cultural administration, including government-funded museums and art museums, to understand data needs and formulate future directions for statistical work. I was the main author of the publication *Arts and Cultural Heritage: An Information Development Plan*, published by the ABS in 2008, which was intended to articulate research directions relevant to public policy debate. I welcome the opportunity to reflect on this work and wish to emphasize that the views expressed here are my own and do not reflect those of the ABS.

THE USE OF DATA IN PUBLIC DEBATE

Political and public debate is peppered with statistical information – debate about museums is no exception. In a democracy, population statistics help to relate policy debate to the citizenry as a whole who ultimately determine public value. Following is a discussion of common statistics used in the context of debate about museums, including:

---

2   Public goods are defined by economists as non-rival and non-excludable. Non-rivalry means that consumption of the good by one individual does not reduce availability of the good for consumption by others; and non-excludability means that no one can be effectively excluded from using the good.

- size – the level of resourcing, size and growth or decline of the museum sector; and
- services – the extent and type of museum services delivered to the citizenry.

DOES SIZE MATTER?

In late 2011 an Australian government media release invited comment on draft directions for a new Australian National Cultural Policy (Crean 2011). The draft policy emphasized the 'arts' and the work of museums or cultural heritage was not so clearly articulated. Nevertheless, it is useful to reflect on how data has been used in the media release for the policy draft, as follows:

15 million Australian adults attend at least one cultural event or performance every year - not including cinema;

More than 285,000 people are employed directly in arts and cultural jobs and Australia's creative industries already contribute over $31 billion to industry gross product;

Labor firmly believes that a creative nation is a productive nation, which is why we invest over $740 million each year directly on the arts and other cultural activities. (Crean 2011, 1)

The statistics used here are derived from ABS data, and I will resist the temptation to critique their use. The key point is that these data are being used to highlight the overall size and importance of arts and culture to the general population and economy. The policy aims to justify why governments 'invest' in 'the arts and other cultural activities'. This is done in tandem with political statements, such as:

A renewed National Cultural Policy will ensure Australia doesn't miss important opportunities to tell our stories, educate and skill our workforce and enable our culture to connect with the rest of the world. (Crean 2011, 1)

Most museums collect statistics on visitors and service use, as well as statistics that describe the size and nature of their heritage collections. The ABS provides standards to guide the collation of these statistics (e.g. number of on-site visits to the organization; number of visits to the organization's website; number of employees; size of the organization's collection) (ABS 2008b).

According to the most recent ABS museums survey, at the end of June 2008 there were 1,184 museum/gallery organizations, operating from 1,456 locations across Australia (ABS 2009). These organizations:

- employed 7,856 people;
- generated income of AUD $998.4m during the 2007–8 financial year;
- incurred expenses of AUD $860.1m for the same period;
- had admissions of 30.7m people for the same period;
- held 52.5m objects in their collections.

Of these 1,184 organizations, 14 per cent were art galleries and the remaining 86 per cent were classified as other museums, including social history museums, historic properties or sites and natural science and other museums.

Museums and cultural heritage organizations use this kind of data to describe the size and therefore relative importance of the sector. Following are examples from two museum sector submissions to the Australian National Cultural Policy Discussion Paper. The first quote is from the Council of Australasian Museum Directors who represent Australian national, state or territory museums around Australia, as well as national museums of New Zealand:

Cultural institutions such as museums are highly popular sources and presenters of cultural knowledge. In the five years to 2009–10 close to 50 million visits were made by members of the Australian public and by visitors from overseas to one of CAMD's member museums in Australia to view an exhibition, listen to a talk, learn about Australia's indigenous, social and natural history, ask a question, participate in a public program or simply to browse the collection … When one combines visitors through the door (over 11.5m to CAMD museums in 2010-11) with visits online (over 32.5m for the same period) and the many hundreds of thousands more reached through touring exhibitions, video conferencing and regional programs, some sense can be garnered of the attraction these cultural institutions hold for the public. (Council of Australasian Museum Directors 2011, 5)

The ABS survey of attendance at cultural venues found that, in 2009–10, more than one-quarter of the Australian population aged 15 years and over (26 per cent or 4.5 million people) had visited a museum[3] in the 12 months prior to interview. This was an increase over the 2005–6 attendance rate of 23 per cent (ABS 2011a). These statements describe what services are being valued, and how many people use or access these services. They assume that bigger numbers represent more value – more people using museums and bigger collections are inherently better – and this presents a persuasive argument in public debate. It is difficult to argue against the public value of a service that is well used by a wide range of people.

Yet, governments must also make decisions about the *relative* value of public investment in a museum – is a hospital, school or arts program more important than a museum? Decisions about the relative value of public services are more complex and seem to be less often publically debated – but this is critical to political and government decision making about what gets funded. In the political context the relative size of a voting constituency is no doubt considered. It is an understandable strategy for all kinds of services, including museums, to 'lobby' politicians in competition for public funds – each service emphasizing the value that they contribute. To what extent does evidence feature in this political process and/or in government advice about priorities? In my view these decisions, even if inherently political, can benefit from improved data.

Size does matter, since the data can be used effectively in public debate. Yet additional data are needed in order to judge the *relative* contribution of museums compared to other public services. This requires an understanding of museum public benefits or outcomes which may be compared across differing services.

---

3   This statistic does not include art galleries, who also had attendance rates of 26 per cent, but could include commercial art galleries depending on the interpretation of the respondent.

In the statement accompanying the draft Australian National Cultural Policy Discussion Paper, there is no commitment to a 'bigger' or 'smaller' culture sector. . Instead, the Australian Minister for Arts at the time, Simon Crean, says that:

> We also need to think creatively about how we can make best use of the considerable resources already in the arts sector to obtain better outcomes for the Australian community. (Crean 2011, 1)

This implies that enough resources ('considerable') are going to the arts – there is no promise of more and no threat of less. There is no specific mention in the draft policy paper about resources to museums. Importantly, this statement emphasizes the need to obtain 'better outcomes' and herein lies the real value.

Before discussing outcomes, we need to know how much public funding is spent on museums, since relative value includes a judgement about the 'bang for your buck' – what outcomes do we get from expenditure public funds? Relevant outcomes are just one element of public accountability (with other dimensions including the efficiency and fairness – not discussed here). .

The ABS Cultural Funding by Government Survey found that in 2009–10 the Australian government provided $90.1m to art museums and a further $295.7m to other museums and cultural heritage, while state and territory governments contributed $187.1m and $371.8m respectively. Local government also provided considerable funding to art museums ($52.4m) and to other museums and cultural heritage ($47.4m). The level of funding from government varies over time, with some increases being experienced for museums between 2007–8 and 2008–9, but more modest growth and even some decline for some states (ABS 2011b, ABS 2011c). More recent data for 2010-11 shows a decline in museum's funding from the Australian government in the past year, with $75.0m to art museums and $219.3m to other museums and cultural heritage (ABS 2012a). In order to be accountable for expenditure of public funds, one must first know how much was spent.

In summary – size matters – measures of the size of the museum sector (their resources, visitors, collections and services) can inform perceptions of public value and provide an essential description of the services being 'valued'. However, public value debate also requires evidence about the benefits derived from the services that museums provide and citizens need for them.

SERVICES TO THE CITIZENRY

To understand the 'public value' of museums it is important to know the extent to which their services extend benefit to the whole citizenry, as well as what is required of them by the 'authorizing environment' of political representatives. Citizens may benefit through direct use of museum services and/or by other indirect benefits, which have been variously categorized as 'use value', 'non-use value', 'instrumental value' and/or 'intrinsic value'. These typologies of value have been written on extensively by others (Holden 2004; Scott 2011) and will not be discussed here.

I want to address the following question – what services or benefits do Australian politicians and citizens expect from museums, and are they being met? What data is used (or could be used) to inform this discussion?

Davison (2001) encapsulated the wide public expectations of museums in Australia, as follows:

> *The new museums face high expectations and, in the politically charged atmosphere surrounding the process of Aboriginal reconciliation, a potentially critical reception. People expect much, possibly too much, of our national museums. They must educate and entertain, inspire and provoke. They must offer exhibitions that compete with the glamour of television and the internet. They must meet expectations of diverse client groups – mainstream politicians, often imposing impossible deadlines, representatives of minority groups demanding endless consultation, commercial sponsors looking for a pay-off, not to mention academic critics. (Davison 2001, 25)*

The context in which museums operate is clearly challenging. In the ABS paper – *Arts and Cultural Heritage: An Information Development Plan* (2008) – an attempt was made to understand the many expectations of government policy and the potential public benefits of arts and cultural heritage services but the task of translating broad cultural policy directions into potentially measurable 'outcomes' (or citizen benefits) was a daunting one.

This is partly because the language of cultural policy is often couched in broad terms that are difficult to define for measurement or research purposes. In addition, there are many overlaps in outcomes – an economic outcome may also have an associated social benefit that is also underpinned by private or intrinsic values (i.e. the joy of museum learning can lead to industry innovation and social participation). In an environment where measures and evidence of performance are increasingly important to politicians as well as to public discussion, it is an important task to construct relevant measures from stated goals or expectations.

The recent draft Australian cultural policy (Department of Regional Australia, Local Government, Arts and Sport 2011, 12) had four broad goals:

1. To ensure that what government supports – and how this support is provided – reflects the diversity of a twenty-first century Australia, and protects and supports indigenous culture.
2. To encourage the use of emerging technologies and new ideas that support the development of new artworks, and that enable more people to access and participate in arts and culture.
3. To support excellence and world-class endeavour, and strengthen the role that the arts play in telling Australian stories both here and overseas.
4. To increase and strengthen the capacity of the arts to contribute to our society and economy.

First, I would add my voice to the many submissions suggesting that this draft cultural policy has an 'arts' bias. It does not capture the cultural goals of museums and heritage organizations at all well.

After stating its goals, the policy articulated more tangible performance expectations – 'we will know if we have reached this goal if ...'. Examples of these expectations relating to the work of museums from the National Cultural Policy Discussion Paper (Department of Regional Australia, Local Government, Arts and Sport 2011) are cited below:

- More Australians from diverse backgrounds and locations have the opportunity to participate in Australia's cultural life – families, young people, people with disabilities, and people in regional areas (2011, 13).
- Australia's institutions and performance companies and artists are increasingly celebrated as being world class (2011, 15).
- Indigenous arts, language and culture continue to attract both domestic and international interest and recognition (2011, 15).
- More international visitors will target Australia as a cultural destination, supporting our economy (2011, 16).

The public value of museums will be, in part, determined by a discussion of whether these expectations have been met. However, these expectations are difficult to report against. What does it mean to 'participate in cultural life'? What is a 'world-class' institution? What kind of 'interest and recognition' is being sought? Indeed, the last point in the list above is the only one that lends itself to some clear definition and measurement, illustrated below.

International visitors that come to Australia to visit a museum add to the economy[4] and significant effort has been put to collecting relevant data or research evidence about this economic outcome for museums. The Council of Australasian Museum Directors provides the following evidence in their submission:

Museums promote Australia as a cultural destination which attracts interstate and overseas tourists and makes a significant contribution to a cultural and heritage tourism market worth over $20 billion dollars a year. In 2009–10 over 3.75m tourists (interstate and overseas) visited CAMD museums in capital cities and major regional centres. In their 2009 Snapshots: Cultural and Heritage Tourism in Australia Tourism Research Australia reported that the two most popular activities undertaken by tourists (both international and domestic) were "visiting heritage buildings sites and monuments" and "visiting museums and art galleries". These types of tourists accounted for more than 150 million visitor nights in Australia each year and contributed strongly to regional economic growth and employment opportunities. Research on Canberra's cultural institutions found that they played a significant role in attracting tourists who spent between $249–255 million per annum in that city. Similarly, the Sovereign Hill Museum sites generate approximately $50 million a year for the Ballarat economy. (Council of Australasian Museum Directors 2011, 25)

These economic arguments are persuasive because they suggest a general benefit to a whole economy, and therefore to the whole citizenry. There appears to be general public pressure on museums to attract large audience numbers and promote their economic benefits (with visitors being entertained, educated and spending money). Blockbuster exhibits get attention in the media. There is some debate about whether an emphasis on blockbuster exhibits may be at the expense of other cultural benefits (Fulton 2011) but at the very least these blockbusters make it easier for museums to gain popularity and meet the expectations of politicians to assist recognition of public value. At best, they can provide a broad cultural experience to many people (Gill 2012).

---

4   Domestic expenditure by local visitors to museums could simply be directed elsewhere within the economy and does not 'add' anything to the economy.

The existence of measures in itself facilitates this public discussion, which in turn supports perceptions of value. Holden (2004) has argued that statistical measures can dangerously oversimplify the public debate, and divert attention from the real value that should be discussed. However, I would argue that measures are important to an informed discussion and the real concern here is that there is only a narrow discussion of 'economy' to the exclusion of other important outcomes for the citizenry as a whole.

The availability of economic data (especially with regard to tourism) may focus the debate of 'public value' in one direction at the expense of other dimensions. So, other types of statistics may be needed on other topics relevant to public expectations of museums. Scott (2011) has provided examples of the many 'intangibles' that are important benefits of museums but are difficult to measure – such as a capacity to learn; innovation; and tolerance of diversity. These aspirations relate to the broad goals set out in the draft Australian cultural policy. The difficulty in defining and describing these aspects of the cultural services of museums with the use of data can lead to a lack of credible public debate around the value of museum services.

RESEARCH DESIGN ISSUES FOR MEASURING BENEFITS OF MUSEUMS

Good research design can overcome the evidence gaps that may be missing from the debate about the public value of museums, particularly as this relates to the 'cultural work' and related citizen benefits of museums. Addressing this gap will take time and effort to overcome. It has taken many decades for modern societies to develop an 'International System of National Accounts' for the measurement of modern economies – but, the economic concepts, units of measurement and data collection methods are now well established.

Recent statistical efforts have focused on the need to measure other dimensions of wellbeing and the progress of societies. The ABS produces *Measures of Australia's Progress* (ABS 2010) which go beyond economic wellbeing to capture other dimensions of social progress such as 'education and learning' and 'family, community and social cohesion'. These goals are highly relevant to museums.

The ABS has undertaken an extensive consultation with Australian people to understand what aspects of progress should be measured in future (ABS 2012b) and the results highlight some important *social* progress goals relevant to museums, including 'learning and knowledge' and 'community connections and diversity'. Globally, this field of statistics is in its infancy. Hence, it is not surprising that the task to provide clear evidence to support the public aspirations of the variously defined concept of the 'cultural' work of museums is a difficult one.

One answer to this problem has been to provide evidence of these museum benefits through research methods which gather up the qualitative testimonials of individuals, in their own words, and to collate museum visitor research. There are many examples of museums effectively using visitor research to inform the development of museums services (e.g. Australian Museum 2011; Kelly 2011; Selwood 2010). Visitor research relies on self-reported satisfaction and testimonials. A testimonial is a statement by an individual about their museum experience – and this type of evidence has its own power, depending on the context.

To illustrate this point, following is the kind of statement that might be made by a regular museum visitor, and it reflects my own sentiments about museums:

I have been visiting museums since I was a child and they inspire me to love life. I have learned so much from museums about different cultures and species and about the earth itself and I have grown to respect all this diversity. Museums make it easy for me to learn and I find enough mystery in them to rouse my curiosity, and enough explanation to inch forward my understanding.

Clearly, this individual gets enormous benefit from their museum experience – but this is a private benefit accruing only to that individual. This statement portrays what Holden (2004) called the 'intrinsic value' of museums. But how useful is this statement as evidence of public value? The extent to which this individual statement reflects public value depends in part on who said it, and in what context.

If the statement were made by a politician then it represents public value by virtue of their political position – as part of the authorizing environment as defined by Moore (1995). If the statement was made by a popularly celebrated sports person it may be very influential in shaping public perception about the value of museums. However, the testimony of one individual visitor in the context of visitor research does not represent evidence of public value, since it does not reflect on the value to the citizenry as a whole. In a democracy, an individual can take action to influence public outcomes through their vote, political lobbying or by volunteering for a museum, or giving museum donations – thereby making a contribution to the 'public sphere' (Benington 2011, 31). Yet the individual statement in the context of visitor research is an expression of private value.

Even if the research is aggregated to conclude that 'of the 2,000 visitors that the museum had during the period, 100 visitors were interviewed and 95 per cent expressed a positive experience of their visit', it is not certain that this reflects evidence of public value. This is an *aggregation* of private values, which may be a useful customer satisfaction measure for that museum, but it does not necessarily relate to the public expectations of museums. As pointed out by Alford and O'Flynn, 'if something is valuable, it is because it is perceived to be valuable by people. Of course, here the people in question constitute a collective – the citizenry – rather than an aggregation of individuals' (Alford and O'Flynn 2008, 7).

These customer satisfaction measures and visitor evaluation studies are essential for the efficient and effective running of a museum, which are important dimensions of public accountability – and they help to shape future museum programmes. However, an efficient museum with high customer satisfaction may still not meet public expectations of value, as determined by the authorizing environment or the citizenry.

This highlights the need for research designed to address questions that are directly relevant to the public expectations of museums. If the public demands the 'instrumental'[5] benefits that Holden (2004) describes then these expectations need to be discussed. In the same way that public economic debate can include a discussion of museum contributions, there is potential for museums to insert themselves into the existing public debate on cultural diversity or social progress – using evidence of course. In Australia, public debate on a range of cultural issues: including migration policy; reconciliation with indigenous populations; productive diversity; skill benefits of a multicultural society; perceived racial tensions or conflict; cross-cultural group attitudes and general social cohesion. There

---

5   Holden (2004) posits that instrumental values are those with a tangible outcome or output, which may be central to a range of other government agendas (education, health, economic) rather than necessarily being cultural work.

is increasing debate around the value of cultural diversity to a nation and its global citizenship and participation in a global economy.

Museums could demonstrate their contribution to a healthy culturally diverse society and to social progress using relevant research and data. , I will focus briefly on the research design process for one example of the cultural work of museums. One outcome distilled from our earlier examination of cultural policy was expressed as follows:

> *Do people develop more tolerant attitudes to different cultures within society through their involvement in or consumption of arts or cultural heritage services? To what extent do people consume arts or cultural heritage services outside their own cultural group, and does this foster cultural awareness? (ABS 2008a, 42)*

This outcome is relevant to the discussion of Goal 1 from the draft Australian cultural policy; 'To ensure that what the government supports – and how this support is provided – reflects the diversity of a 21st Century Australia, and protects and supports Indigenous culture' (Department of Regional Australia, Local Government, Arts and Sport 2011, 14). The policy document also makes a reference to the link between 'education and social cohesion' although the focus of this discussion is on arts education. These goals are also relevant to the wider social progress goals of 'learning and knowledge' and 'community connections and diversity' (ABS 2012), for which national benchmark measures will be developed.

The idea of a cohesive or civil society which embraces an acceptance of diversity is something in which museums have often claimed to have a role (Sandell 2002). This is necessarily underpinned by individuals learning about Australian society, indigenous culture and other diverse cultures from their interaction with museums. The Ministry for Culture and Heritage, New Zealand (2009) has identified social cohesion as a theme requiring development of relevant indicators, although no data has yet been collected to measure these.

Some Australian museums undertake audience research and specific programme evaluation (Kelly and Gordon 2002) with participants. Such studies can provide good evidence that people learn about other cultures from their engagement with museum programmes – such as Australian Aboriginal and Torres Strait Islander cultures or the various cultures of immigrant groups to Australia. This evidence of cross-cultural learning is a first step in demonstrating the public value of museums in contributing to the social cohesion outcome. This research is understandably limited to smaller studies of visitors to particular museums or participants of particular museum programmes. It is expensive to design and run large-scale research projects that consider a wider spectrum of 'public' response – either for *all* Australian visitors to museums (around 26 per cent of the population) or to the *population* as whole (who may not directly interact with museum services, but may nevertheless be influenced by the cultural content reproduced and reused in the population).

Current ABS population surveys provide data on the numbers of people (children and adults) attending museums, but do not ask about their learning from museums, nor exposure to cultural knowledge. The design of relevant interview questions is not a simple process, but it could be done by including questions on population surveys. Population data on museum learning and cultural knowledge may be powerful evidence in public debate – but it risks being focused again on the 'size' of museum services (i.e.

the reach of museum services). In order to demonstrate public value, we need data that is comparable to the social progress measures used in other areas of public service (e.g. education services), so that the *relative* contribution of museums to the citizenry as a whole can be judged.

With economic analysis relative contributions of different services can be judged easily since the measures are all expressed in dollar terms – the economic value generated by a museum can be compared to that of a theatre, car race or football game. There have been attempts to convert other intangible outcomes into dollar measures, such as through 'willingness to pay' or 'contingent valuation' studies (Throsby 2003) and I will not debate these here. Suffice to say that if it is feasible to measure a social outcome more directly then that is preferable – and the field of social statistics is developing to this end (ABS 2004; Rajulton, Ravanera and Beaujot 2007). As a starting point, the research design process requires a definition of culture, and a definition of the cultural services of museums, since this can help define the scope of the museum services from which public benefits may accrue. In response to the Australian National Cultural Policy Discussion Paper, a majority of the submissions from the museums sector expressed a strong need for a definition of culture, and more explicit recognition of the work of museums in preserving and/or shaping culture. As noted by one submission:

The question of definition is a perennial one in discussions of cultural policy. Nevertheless, addressing the "what is culture?" question remains the key challenge in formulating a national cultural policy. (University of Western Sydney Centre for Cultural Research 2011, 1)

The Council of Australasian Museum Directors have made the following recommendation to the Australian government to:

reconfigure policy approaches in line with a broader concept of culture which acknowledges the importance to cultural and creative life, of "cultural memory" and the heritage collections, institutions and organisations which sustain and develop it. (Council of Australasian Museum Directors 2011, 4)

These conceptions of museums' role in culture are multi-faceted and provide a difficult basis for research design. A good definition for measurement purposes needs to enable recognition of the unit (or units) of measurement and attributes of that unit (or units). The ABS (2008a) has provided a definition of culture as follows:

Culture is used to describe particular ways of life, whether for a group of people or a period of time. A way of life can be known as a "culture" if there are collectively understood representations of customs, traditions, beliefs or values shared by a group or prevailing during a period. Culture may be represented in various ways including (but not limited to) art forms. (ABS 2008a, 3)

In this definition the units of measurement would be the 'group of people' or 'period of time' that own the culture. The cultural attributes of these units are the shared 'way of life' which may be represented in customs, traditions, beliefs and values as well as through art works, texts, performances or materials of everyday living. Following from this, a definition of cultural heritage[6] was also provided:

> *The preservation of culture through the collection and management of objects and ideas that represent ways of life of particular groups of people. The sphere of cultural heritage activities includes activities generally associated with museums, art museums, libraries and archives. (ABS 2008a, 3)*

Culture is maintained and preserved by the groups of people who own or share a 'way of life'. Museums may have been perceived as repositories of historical artefacts of culture, yet now also have a role to actively assist particular groups to maintain their living culture, as has been done in recent decades with indigenous Australians (Kelly and Gordon 2002). So, evidence about how this cultural work of museums is contributing to wider reconciliation objectives and social cohesion (valuing cultural diversity) could be a good basis for demonstrating public value of museums. This definition is just a broad starting point, and there is still more definitional work to do.

The ABS *Arts and Cultural Heritage: Information Development Plan* (2008a) provided a range of research directions relevant to public policy and debate about the potential benefits of arts and museum public services. These research directions take account of how the work of museums interacts with other public agendas like education, immigration and reconciliation. In setting a research agenda it will be useful to draw on the research methods already being developed to assess social progress for Australia (ABS 2012b). If museums can provide comparable relevant measures then this will support public debate about the public value of museums to the citizenry relative to other public services. This use of comparable data does not need to invoke a debate about competition with other services, like educational institutions or performing arts programs, but can be used to show how museums complement other services to provide additional public value. A collaborative approach to setting a research agenda across Australian museums would be important in order to galvanize research activity across the museum sector, and to create more possibilities for entering into the public and political discourse on the value of museums.

Conclusion

The difficulty in defining and describing the core cultural services and outcomes of museums, including with the use of data, leads to a gap in the public debate around the public value of museums. This chapter has illustrated how data about the 'size' of museums has been used effectively in public debate. Size matters because public value requires museums to reach out to the citizenry as a whole. Ultimately the question of whether big is better requires political judgment that also weighs up the *relative* value of museum services compared to other public services.

Where there are well established methods for measurement, such as in providing economic measures analysing cultural tourism (ABS 2001; Foo and Rossetto 1998) these outcomes seem more likely to feature in discussion of public value. The economic

---

6   Cultural heritage is only one aspect of museum services, with natural heritage also being important.

contribution of museums is a fundamental expectation that is likely to remain important. However, more effort could be directed to defining the important 'cultural' work of museums and their contribution to 'social progress' as measured for the Australian nation as a whole (ABS 2012b). With good definitions, population studies may be designed to provide meaningful results for comparing museums and other public services on social outcomes relevant to cultural learning and cultural diversity.

Measures enable discussion about a complex reality which can help citizens and politicians to discuss the public value of museums. Statistics are powerful because they represent a population or wider citizenry. Once measures are established and well understood (which takes time and resources), they may be easily communicated and used. Public discussion may also use evidence derived from case studies and illustrative 'stories' (as many journalists do), but their potency in public debate will depend on the context of the story and story teller.

Regardless of the source of evidence, it will only contribute to an understanding of public value if it is used effectively in public debate – whether that is in political statements, public reports, museum journals, online forums or media articles. Ultimately the public value of museums will be determined by citizens and their elected representatives, but hopefully their judgments will be well informed by relevant, credible and meaningful data.

References

Alford, J. and O'Flynn, J. 2008. *Public Value: A Stocktake of a Concept.* Paper presented to the Twelfth Annual conference of the International Research Society for Public Management (March 2008, Brisbane, Australia).

Australian Bureau of Statistics (ABS) 2001. *Cultural Tourism Statistics.* Report prepared for the Cultural Ministers Council. [Online]. Available at: http://www.culturaldata.gov.au/publications/statistics_working_group/cultural_tourism/cultural_tourism_statistics [accessed 21 July 2012].

Australian Bureau of Statistics (ABS) 2004. *Information Paper: Measuring Social Capital – An Australian Framework and Indicators*; cat. no. 1378.0. Canberra: Commonwealth of Australia.

Australian Bureau of Statistics (ABS) 2008a. *Arts and Cultural Heritage – an Information Development Plan, ABS Information Paper*; cat. no. 4915.0.55.002. Canberra: Commonwealth of Australia.

Australian Bureau of Statistics (ABS) 2008b. *Towards Comparable Statistics for Cultural Heritage Organisations, ABS Information Paper*; cat. no. 4916.0. Canberra: Commonwealth of Australia. [Online]. Available at: http://www.abs.gov.au/AUSSTATS/abs@.nsf/DetailsPage/4916.02008 [accessed 21 July 2012].

Australian Bureau of Statistics (ABS) 2008c. *Australian Culture and Leisure Classification, Second Edition*; cat. no. 4902.0. Canberra: Commonwealth of Australia. [Online]. Available at: http://www.abs.gov.au/ausstats/abs@.nsf/mf/4902.0 [accessed 21 July 2012].

Australian Bureau of Statistics (ABS) 2009. *Museums, Australia, 2007–08*; cat. no. 8560.0. Canberra: Commonwealth of Australia. [Online]. Available at: http://www.abs.gov.au/ausstats/abs@.nsf/Latestproducts/8560.0Main%20Features22007-08?opendocument&tabname=Summary&prodno=8560.0&issue=2007-08&num=&view= [accessed 21 July 2012].

Australian Bureau of Statistics (ABS) 2010. *Measures of Australia's Progress*; cat. no. 1370.0. Canberra: Commonwealth of Australia.

Australian Bureau of Statistics (ABS) 2011a. *Attendance at Selected Cultural Venues and Events, Australia, 2009–10*; cat. no. 4114.0. Canberra: Commonwealth of Australia.

Australian Bureau of Statistics (ABS) 2011b. *Art Gallery and Museum Attendance, in Perspectives on Culture*; cat. no. 4172.0.55.001. Canberra: Commonwealth of Australia.

Australian Bureau of Statistics (ABS) 2011c. *Cultural Funding by Government, Australia, 2009–10*, cat. no. 4183. Canberra: Commonwealth of Australia.

Australian Bureau of Statistics (ABS) 2012a. *Cultural Funding by Government, Australia, 2010–11*, cat. no. 4183. Canberra: Commonwealth of Australia.

Australian Bureau of Statistics (ABS) 2012b. *Measures of Australia's Progress – Aspirations for our Nation: A Conversation with Australians about Progress, 2011-12*, cat. no. 1370.0.00.002. Canberra: Commonwealth of Australia.

Australian Museum. 2011. *Australian Museum Visitor Profile, 2008–2011*. [Online]. Available at: http://www.australianmuseum.net.au/document/Australian-Museum-Visitor-Profile-2008-2011 [accessed 9 December 2012].

Benington, J. 2011. From Private Choice to Public Value?, in *Public Value Theory and Practice*, edited by J. Benington and M. Moore. UK: Palgrave Macmillan. 31–51.

Council of Australasian Museum Directors. 2011. *Submission to the Australian National Cultural Policy Discussion Paper*. [Online]. Available at: http://culture.arts.gov.au/sites/default/files/submissions/council-of-australasian-museum-directors.pdf [accessed 4 February 2012].

Crean, S. 2011. Minister for Arts, *National Cultural Policy Media Release*, 11 August. [Online]. Available at: http://www.minister.regional.gov.au/sc/releases/2011/august/sc099_2011.aspx [accessed 12 December 2012].

Davison, G. 2001. National Museums in a Global Age: Observations Abroad and Reflections at Home, in *National Museums Negotiating Histories, Conference Proceedings*, edited by D. McIntyre and K. Wehner. Canberra: National Museum of Australia, 12–28.

Department of Regional Australia, Local Government, Arts and Sport. 2011. National Cultural Policy Discussion Paper. [Online]. Available at: http://culture.arts.gov.au/discussion-paper/ [accessed 12 December 2011].

Foo, L.M. and Rossetto, A. 1998. *Cultural Tourism in Australia – Characteristics and Motivations*. Canberra: Bureau of Tourism Research, Commonwealth of Australia. [Online]. Available at: http://ret.gov.au/tourism/Documents/tra/Snapshots%20and%20Factsheets/OP27.pdf [accessed 21 July 2012].

Fulton, A. 2011. Mass Appeal is a Monster Success at Museums, *The Age*, 26 September. [Online]. Available at: http://www.theage.com.au/entertainment/art-and-design/mass-appeal-is-a-monster-success-at-museums-20110925-1kril.html#ixzz1q1oDSEqk [accessed 30 March 2012].

Gill, R. 2012. Culture Vulture: Blockbusters, *The Age*, 10 March. [Online]. Available at: http://www.theage.com.au/entertainment/art-and-design/culture-vulture-blockbusters-20120309-1up1k.html [accessed 21 July 2012].

Holden, J. 2004. *Capturing Cultural Value: How Culture has Become a Tool of Government Policy*. London: DEMOS.

Kelly, L. 2011. Family Visitors to Museums in Australia, in *Understanding Museums: Australian Museums and Museology*, edited by D. Griffin and L. Paroissien. [Online]. Available at: http://nma.gov.au/research/understanding-museums/index.html [accessed 9 December 2012].

Kelly, L. and Gordon, P. 2002. Developing a Community of Practice: Museums and Reconciliation in Australia, in *Museums, Society and Inequality*, edited by R. Sandell. London and New York: Routledge, 153–74.

Ministry for Cultural Heritage, New Zealand. 2009. *Cultural Indicators for New Zealand, Tohu Ahurea mō Aotearoa.* [Online]. Available at: http://www.mch.govt.nz/files/CulturalIndicatorsReport.pdf [accessed 21 July 2012].

Moore, M. 1995. *Creating Public Value: Strategic Management in Government.* Cambridge, MA: Harvard University Press.

Rajulton, F., Ravanera, Z. and Beaujot, R. 2007. Measuring Social Cohesion: An Experiment using the Canadian National Survey of Giving, Volunteering, and Participation. *Social Indicators Research*, 80(3), 461–92.

Sandell, R. 2002. Museums and the Combating of Social Inequality: Roles, Responsibilities and Resistance, in *Museums, Society, Inequality (Museum Meanings)*, edited by R. Sandell. London and New York: Routledge.

Scott, C. 2011. *Measuring the Immeasurable: Capturing Intangible Values*, Conference keynote to the Marketing and Public Relations International Committee of International Council of Museums, September 2011, Brno Czech Republic. [Online]. Available at: http://network.icom.museum/fileadmin/user_upload/minisites/mpr/papers/2011-Scott.pdf [accessed 30 March 2012].

Selwood, S. 2010. *Making a Difference: Understanding the Cultural Impact of Museums.* Essay for the National Museums Directors Conference (UK). [Online]. Available at: http://www.nationalmuseums.org.uk/media/documents/publications/cultural_impact_final.pdf [accessed 30 March 2012].

Throsby, D. 2003. Determining the Value of Cultural Goods How Much (or How little) Does Contingent Valuation Tell Us. *Journal of Cultural Economics*, 27, 275–85.

University of Western Sydney Centre for Cultural Research. 2011. Submission to the Australian National Cultural Policy Discussion Paper. [Online]. Available at: http://culture.arts.gov.au/sites/default/files/submissions/uws-the-centre-for-cultural-research.pdf [accessed 20 February 2012].

9 Museums and Public Value: A US Cultural Agency Example

MARSHA L. SEMMEL

Introduction

The Institute of Museum and Library Services (IMLS) is a US federal agency that works at a national level supporting museums and libraries of all types through grants, research, policy development, and facilitating collaborative work across national, state and local instrumentalities. It has a strong commitment to both fostering public value in the programmes that it funds and demonstrating the public value of the museum and library sectors. This chapter situates the current work of the IMLS within a broader ecology of US government policy and ongoing public and private debates about defining and measuring public value.

Public Value and Policy in the United States: Shifting Ecologies

In the United States today, across the public (governmental) and private sectors, the issue of 'public value' is under scrutiny and the topic of much debate. The Obama administration has made jobs, education, early learning, infrastructure, diffusion of technology, health and wellness, economically sustainable neighbourhoods, tax reform and energy top domestic priorities. In his 2012 State of the Union address and in a pivotal December 2011 speech in Osawatomie, Kansas, the president addressed the role of the government – working with the private sector – to support the values that built and nourished the American dream – an America where 'everyone gets a fair chance'.

While most Americans subscribe to the importance of the 'American dream', not all agree with the Obama administration's priorities, nor with its assumptions about the role of government in achieving it. A current economic, social and cultural 'churn' prevails. Conflicting and increasingly polarized views about the widening gap between rich and poor, immigration and immigration 'reform', global warming and the urgency of environmental regulation, the rising costs of – and access to – health care, gay rights and an escalating high school dropout rate are amplified by the 24/7, multi-platform media, which keeps often strident voices in headlines, blogs and tweets.

At the federal level, these debates are reflected most persistently in Congressional gridlock over legislation and budget allocations. Positions have been staked on the proper and appropriate role of government in supporting public services and about what those services should be. The tone and tenor of the discourse have intensified as issues of public value have clashed with concerns about the mounting US budgetary deficit.

At the state and local levels, municipal officials have also had to make hard choices – again based on budgets, priorities, and, yes, values – as they allocate resources. Where should the investments be made, which populations and which institutions should be making sacrifices, how can public funds be leveraged effectively, and what should be the evidence of this effectiveness?

Up for consideration are the full range of civic and cultural activities and expenditures, from the size, nature and compensation of the federal (and municipal) work forces, to highway infrastructure, health care (including women's health), voting rights and regulations, and public funding for libraries, education and other social services. In addition, potential regulatory changes and tax code amendments are also 'on the table'. Museums are not immune from any of these shifts.

These government-based resourcing discussions are occurring in a dynamic and transformed funding environment, with ever blurring boundaries between public investments and private philanthropy. In her annual philanthropic forecast, *Philanthropy and Social Investing: Blueprint 2012*, Lucy Bernholz cites the social economy as the biggest shift in philanthropy today. The social economy 'is a more accurate and inclusive term for the mix of revenues, structures, and physical and virtual networks that we use to apply private resources to public good' (Bernholz 2011, 14). This economy is integrally linked to public priorities: 'The decisions we make about our private resources are shaped – overtly or not – by public priorities and our public resources ... The social economy lives alongside government funding and is regulated by government laws' (Bernholz 2011, 5).

This joined-at-the-hip phenomenon is reflected in US government practice today; for example, the president's Domestic Policy Council has focused its public value efforts since 2009 on community service, social investment and public/private partnerships.

Porter and Kramer (2011, 72) in their article, 'Creating Shared Value', state that

> the principles of shared value creation cut across the traditional divide between the responsibilities of business and those of government and civil society. From society's perspective, it does not matter what types of organizations created the value. What matters is that benefits are delivered by those organizations-or combinations of organizations-that are best positioned to achieve the most impact for the least cost.

To that end, corporations and new private sector venture investment organizations are developing new methodologies and metrics to demonstrate evidence of sound and efficient philanthropy and public value outcomes.[1]

This new funding ecology, which includes shifts in funding models, blurring of public/private sector boundaries, and new expectations for social change and impact measurement, has significant implications for the entire US nonprofit sector (which includes most US museums). Institutions are operating in an environment that increasingly privileges greater collaboration, tangible and shared measures of effectiveness, and alignment of

---

1   Kaplan and Grossman's article on 'The Emerging Capital Market for Nonprofits' (2010) describes this phenomenon and provides examples of the value-creation and impact measurement tools in this area, for both direct impact on the organization and its audiences and 'systemic impact'.

goals to achieve system-wide change. Institutions, including museums, cannot afford to be 'islands', attentive only to their own, unique measures of success.

Such non-partisan US-based organizations as United Way Worldwide, America's Promise, the Local Investment Service Corporation (LISC), Grantmakers for Effective Organizations, Grantmakers for Education, and Habitat for Humanity are creating cross-sector alliances and initiatives that are aimed at sharing promising practice, gathering sound and reliable data and evidence, and fomenting systemic change for public benefit.[2]

And where is the American public? In polls, presidential primaries, local referenda and social media sites, we see an increasingly cynical, discouraged and distrustful American public that gives its legislators – and many long-trusted institutions – historically low votes of confidence. The Harwood Institute's 2011 *Citizens and Politics: A View from Main Street America* study surfaced deep-seated doubts in people's faith in the American dream of equal opportunity, a hunger for individuals and institutions that will deliver on their promises, and a longing for acts of compassion and 'small things' that will help 'restore faith in ourselves to get things done'.

One could argue that this situation provides ample room for such traditionally trusted institutions as museums and libraries to fulfil their potential as boundary-spanning organizations that make a positive difference in people's lives. Indeed, a recurring contemporary refrain in the museum sector calls for museums to move from being 'nice to have' to being 'necessary' for the public good. Museums, like other cultural and social organizations, are under more pressure than ever to demonstrate their public value, whether their main source of support comes from the public or the private sector. *The Chronicle of Philanthropy's* Outlook 2012 identified 'more demands to show results' as one of the top five challenges for nonprofit leaders: 'in 2012, all nonprofits should be prepared to answer this question: What impact are you having?'.

This belief is echoed in Mario Morino's *Leap of Reason: Managing to Outcomes in an Era of Scarcity* (2011). Although he does not focus on museums per se, Morino (a former software entrepreneur turned philanthropist) notes:

> *For the entire sixteen years I've been working full-time in the social sector, a problem has been gnawing at me, sometimes literally keeping me up at night. Here's the problem in a nutshell:* ***We don't manage to outcomes, thus greatly diminishing our collective impact … The problem is not new, but it is growing in urgency.*** *The cold reality is that in our present era of unsustainable debts and deficits, our nation simply will not be able to justify huge subsidies for social sector activities and entities without more assurance that they're on track to realize results. Public funders-and eventually private funders as well-will migrate away from organizations with stirring stories alone, toward well-managed organizations that can also demonstrate meaningful, lasting impact. (Morino 2011, 1)*

In this ever more demanding funding and accountability environment, cultural sector leaders may find the strategic triangle proposed by Mark H. Moore of use. The three sides of the triangle – representing an organization's operations, the authorizing environment that provides support, and its citizen/customers – must be maintained in vigilant and

---

2   Grantmakers for Education's Vision 2025; Change the Equation (a nonprofit 'dedicated to mobilizing the business community to improve the quality of STEM learning in the United States'); Grantmakers for Effective Organizations (2011); America's Promise's *Grad Nation*; and Annie E. Casey Foundation's Campaign for Grade-Level Reading are only some of the collective, museum-relevant, efforts to 'move the needle' on pressing national matters.

dynamic equilibrium. The triangle, originally developed for units of government, has equal application in the world of nonprofits. With dwindling public resources, increasing sources of competition for audiences' attention, and doubts about the viability of traditional business models, all organizations need to consider the three sides of the triangle as they seek to fulfil their public good missions.

What are some implications of these changing demands for accountability and results on the US federal cultural agencies, with specific attention to the Institute of Museum and Library Services?

US Cultural Agencies and Public Value

In the United States, there is no cultural ministry. At the federal level, much cultural support occurs through three independent agencies under the auspices of the Federal Council on the Arts and the Humanities, the National Endowment for the Arts (NEA), the National Endowment for the Humanities (NEH) and the Institute of Museum and Library Services (IMLS).[3] How are these three agencies, each of which supports museum activities, addressing public value?

In the legislation that enabled the creation of the NEA and NEH, the US Congress affirmed its belief that 'the encouragement and support of national progress and scholarship in the humanities and the arts, while primarily a matter for private and local initiative, are also appropriate matters of concern to the Federal Government'.[4] The declaration of purpose states that 'democracy demands wisdom and vision in its citizens' and focuses federal support on access, education, models of excellence and the preservation of the country's multicultural heritage.

The IMLS, NEA and NEH conduct their work principally through grant making and special leadership initiatives, with the IMLS and NEA having increasingly robust research functions. Each is part of the executive branch of the US government and is thereby subject to the accountability requirements imposed by the Office of Management and Budget (OMB), which include increasingly rigorous guidelines for performance-based and mission-driven strategic plans as well as evidence of impact for each agency (and each programme within each agency). Each year, every federal agency receives budgetary guidance from the OMB that informs and shapes the agency's annual budgetary request. Over several months, members of the OMB staff review and evaluate agency submissions and make decisions on annual appropriations requests, in accord with the Government Performance and Results Act (GPRA). In brief, the GPRA articulates the US government's performance management framework and emphasizes the importance of improving effectiveness and efficiency to achieve measurable outcomes. In addition, it requires the federal government to adopt a limited number of cross-cutting goals. These goals address broad policy issues as well as government-wide management objectives. Among the priorities for fiscal year 2013 are job creation, education and skills for American workers,

---

3   Other federal entities playing important cultural roles include the Smithsonian Institution, the Library of Congress, the National Gallery of Art and the National Park Service, with specific programmes also at the US departments of state, defence and transportation.

4   20 USC 951, Declaration of findings and purpose, Federal Council on the Arts and the Humanities, 1965.

American innovation and manufacturing, and *Build America: A 21st Century Infrastructure*, as well as a leaner and more streamlined federal government.

The Congress then evaluates and amends the president's budgetary submission and makes the appropriations decisions for each agency. Pursuant to their missions and legislative mandates, the NEH, NEA and IMLS develop strategic foci (grant opportunities, special initiatives) and concomitant operations plans that address these critical national challenges and government directives. Reflecting the changing public value environment and the new funding ecology, each federal cultural agency has also been encouraged to develop and support appropriate public/private partnerships.

It is worth noting that while each agency provides discretionary grants to eligible entities through Washington-DC-directed programmes, each agency also allocates a significant portion of funds to state organizations. These state-based organizations must therefore also navigate the shoals of public value issues.[5]

In Focus: The Institute of Museum and Library Services

THE MEANING OF PUBLIC VALUE AT THE IMLS: 2010 RE-AUTHORIZATION AND 2012 STRATEGIC PLAN

The Institute of Museum and Library Services (IMLS) supports capacity-building activities in museums of all kinds, including aquariums, arboretums, botanical gardens, art museums, children's museums, general museums, historic houses and history museums, nature centres, natural history and anthropology museums, planetariums, science and technology centres, specialized museums and zoos. As noted above, the Congress ultimately determines the agency's authorization and annual appropriations.

Since 1976, when Congress passed the Museum Services Act that created the Institute of Museum Services (IMS), the precursor to the IMLS, the US government has provided support and technical assistance for basic museum operations and conservation project support. The original legislation mandated the IMS to encourage and assist museums in their educational, preservation, stewardship and management roles.

The Congress created the IMLS in 1996, combining two existing government programmes – the IMS and the federal library grants authorized by the Library Services and Technology Act formerly housed at the US Department of Education. In this new form, the agency's museum-related responsibilities evolved to include national leadership grants (including funding for research, beginning in 2005), enhanced focus on integrating new technologies into museum practice, museum–library collaborations, and an emphasis on community impact. From its inception, federal support for museums has been based on their *public service* role of connecting society to 'the cultural, artistic, historic, natural, and scientific understandings that constitute our heritage', providing stewardship for important collections, and serving as core centres of learning and education (Museum and Library Services Act of 2003, 5).

The IMLS has been re-authorized by Congress in 2003 and 2010. Each re-authorization has underscored the original purposes of the agency and refined and increased its

---

5   In the case of the NEA and IMLS, there are allotments to state arts agencies and state library administrative agencies that also receive state funds; the state-based humanities councils are nonprofits, with different levels of public support.

authority and mandate. The 2010 statute gives additional focus to museums as agents of economic development and community revitalization.

Since 2003, the IMLS has had an enhanced responsibility for research, data collection and policy-making. The 2010 re-authorization notes that 'The Director shall annually conduct policy research, analysis, and data collection to extend and improve the Nation's museum, library, and information services' (Museum and Library Services Act of 2010, 5). Further, these activities

> shall be used to identify national needs for and trends in museum, library, and information services; measure and report on the impact and effectiveness of museum, library and information services throughout the United States ... identify best practices; and develop plans to improve ... services ... and to strengthen national, State, local, regional, and international communications and cooperative networks.[6] (Museum and Library Services Act of 2010, 19)

Current IMLS data-gathering and research activities fulfil this requirement for the field and also enable the agency to address the performance requirements of the GPRA.

The 2010 re-authorization also directs the agency head to coordinate the IMLS work with other federal agencies in areas associated with such national priorities as economic and community development, workforce investment, education, early childhood, improving digital literacy skills and disseminating health information. This emphasis is highlighted in the new IMLS strategic plan, published in January 2012.

Although there is a long history of collaboration with the 'sister' cultural agencies, the National Endowments of the Arts and the Humanities, new library-focused alliances have occurred between the IMLS and the Department of Labor, the Federal Communications Commission and the Administration for Children and Families in the Department of Health and Human Services that are focused on these national priorities.[7]

How does the public value concept translate at the IMLS? Consider the Moore strategic triangle. The IMLS authorizing environment comprises the executive Office of Management and Budget and the Congress. The nation's more than 100,000 libraries and more than 17,500 museums are the principal customers. IMLS programmes and initiatives empower these institutions to respond effectively to the needs of the American public. Finally, in this era of limited federal resources – and accompanying directives for greater streamlining – IMLS operations are monitored closely, with the implementation of a variety of efficiencies covering the full range of administrative expenses.

The IMLS also *models and incentivizes* public value among our constituent organizations by shaping grant programmes and special initiatives to respond to

---

6   Because the library data collection activities have a longer history (a legacy of the federal library programme pre-dating the establishment of the agency), the IMLS Office of Planning, Research, and Evaluation has issued more research and data briefs on library-related topics, including workforce development, early learning and the impact of public accessing computing in libraries, than on museum-focused topics.

7   Current inter-agency coordination includes long-standing and new partnerships with NEA and NEH, such as the National Arts and Humanities Youth Program awards, a research/practice partnership on 'The Arts and Human Development' (with the Department of Health and Human Services) and updating *Design for Accessibility: A Cultural Administrator's Toolkit*, a resource that aligns with accessibility and compliance requirements of US government regulations, including Section 504 of the Rehabilitation Act and the Americans with Disabilities Act (ADA). The agency has issued a Training and Employment Notice with the Department of Labor Employment and Training Administration, an Information Memorandum with the Administration for Children and Families of the Department of Health and Human Services, and is tasked with certain responsibilities in the Federal Communications Commission's National Broadband Plan. These focus on library services.

national priorities and requiring grantees to define and demonstrate evidence of impact. The new IMLS strategic plan for 2012–16, *Creating a Nation of Learners*, reflects the agency's current public value focus.

The plan was developed under the leadership of IMLS Director, Susan Hildreth, who was appointed by President Obama for a four-year term beginning in January 2011. Through discussions with the presidentially-appointed, Senate-confirmed, National Museum and Library Services Board and public meetings with IMLS stakeholders (such as the various library and museum service organizations), the agency developed strategic questions to help structure the plan and envision future IMLS services. The IMLS then used an online social media tool, *Ideascale*, to engage more than 1,400 individuals (principally members of the US library and museum community) during the summer of 2011. The participants articulated and prioritized their issues, which ranged from institution-centric to social and educational impact.

The resulting plan, with its goals, objectives and measures of impact, therefore reflects the agency's statutory mandate and responds to stakeholder needs. Its vision is 'A democratic society where communities and individuals thrive, with broad public access to knowledge, cultural heritage, and lifelong learning'. Each of the five IMLS strategic goals contains an outcome focused on adding value to the public sphere and contributing to the development of citizenship amongst individuals:

1. The IMLS places the learner at the centre and supports engaging experiences in libraries and museums that prepare people to be full participants in their local communities and our global society.
2. The IMLS promotes museums and libraries as strong community anchors that enhance civic engagement, cultural opportunities and economic vitality.
3. The IMLS supports exemplary stewardship of museum and library collections and promotes the use of technology to facilitate discovery of knowledge and cultural heritage.
4. The IMLS advises the president and Congress on plans, policies and activities to sustain and increase public access to information and ideas.
5. The IMLS achieves excellence in public management and performs as a model organization through strategic alignment of IMLS resources and prioritization of programmatic activities, maximizing value for the American public.

Further, each goal has a set of tangible objectives and measures that create a roadmap for action and evidence of performance. A performance improvement model describes the theory of change and links activities and strategies to outcomes (see Figure 9.1).

As of this writing, specific impact measures for each strategic goal are still being finalized. Steps towards measuring and documenting impact have occurred, however, and others are in the works. All grants made since 2009 have been 'tagged' by issue area, such as health, environment, civic engagement, workforce development, twenty-first century skills, and economic/community development; visitors to the IMLS website can find tagged grant descriptions and related materials. The FY2013 budgetary request to Congress graphed the full scope of FY2009–FY2011 grant-making activity, for every programme, according to these issue areas.[8]

---

8   Institute of Museum and Library Services (2012b).

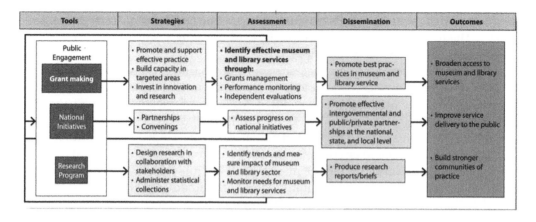

Figure 9.1 IMLS performance improvement model
Source: Creating a Nation of Learners, 2012.

Future grant competitions will require applicants to link funding requests to one of the IMLS strategic goals. Revisions are also underway to the grantee reporting requirements that would provide more specific guidance for measuring value and impact. For the next five-year plans required from each State Library Administrative Agency for their annual, population-based, formula grants (FY2012–FY2016), the IMLS Office of Planning, Research, and Evaluation (OPRE) has developed, in concert with each state agency, a new system of metrics, 'Measuring Success', which will be used to evaluate impact and inform future resource allocation.

THE IMLS AND MEASURING THE PUBLIC VALUE OF MUSEUMS

The IMLS emphasis on outcomes and evaluation dates back to 2000. Many institutions had their first experiences with logic models through IMLS-supported publications, workshops and tools. In 2006, the IMLS supported the development of *Shaping Outcomes: Making a Difference in Libraries and Museums*, a tutorial on outcomes based planning and evaluation, working with Indiana University Purdue University Indianapolis (IUPUI). These efforts focused principally on supporting outcome-based planning and evaluation activities for specific projects and programmes.

In support of the agency's expanded statutory mandate for policy research, analysis and data collection, the OPRE oversees two national data collections efforts for libraries; the Public Libraries in the United States Survey and the State Library Agency Survey. The IMLS website posts data from these surveys, other research and data collection projects, and a growing number of research briefs drawn from them. The OPRE is also managing new data collection projects that will provide current and public information on the US museum sector. The agency has been working with the museum field, researchers and other organizations to develop the first museum-focused data collection and research presence in the federal government.

An important early milestone was *Exhibiting Public Value: Government Funding for Museums in the United States*, the first-ever comprehensive examination of the ways in which government at all levels supports the museum sector, which was published in 2008 (Manjarrez et al. 2008). *Museums Count*, an open-source, web-based census of US museums, is currently under development. A 2010–11 contract with the American Association of Museums and the White Oak Institute helped to facilitate the development of standard data definitions in collaboration with the museum field. Concurrently, work has proceeded with International Information Associates to create the *Museums Count* information architecture. The *Museums Count* survey will gather data on museum location and type; governance; collections and collections care; programmes, visitation and services; partnerships, staffing and funding. As of this writing, the draft survey instrument is undergoing review. Plans call for public deployment before the end of calendar 2012. The resulting data, the first of its kind in the federal sector, will be available to researchers, policy-makers and practitioners and will build a picture of the public value of museums across a range of indices.

To get a more informed picture of the American public's perceptions of our constituent institutions, the OPRE is also developing a household survey that will gauge public knowledge, attitudes and beliefs about, as well as usage of, museums and libraries. The survey will be targeted to reach 4,500 US households and gain information on users and non-users of museum and library services.

MUSEUM GRANT PROGRAMMES

Although IMLS museum grants support a broad variety of capacity-building and community-strengthening activities, the largest programme, *Museums for America*, is perhaps the one linked most directly with public value.

Applicants must have current strategic plans that support the museum's community role, with the proposed project linked to a specific goal in that plan. The programme provided $123 million in grant support to museums from 2004 to 2010. Successful proposals in this category (and others) typically include community needs assessments, evidence of stakeholder involvement in programme development and evaluation plans with proposed outcomes.

A recent formal external evaluation of Museums for America, *Supporting Museums— Serving Communities: An Evaluation of the Museums for America Program* (Apley et al. 2011) does not address long-term impact on museum audiences, but it does provide useful data about how museums are valued by the public and other stakeholders, specifically in the areas of increased and deepened audience engagement, new audiences reached, and the development of sustained relationships with non-museum community partners, such as schools, health and social service organizations. Seventy per cent of surveyed museums worked with formal or informal partners. The report's 20 profiles and six short case study videos illustrate how museums used MFA funds to address such issues as civic engagement, environmental awareness, cross-cultural understanding and technological literacy.

SPECIAL INITIATIVES

From its inception, the IMLS has identified specific initiatives that are designed to promote national priorities and public value. These initiatives typically involve research, convenings, grant opportunities, case studies and sharing 'what works'. Each has been designed to link museum practice with broader community issues, with implications for practitioners and policy-makers. Current initiatives, therefore, respond to the 'cross-cutting priorities' identified by the Obama administration and endorsed by other stakeholders.

MUSEUMS, LIBRARIES AND TWENTY-FIRST CENTURY SKILLS

The United States is part of the global conversation about the twenty-first century skills required to achieve success in life and in work. President Obama has counselled students:

> *You'll need the knowledge and problem-solving skills you learn in science and math to cure diseases like cancer and AIDS, and to develop new energy technologies and protect our environment. You'll need to insights and critical-thinking skills you gain in history and social studies to fight poverty and homelessness, crime and discrimination, and make our nation more fair and more free. You'll need the creativity and ingenuity you develop in all your classes to build new companies that will create new jobs and boost our economy. (President Barack Obama, September 2009)*

In their 2011 book, *That Used to Be Us: How America Fell Behind in the World It Invented and How We Can Come Back*, Thomas L. Friedman and Michael Mandelbaum note that 'In a hyper-connected world where innovation takes place ever more rapidly, what a person knows today will be outdated tomorrow. In such a world one of the most important life skills will be the ability and desire to be a lifelong learner' (2011, 138–9). Friedman and Mandelbaum join other scholars, business and labour leaders, legislators and foundations in promoting such twenty-first century skills as creativity and imagination, critical thinking, effective oral and written communication, and collaboration.[9]

Believing that museums and libraries have critical roles to play in promoting these skills, the IMLS produced *Museums, Libraries and 21st Century Skills* in August 2009. Created with a national task force of library and museum leaders, the report anchors an agency-wide initiative that situates museums and libraries in the evolving transformation of learning, education and workforce development. It documents societal changes, defines twenty-first century skills, and identifies newly important literacies, including financial literacy, civic literacy, environmental literacy and global awareness, which are required currency to navigate and address today's challenges.

Until the IMLS report, US museums and libraries had been largely absent from this urgent national discourse. With its various components, including grant-funded projects, a robust website, a series of community forums, and presentations at state, regional and national professional conferences – the IMLS-led initiative has changed that understanding. Approximately 13,000 copies of the report have been distributed, and the agency has collected numerous examples of museums using it as the basis for major organizational change. This work undergirds goal one of the IMLS strategic plan, and it has enhanced the agency's presence (and the role of museums and libraries) with other public and private entities, including the US Department of Education and Grantmakers for Education, a consortium of more than 200 education-focused foundations.

An important outcome of this work is a formal IMLS–John T. and Catherine C. MacArthur Foundation partnership, under the auspices of the Obama administration's

---

9   See also Fadel and Trilling and the Partnership for 21st Century Skills (2009).

Educate to Innovate initiative, to fund the planning and design of up to 30 teen-focused learning labs in libraries and museums that will promote 'connected' site- and online-based learning and nurture a national community of practice around re-imagined museum and library spaces for youth that nurture STEM (science, technology, engineering and math) learning and twenty-first century skills.

The IMLS is also working with the Partnership for 21st Century Skills, a large and still growing coalition of educational associations, foundations, corporations, publishers and nonprofits that focuses on a state-based approach to incorporating twenty-first century skills in K-12 curricula, assessment and practice, on a new 'Beyond School' project that will align goals, resources, competencies and outcome measurement across the in- and out-of-school communities. In sum, museums and libraries have enhanced national visibility as central to the emerging twenty-first century, learning ecosystem.

LET'S MOVE MUSEUMS AND GARDENS

'The physical and emotional health of an entire generation and the economic health and security of our nation is at stake' (First Lady Mrs Michelle Obama, 9 February 2010).

In the past 30 years, childhood obesity rates in the United States have tripled, with an ominous forecast of a future diabetes epidemic and growth in such obesity-related health problems as heart disease, high blood pressure, cancer and asthma. First Lady Mrs Michelle Obama has joined other government officials, health professionals and civic leaders in calling national attention to a growing national problem with her *Let's Move!* initiative.

In May 2011, the IMLS joined with seven major US museum service organizations[10] to launch *Let's Move! Museums and Gardens*, calling for museums and gardens to strengthen their role in fighting childhood obesity and fostering nutritious habits and healthy behaviours among families and children. This public–private partnership aligns museums with the *Let's Move!* campaign, marshalling their resources and strengths to address this growing national crisis.

As of February 2012, more than 530 museums and gardens in all 50 states have made commitments to at least two of the four *Let's Move! Museums and Gardens* action steps that are tracking relevant exhibits, youth and family programmes, food service choices, and information on nutrition at museum food service operations.

MUSEUMS, LIBRARIES AND EARLY LEARNING

Another issue attracting broad bipartisan, public and private support is the importance of learning in the first years (0–8) of life. Recent research on the cognitive, social, behavioural and neurological aspects of learning has led to a growing policy awareness of the need to address early learning gaps and occasioned many new efforts throughout the public and private sector. This research has shown the economic and social costs of the growing numbers of children unprepared for the transition from 'learning to read' to 'reading to learn', typically at third-grade level in the United States. (Currently, two-

---

10   Association of Children's Museums, American Public Gardens Association, American Association of Museums, American Association for State and Local History, Association of African American Museums, Association of Science and Technology Centers, Association of Zoos and Aquariums.

thirds of US fourth graders are not proficient, according to national assessment data; Campaign for Grade-Level Reading, 2012.) President Obama has stated, 'Learning begins at birth', and in 2009 established an Interagency Policy Board focusing on the need for family engagement, developing benchmarks and evidence of effective practice, targeted research, and a coordinated and integrated early learning system that includes home, school and community. In addition to increased support at the federal level, important state-based initiatives are occurring throughout the country, with the leadership of the National Governors Association and other entities.

Building on several other foundation-led investments and uniting the private philanthropic sector in new ways, the Campaign for Grade-Level Reading is a national effort launched in February 2011 by the Annie E. Casey Foundation and joined by more than 90 foundations, to promote school readiness and third-grade reading proficiency. The Campaign promotes better coordination of early learning services and programmes, improved instruction and evaluation, and promulgation of proven effective practice. Using a community lens and projecting a 10-year timespan, the Campaign aims to have hundreds of US cities and towns work together to meet today's early learning challenges. The IMLS has joined with the administration and the Campaign to leverage the library and museum infrastructure in support of these ambitious, long-term goals.

The agency has long supported library- and museum-based programmes for young children, their parents and caregivers. In 2003, the IMLS funded '*The 21st Century Learner: The Continuum Begins with Early Learning*', a symposium and publication co-organized by the Association of Children's Museums and the Association for Library Service to Children. Millions of dollars in grants to libraries and museums have focused on programmes and services for this audience. In FY2012 and FY2013,[11] the IMLS is calling for proposals from museums and libraries that will align and integrate their institution's early learning projects with broader, community-wide goals. In addition, the agency is preparing a report for policy-makers on the role of museums and libraries in promoting sound and effective early learning programmes, especially through inter-generational programmes that include children and their parents and caregivers.

DIGITAL INCLUSION: AN UNTAPPED PUBLIC VALUE ISSUE FOR MUSEUMS

> *Broadband is the great infrastructure challenge of the early 21st century. Like electricity a century ago, broadband is a foundation for economic growth, job creation, global competitiveness and a better way of life ... It is changing how we educate children, deliver health care, manage energy, ensure public safety, engage government, and access, organize and disseminate knowledge. (National Broadband Plan 2010, 1)*

The March 2010 publication of the *National Broadband Plan: Connecting America* by the US Federal Communications Commission signalled another important US government priority with relevance to the library and museum sector. The report highlights the urgency of accessibility for all Americans to educational content, health and employment data, and other vital information and opportunities via digital technologies and broadband. In 2011, acting on a mandate in the National Broadband Plan, the IMLS partnered with

---

11   The agency's National Leadership Grant category for Library/Museum Collaboration projects has made library and museum community efforts in alignment with the Campaign's goals a funding priority.

the University of Washington Information School and the International City/County Management Association to create *Building Digital Communities: Getting Started*, a guide that defines 'digital inclusion', establishes some core access and adoption principles, and identifies the strategic areas of education, workforce development, health care, public safety, civic engagement and social connections as focal points for community digital inclusion efforts. The guide was developed with a national group of community-based advisors and informed by several community listening sessions held around the United States.

While libraries have been central to this national conversation, museums have remained on the sidelines. Yet they have much to offer. Museums are currently classified among many different types of Community-Based Organizations (CBOs). Their unique value-added has not been articulated for policy-makers. The IMLS has supported many individual museum grant projects that can provide a foundation for more coordinated and visible articulation of museums' public value in this arena.

Conclusion: Observations on Museums and Public Value

In the United States today, all public institutions, including museums, are facing continuing questions of relevance and value. Few are immune from changing audience expectations, differing priorities for public funds, and increased demands for accountability and outcomes. Our media are awash with turbulent and often contentious debates at various governmental levels about urgent needs, institutional worthiness, resource allocation, and evidence of effective impact for the public good. If our museums are indeed necessary to the wellbeing and vitality of our communities, they need to be able to provide credible evidence that this is the case. The wisdom and acuity of the observations of the late museum scholar Stephen Weil, in such pieces as the 2005 'A Success/Failure Matrix for Museums' (Weil 2005) continue to hold true. In that essay, his last, Weil wrote that 'purpose isn't the most important thing in the museum. It's the only thing' (Weil 2005, 38). And that purpose must have some demonstrable social value.

Through our grant programmes, special initiatives, data gathering and research, and respective 'bully pulpits', US federal cultural agencies like the Institute of Museum and Library Services are doing their best to encourage, document and support museums' worthy efforts at serving their respective publics and providing demonstrable public value for their authorizers and constituents.

All comments within are those of the author and do not represent the views of the Institute of Museum and Library Services.

References

Apley, A., Frankel, S., Goldman, E. and Streitburger, K. 2011. *Supporting Museums—Serving Communities: An Evaluation of the Museums for America Program*. Washington, DC: Institute of Museum and Library Services.

ArtPlace America. [Online]. Available at: http://www.artplaceamerica.org [accessed 10 March 2012].

Association of Children's Museums. 2004. *The 21st Century Learner: The Continuum Begins with Early Learning.* Washington, DC: Association of Children's Museums.

Bernholz, L. 2011. *Philanthropy and Social Investing: Blueprint 2012.* Stanford: Stanford Social Innovation Review.

Campaign for Grade-Level Reading. 2012. [Online]. Available at: http://gradelevelreading.net [accessed 12 June 2012].

Change the Equation. 2012. [Online]. Available at: www.changetheequation.org [accessed 10 March 2012].

Delivering on the Accountable Government Initiative and Implementing the GPRA Modernization Act of 2010. 2011. Washington, DC: Executive Office of the President. Office of Management and Budget.

DiConsiglio, J. 2010. *Connecting to Collections: A Report to the Nation.* Washington, DC: Institute of Museum and Library Services.

Downs, M. 2008. *Nine to Nineteen: Youth in Museums and Libraries: A Practitioner's Guide.* Washington, DC: Institute of Museum and Library Services.

Federal Communications Commission. 2010. *The National Broadband Plan: Connecting America.* Washington, DC: Federal Communications Commission.

Friedman, T.L. and Mandelbaum, M. 2011. *That Used to Be Us: How America Fell Behind in the World It Invented and How We Can Come Back.* New York: Farrar, Straus and Giroux.

Grantmakers for Education. 2011. *Innovation 2.0: Grantmaking to Transform America's Education Systems.* [Online]. Available at: www.edfunders.org [accessed 24 June 2012].

Grantmakers for Effective Organizations. 2011. *Catalyzing Networks for Social Change: A Funder's Guide.* Washington, DC: Grantmakers for Effective Organizations.

Harwood Institute, The. 2012. [Online]. Available at: http://www.theharwoodinstitute.org/index.php?ht=d/Blogger/archive [accessed 24 June 2012].

Harwood, R.C. 2012. *The Work of Hope: How Individuals and Organizations Can Authentically Do Good.* Washington, DC: The Harwood Institute.

Indiana University Purdue University Indianapolis and Institute of Museum and Library Services. 2006. *Shaping Outcomes: Making a Difference in Libraries and Museums.* [Online]. Available at: www.shapingoutcomes.org [accessed 24 June 2012].

Institute of Museum and Library Services. 2000. *Perspectives on Outcome-Based Evaluation for Museums and Libraries.* Washington, DC: Institute of Museum and Library Services.

Institute of Museum and Library Services. 2004. *Charting the Landscape, Mapping New Paths: Museums, Libraries and K-12 Learning.* Washington, DC: Institute of Museum and Library Services.

Institute of Museum and Library Services. 2009. *Museums, Libraries and 21st Century Skills.* Washington, DC: Institute of Museum and Library Services.

Institute of Museum and Library Services. 2010. Learning Labs for Libraries and Museums. [Online]. Available at: http://www.imls.gov/about/learning_labs.aspx [accessed 24 June 2012].

Institute of Museum and Library Services. 2011. *Let's Move! Museums and Gardens.* [Online]. Available at: http://www.imls.gov/about/letsmove.aspx [accessed 24 June 2012].

Institute of Museum and Library Services. 2012a. *Creating a Nation of Learners: Strategic Plan 2012–2016.* Washington, DC: Institute of Museum and Library Services.

Institute of Museum and Library Services. 2012b. *Fiscal Year 2013 Appropriations Request to the United States Congress.* Washington, DC: Institute of Museum and Library Services.

Institute of Museum and Library Services, University of Washington Technology and Social Change Group, International City/County Management Association. 2012. *Building Digital Communities.* Washington, DC: The Institute of Museum and Library Services.

John S. and James L. Knight Foundation. 2010. *Knight Soul of the Community 2010*. Miami: John S. and James L. Miami, Fld: Knight Foundation in partnership with Gallup, Inc.

Kaplan, R.S. and Grossman, A.S. 2010. The Emerging Capital Market for Nonprofits. *Harvard Business Review*, 88(10), 111–18.

Manjarrez, C., Rosenstein, C., Colgan, C. and Pastore, E. 2008. *Exhibiting Public Value: Museum Public Finance in the United States*. Washington, DC: Institute of Museum and Library Services.

Moore, M.H. 1995. *Creating Public Value: Strategic Management in Government*. Cambridge, MA: Harvard University Press.

Markusen, A. and Gadwa, A. 2010. *Creative Placemaking*. Washington, DC: National Endowment for the Arts.

Morino, M. 2011. *Leap of Reason: Managing to Outcomes in an Era of Scarcity*. Washington, DC: Venture Philanthropy Partners.

National Endowment for the Arts. 2003. *Design for Accessibility: A Cultural Administrator's Toolkit*. [Online]. Available at: http://www.nea.gov/resources/accessibility/pubs/DesignAccessibility.html [accessed 10 March 2012].

National Endowment for the Arts. 2010. *Art Works for America*. Washington, DC: National Endowment for the Arts.

National Endowment for the Arts. 2011. *The Arts and Human Development: Framing a National Research Agenda for the Arts, Lifelong Learning, and Individual Well-Being*. White paper based on 'The Arts and Human Development: Learning Across the Lifespan'. Convening on 14 March 2011. [Online]. Available at: www.nea.gov/pub/TheArtsAndHumanDev.pdf [accessed 24 June 2012].

National Endowment for the Arts. 2012. *Task Force on the Arts and Human Development*. [Online]. Available at: www.nea.gov/research/taskforce/arts-and-human-development.html [accessed 10 March 2012].

Outlook 2012. *Chronicle of Philanthropy*, 19 January, 7.

Partnership for 21st Century Skills. [Online]. Available at: http://www.p21.org/ [accessed 24 June 2012].

Porter, M.E. and Kramer, M.R. 2011. Creating Shared Value. *Harvard Business Review*, 89(11), 63–77.

Semmel, M.L. 2012. An Opportune Moment: Museums in the National Conversation on Early Learning. *Journal of Museum Education*, 37(1), 17–28.

Trilling, B. and Fadel, C. 2009. *21st Century Skills: Learning for Life in Our Times*. San Francisco: Jossey-Bass.

US Department of Education. 2010. *Early Learning Initiative*. [Online]. Available at: http://www.ed.gov/early-learning [accessed October 2011].

US Department of Education. 2010. *Learning Powered by Technology: The National Education Technology Plan*. Washington, DC: US Department of Education.

US Senate and House of Representatives. 1976. *Museum Services Act of 1976, Title II of the Arts, Humanities, and Cultural Affairs Act of 1976* (P.L. 94-462). Washington, DC.

US Senate and House of Representatives. 2003. *Museum and Library Services Act of 2003*, Public Law 108-81. 108th Cong., 1st session. Washington, DC: US Senate and House of Representatives.

US Senate and House of Representatives. 2010. *Museum and Library Services Act of 2010*, Public Law 111.340, 111th Cong., 2nd session. Washington, DC: US Senate and House of Representatives.

Weil, Stephen E. 2005. A Success/Failure Matrix for Museums. *Museum News*, 84(1), 36–40.

White House, The. 2009. *President Obama's Message for America's Students*. [Online]. Available at: http://www.whitehouse.gov/video/President-Obamas-Message-for-Americas-Students [accessed 24 June 2012].

White House, The. 2010. *Let's Move!* [Online]. Available at: http://www.letsmove.gov/ [accessed 24 June 2012].

White House, The. 2011. *Remarks by the President on the Economy at Osawatomie, Kansas.* Washington, DC, 6 December.

White House, The. 2012. *Remarks by the President in State of the Union Address.* Washington, DC, 24 January.

White House, The. Office of Management and Budget. 2012. *The Budget for Fiscal Year 2013.* Budget Overview, 13 February.

10 Public Value and Public Policy in Britain: Prospects and Perspectives

DAVID O'BRIEN

Introduction

Museums are contested sites. When the new Museum of Liverpool opened in the summer of 2011 it attracted 250,000 visitors in its first month (NML 2011). However, the build up to the opening was beset by arguments over funding, costs and content, suggesting a clash of not just technical approaches to dealing with managing the project, but also of the meaning and worth of the project itself. The museum was a site for contests and controversies over value. The visitor numbers suggest the museum was a great success, with an obvious *use* value for the visitors, but museums, along with the rest of the cultural sector, do not see their value narrowly defined in the numbers making use of their institutions as visitor attractions. Rather they have a range of functions that are narrated in terms of differing values. These functions are carried out against the position of the museum as a site for the conflict of values, a place where issues of representation and identity, ethics and morality are to be struggled with and struggled over. In Liverpool, an important aspect of the museum is to engage with the tragedies of Liverpool's past, attempting to deal with issues of racism, sexism and homophobia, along with class and religious conflicts, in a way that both represents these issues but also renders them accessible (as well as palatable) for differentiated visitors, with their range of motivations for attending. The conflicts and accords of morals and ethics, perspectives and personalities, are intertwined with the value of the visitor numbers. The pressing question over the last 20 years, in the UK and elsewhere, has become how best to measure the value of the funding, the visitor experience, and the institution's performance. Public value, since the beginning of the twenty-first century, seemed to offer a way to do exactly that.

This chapter historicizes public value, contributing three perspectives to our understanding of the term. First, that the term public value has lost currency in the UK as a result of political changes associated with the election of the Coalition government in 2010. Second, that there is a theoretical uncertainly surrounding the meaning of public value, an uncertainty which was closely related to public value's success in capturing the imagination of key think tanks, academics and parts of the British state. Finally, that the empirical limits of public value as a measurement framework, as compared with forms of economic valuation useful for the cost–benefit analysis associated with UK central government decision-making, have been reached.

To begin, the chapter explores the meaning of public value, before turning to describe three case studies of its use by cultural organizations. The chapter places these case studies in the broader context of the search for ways of measuring within the cultural sector, particularly the economic valuation techniques associated with the UK's Department for Culture, Media and Sport's (DCMS) Measuring Cultural Value programme. The chapter concludes with an assessment of public value as a concept that, as a result of its association with New Labour and the ongoing financial crisis facing the UK, will have a limited usefulness for the cultural sector under the Coalition government currently in power in the UK. That is not to deny the importance of the ideas associated with public value, but rather that the chapter is framed by a scepticism of public value's broader prospects of capturing the current public policy agenda. The chapter suggests caution over the prospects that pubic value is the right language and approach for a cultural sector grappling with the problem of representing value whilst demonstrating the efficient and effective use of the public funds they receive.

The Transatlantic Career of Public Value

Ideas have careers. Some ideas travel, travel well and travel light (Miller 2011), whilst others are confined to academic debates, think tank pamphlets or government departments at singular times and in singular places. Public value is an idea that has enjoyed a remarkable itinerary.

Alford and O'Flynn, in an excellent (2009) overview of public value, identify several meanings and uses of the term, ranging from an overarching policy paradigm responding to New Public Management (NPM);[1] a rhetorical strategy for under-fire bureaucracies and public managers; a narrative or ethnographic account of the world and practices of public managers; and as a framework for measuring the performance of organizations and staff that moves beyond the narrowly managerialist focus of much NPM.

The uses of public value are united by a concern with identifying the unique and particular forms of value created by public organizations, a concern largely ignored and neglected by theories of NPM that were dominant within Western, English-speaking democracies, particularly the United States, UK and Australia, during the 1980s and 1990s, as well as within supra-national institutions such as the OECD. Public value was initially a *corrective* to the perceived excesses of NPM's overly reductive focus on both private sector management techniques and the economic value associated with those approaches (Meynhardt 2009). A corrective that then became much more widely associated with issues of legitimacy, defence of institutional positions and an extra-economic framework for measuring performance.

The various uses of the term are the major discussion point when considering public value, because of the lack of coherence associated with the term. The many uses of public value have made it easy to diffuse the idea, made it possible for the concept to be taken up in a range of contexts (often in surprisingly contradictory ways) and provoked sustained engagement, attachment and critique from an array of different sources. Since it was first

---

1   New Public Management is a broad and disputed term, but is generally taken to encapsulate a variety of policies including privatization and denationalization of state-owned industries, the introduction of markets into public service provision, the use of commercial business management techniques within public management and a reconfiguration of the relationship between state and citizen.

set out by Mark Moore in the mid-1990s, public value has received a variety of receptions: from the enthusiastic embrace of public managers to the, at best, intrigued reaction or, at worst, outright hostility, of the academic community (Alford and O'Flynn 2009).

Academic discussion has offered a selection of problems surrounding questions of public value's limits and implications. Rhodes and Wanna (2007, 2009) emphasize that public value is a threat to the public manager by asking them to act in overtly political ways, by becoming entrepreneurial, on the one hand, and acting as self-appointed interpreters and thus guardians of the public interest. For Rhodes and Wanna there is an overly benign view of public organizations implicit in public value, missing the crucial fact that public institutions often act in coercive ways, exercising power and sometimes violence to compel citizens' actions. Most importantly Rhodes and Wanna see public value as a fundamentally American idea, one which is grounded in Moore's experiences at Harvard and working with American public bureaucracy, which is influenced by a much more entrepreneurial managerial tradition compared to the Westminster system. In particular the UK does not offer the space for the entrepreneurial public official as a result of the strong forms of control within UK administration, the dominance of the party system and the civil service's status as a permanent part of the constitutional bureaucracy (Rhodes and Wanna 2009).

In contrast to Rhodes and Wanna's defence of the role of public officials in Westminster systems, criticism associated with thinkers from the right of the political spectrum has seen public value as a further extension of those aspects of bureaucracy critiqued by public choice approaches (Eriksson 2011) to public administration. These critiques see public value as a *defensive* tactic for institutions struggling with criticism about their place in public life and seeking to reinforce privileged positions (Elstein 2004).

The most obvious difficulty for public value has been locating it within the normative/positive divide within public administration.[2] Whilst there is clearly a normative aspect for those advocating the 'public value' of a given state institution or practice, this advocacy seems to have been fused with an attempt to construct an empirically grounded description of the activities of public sector organizations and employees. This is both a weakness of public value as a category (Rhodes and Wanna 2007) but also a strength of the term as it has enabled public value to be *both* a form of advocacy and a description of practice. The pragmatic nature of public value, illustrated by its dual nature, is crucial to understand its success and perhaps its potential limits. Work from the UK, particularly associated with the Cabinet Office and subsequently several think tanks, which had considerable crossover with senior advisors to New Labour, constructed public value for the British context to become

> an overarching framework in which questions of legitimacy, resources allocation and measurement can be made. (Horner and Hazel 2005, 243, cited in Alford and O'Flynn 2009)

Within this framework, there is a specific aspect of public value that can be particularly useful, not just for museums but also for organizations across the public sector. Public value suggests organizations focus on the public. Whereas public service provision was

---

2   Although not a strict divide, the division is broadly between positivistic scholars seeking to offer descriptive accounts of the functioning of public administration systems and those scholars offering normative work that argues for the value of public administration, particularly as a contrast to NPM-influenced critics.

traditionally dominated by professional interests (subject to critiques from left- and right-wing commentators) public value urges a focus on the citizen, rather than just the expert or the politician (Benington 2009). For the museum this presents both an opportunity and threat, drawing on critics from a museological perspective questioning the validity of imperialistic or elite narratives within the museum (Woodward 2012), whilst also offering the institution emerging techniques of audience research to understand potential new visitors, to open new revenue streams and to ensure institutional sustainability by repeat attendance or closer relationships with a wider range of people.

The Work Foundation's (Horner et al. 2007) discussion of the way London's Victoria and Albert (V&A) Museum creates public value is instructive here, suggesting value is created across a range of practices, around access, world leader status and creativity, evaluated by a range of key performance indicators and research projects. This description of the V&A draws on public value as practice, normative category and advocacy tool. Whilst the limitations of measurement frameworks are robustly recognized (Horner et al. 2007, 26), the institution is presented as balancing expertise with consultation. The V&A is seen to be a world leading institution with awareness of the importance of a relationship with the general public.

The V&A shows how public value has been employed by cultural organizations by combining some of the ways outlined in Alford and O'Flynn's (2009) summary. As subsequent parts of the chapter will show, the failure to disentangle the various meanings of public value, as it has been adopted across the cultural sector, have prevented a clear conception of public value from gaining traction. In the first instance this will mean performance measurement frameworks associated with public value will carry traces of the narrative, paradigmatic and rhetorical aspects of public value which may not cohere with conceptions of public management and the role of the state held by politicians in the post-New Labour era. Second the continued lack of clarity offers the opportunity to agree with Benington's (2009, 233) assertion that there is a clear tension within the meanings associated with public value and that

> *there is a danger in the UK at least, of public value getting used loosely, as a broad portmanteau phrase expressing ideals and aspirations about public service, but capable of meaning many different things to many different people.*

From Public Value to Cultural Value

Public value has been taken up by the cultural sector in several ways, most obviously as 'cultural value' (Holden 2004). 'Cultural value' has a complex history and has evolved to encompass a series of intertwined forms of value created by artistic and cultural organizations, as well as becoming associated with important research agendas in the UK. Although first used in a speech by Ellis (2003), the term is most notably associated with the work of John Holden. In Holden's (2004) work the value created by cultural organizations takes three forms, including the intrinsic value of the experiences generated by the organizations, the instrumental value created for public policy purposes and the institutional value created by the bonds between organizations and their various publics. Institutional value maps most closely to the public value tradition described previously in this chapter.

The development of a tripartite theory of public value for the cultural sector, with specific forms of cultural value associated with, but not exclusively mapping onto, Holden's vision of intrinsic value was the basis for various conferences, speeches and papers from both politicians (Jowell 2004) and think tanks associated with New Labour (Hewison 2006) which would culminate (Edgar 2012) in the attempt to develop a framework for cultural policy grounded in the peer-review system proposed by the McMaster review (McMaster 2008).

The great tension, as identified in the Demos adaptation of public value for the cultural sector, is between the intrinsic value associated with visitor and participant experiences, linked to conceptions of excellence, and the wider forms of value associated with democracy and accountability (forms of value which cut across both institutional and instrumental values). As Jancovich (2011, 272) notes, many cultural organizations' work encounters this tension, between 'those who believed that cultural policy needed to directly consider the needs of its public and those who championed the need for artistic independence, to work outside the constraints of such accountability'. Public value was seen to be a way to understand the need for organizations to affirm their institutional and instrumental value, whilst narrating the 'intrinsic' commitments to excellence in measurable ways.

The importance of excellence to cultural organizations as an essential part of their activity is bound up with the adaptation of public value as a framework for measurement of the added value of cultural activity that goes beyond NPM conceptions of value. The assertion of the uniqueness or difference of cultural organizations, as compared with other areas of public policy, is grounded in the supposedly unquantifiable nature of the benefits of culture, an unquantifiability often defended by modernist and romantic conceptions of the transformative power of cultural experience (Carey 2005).

The unquantifiable nature of culture is taken to mean that forms of decision-making associated with modern government are not applicable. The 'audit society' (Power 1997) of accounting and management techniques founded on the commensurability of differing policy interventions to a single monetary metric, to be compared and contrasted with other policy options, finds no place for the museum, the gallery, the theatre or the concert hall. Indeed, in the early debates surrounding the birth of cultural value statements such as that by Adrian Ellis were typical:

the current language of performance and its quantification is unlikely to be jettisoned by this or any future administration. But it needs to accommodate the vocabulary of cultural value. Unless a common and public language can be found in which to discuss cultural purposes and intrinsic – alongside instrumental – value, then funders will tend to focus on a partial view of cultural institutions and the funded will chaff and sulk, dependent through they are on the public purse. So policy makers and the cultural community have an opportunity to face a common set of challenges on common ground. (Ellis 2003)

Comments such as those by Ellis provided the context for the operationalization of the rhetorical aspects of public value as a defence of cultural organizations into a measurement framework to articulate value to both policy and the public.[3]

The Career of Public Value in Arts and Culture: Three Case Studies

The most well developed use of public value within the UK's cultural sector is associated with the Heritage Lottery Fund (HLF). The HLF is responsible for administering and distributing funding from the UK's National Lottery to a wide variety of heritage projects, where heritage is viewed in a broad sense, encompassing both museums, historic buildings and intangible forms of heritage.

The HLF, in partnership with Demos, the think tank that had developed public value into the cultural value framework, constructed a sophisticated evaluation tool to understand the impact, management and future development of its major funding streams. The HLF sought to identify the different forms of value its investments created, most notably the kind of value unique or specific to HLF funded projects. The Demos framework, of intrinsic, instrumental and institutional value, was adapted to develop measurement tools around key concepts, for example intrinsic values were associated with the HLF's work as managers and conservers of heritage (Clark and Maeer 2008).

However this process was not without teething problems as, in accord with criticisms of Moore's original conception of public value discussed above, the HLF was required to operationalize Demos' framework into specific research questions, measurements and indictors. Clark and Maeer (2008) describe the benefits and limitations of employing the framework, focusing on the benefits for the organization as it gathered data that enabled the HLF to understand its role, its functions and its relationships in a clearer (and more clearly evidenced) way. Thus, in the HLF's conception, public value became a framework for measurement, for organizational learning, and for accountability. This framework was in keeping with attempts to develop measurement for the cultural sector since the 1980s, remaining subject to the same empirical and conceptual problems, particularly over measuring the social impact aspect of its instrumental value (Selwood 2010).

The second case study comes from the Arts Council England (ACE). The ACE is the non-departmental public body that administers a significant slice of public funding for the arts and, following the closure of the Museums, Libraries and Archives Council as a separate entity after the election of the Coalition in 2010, an important part of the museums sector.

The ACE's work was based on a consultation exercise to 'debate about the value of the arts and the role of public funding. In particular, the arts debate sought to explore how public value is currently created by the arts today and what it would mean for the Arts Council and the individuals and organisations we fund to create public value' (Bunting 2007, 4). The programme employed a variety of consultative methods, including focus groups and in-depth interviews with ACE staff, members of the public, arts professionals

---

3   Most notably in the development of Holden's (2004) and Hewison's (2006) creation of the value triangle and attempts to apply public value in the context of the Heritage Lottery Fund. This saw the evolution of public value as a way of describing cultural value to a way of measuring organizational performance when applied to the HLF.

and administrators (Bunting 2007). The results suggested a series of topics for debate, around excellence, innovation, transparency of decision-making and the uniqueness of the experiences and the benefits of ACE-funded activities. The debate has done much to inform the ACE's most recent strategy, *Achieving Great Art for Everyone* (ACE 2010), with a recognition that the ACE has responded to the insights gained from its interpretation of public value as a form of research and consultation.

The most pertinent point about the ACE's use of public value is not the extent to which the concept has, or has not, affected organizational practice. Indeed, the consultation gave the ACE a rich picture of a very well informed and nuanced arts audience. Rather the ACE's version of public value illustrates the flexibility (and thus potential incoherence) of public value, along with the limitations of public value when employed as research and consultation. Gray's (2008) analysis of the ACE's understanding of public value makes it clear that the problem of an overly managerial version of public value manifests itself most obviously in relation to the question of who exactly are the public. Although the ACE's research work was robust, for Gray it focused on giving too much weight to the views of ACE staff, ACE funded organizations and the cultural sector. This focus gave the critical question of what the public value of cultural activity is comparatively little importance, compared with the need to assert that cultural activity was certainly of public value, an idea seemingly self-evident to large sections of the consultation (Gray 2008, 9). Public value is here 'a management device to investigate how the goods and services ACE delivers could be more effetely managed and targeted at existing users', but framed within the broader discourses associated with public value suggesting the idea is 'intended to provide the basis for re-thinking about, and re-designing, what ACE is doing in terms of service delivery for the population of England' (Gray 2008, 11).

Whilst emphasizing different aspects of the use of public value by the ACE, Lee et al. (2011) are supportive of Gray's (2008) critique of public value as conceived by the ACE, that, in effect, the process justified the ACE's current management practices with very little consideration of the problems associated with the 'institutional' value (Holden 2004) created by the ACE. This critique exactly parallels the broader charges levelled at public value by Rhodes and Wanna (2007, 2009), that public value ignores the problematic and contested nature of public decision-making, forgetting the important political oversight constraining public managers. The ACE's use of public value further illustrates how the idea has travelled and been adapted to differing institutions. For the HLF, public value was a framework to measure performance. For the ACE, public value was a way to support its existing status.

These two uses of public value are present in the third major use of public value in the cultural sector, by the British Broadcasting Corporation (BBC). The BBC is publically funded through a license fee payable by the general population of television users, subject to exemptions for specific groups. This method of funding the state broadcaster in the UK has been controversial, particularly so since the 1980s, when the-then Thatcher government was suspicious of this funding method for reasons associated with economic theory and assumptions about the ideology prevailing within the BBC itself.

The BBC was subject to significant institutional change during the 1980s and 1990s, a change well documented by Born (2004). By the mid-2000s, following almost two decades of restructuring and the exposure of archaic governance practices following the Hutton inquiry into the death of Dr David Kelly, the BBC faced challenges over its funding, its services and its governance (Lee et al. 2011). Against this backdrop public value, for the BBC, was a way to move beyond a narrow conception of the function of public organizations and to assert the BBC's unique status as a public service broadcaster (much like the public service ethos of the civil servant).

Public value for the BBC took three forms. In its current guise public value has evolved as a 'test' to inform the BBC Trust's scrutiny of the Corporation's decisions (Coyle and Woollard 2010). However recent literature (particularly Lee et al. 2011) has questioned the extent to which the public value test has moved beyond the dual nature of public value's initial use by the BBC. In the first instance it was associated with a broad programme of market research on consumers' relationships with the BBC. Second it was mobilized to make an economic argument about the necessity of licence fee funding for the BBC, an economic argument which seemed in tension with the forms of public value associated with the first use of the term by the BBC. A combination of the two uses suggested a focus on those benefits, or value, which were not reducible to the economic, in keeping with the way public value has been received in the UK. However, in contrast with the Arts Council, the consumer research and some of the narratives of value were precisely concerned with the economic value of the BBC measured in willingness to pay surveys. Thus the primary use of public value was rhetorical, constructing a narrative of the worth, importance and status of the BBC whilst employing the tools of HM Treasury to make an economic case to Whitehall.

From Measuring Impact to Measuring Value

The use of economic techniques to bolster the narrative of the BBC's case for funding is an example of the move away from measurement of the impact of activities as a method of making funding cases, towards methods that are more concerned with valuation in financial terms, based on guidance from central government. This move has its roots in a much longer term battle to find ways of articulating the value of cultural funding, a battle public value was supposed to have won.

From the end of the Second World War and into the 1970s the question of measurement in the cultural sector was not a major issue. The combination of Keynes' vision for the Arts Council (Upchurch 2004), the rise of working class arts education (Hewison 1995), the national identity and subsequent national prestige fostered by elite forms of cultural practice, along with the Victorian-inflected civilizing power of those forms, all contributed to a cultural settlement where measurement was a low priority.

This consensus ended in the 1980s, concurrent with the rise of NPM (Hood 2008) in the UK. During the 1980s and into the 1990s, as the state sought to roll back its funds and its direct provision, measurement in the cultural sector was grounded in the contribution the cultural sector could make to social and economic goals. Impact studies, initially quantifying economic impact, then developing to measure social impacts (culminating in frameworks such as the Generic Learning and Social Outcomes indicators developed by the Museums, Libraries and Archives Council) were the dominant framework for making the case for the sector and were entrenched as part of New Labour's cultural policy. Under Labour their importance accelerated as successive culture secretaries began to attach cultural programmes to a range of other policies, including health and criminal justice (Gray 2009).

Economic impact has been used as a way of trying to fit cultural policies into a cost–benefit analysis framework. As a vast range of commentators (e.g. Cowen 2006, 15) have identified, this risks reducing culture to a range of benefits that are provided by other sectors of government intervention and fails to capture the full benefits of culture to individuals, their communities and to society. Thus the problem of valuing culture has become how best to fit the unique aspects of culture, outside of the social and economic impacts, into the economic language of the welfare economic paradigm used by NPM influenced central government in the UK. This problem has become especially pressing given the increasing demands on decreasing resources expected across the public sector for the foreseeable future (Selwood 2010).

The DCMS has recently published discussion papers on how to adapt the language of economic value for the cultural sector, to move beyond narratives of 'impact' (O'Brien 2010), but without the public value paradigm. Economic value is grounded in individual utility and preference satisfaction, as expressed in what people are willing to pay for a good or service (Throsby 2001, 19). This is often reflected in market prices, although people may often be willing to pay more than the price for a good or service and the difference between price and willingness to pay is referred to as consumer surplus. Where there is no market for a good or service and therefore no price, e.g. in the context of museums free at the point of use in the UK, value can be seen in the opportunity cost of that good or service, whether in terms of willingness to pay money or willingness to give up resources, such as time (Mulgan et al. 2006). This understanding of value, as the reflection of individual utility, usually expressed in their preferences, is at the root of the UK government's conception of value for use in decision-making.

There are two main forms of economic valuation methods that fit in with central government's understanding of value; methods that derive value by attempting to understand people's preferences, whether stated or revealed; and methods that attempt to valuations based on the utility people derive from engagements with the cultural sector, shown in the impact of that engagement on individual's subjective well-being (O'Brien 2010). This debate is still ongoing, as these techniques leave little room for the expertise of organizations' staff because they focus on the consumer's viewpoint, although they do satisfy central government's prevailing decision-making discourse. It is somewhat inevitable that the dialectic between forms of measurement that make different practices and values commensurable, as opposed to those practices, artefacts and institutions valued precisely for their *incommensurability* (Espeland and Stevens 1998) will continue, with both economic valuation and those measurement systems based on public value playing a part in the search for a solution to the question of how best to value culture.

Perspectives and Prospects for Public Value in the Post-New Labour Era

If it is the case that the debate over forms of impact has now moved to the problem of measuring value, primarily in economic terms, where does this leave public value, for the cultural sector and more widely within contemporary politics?

There is predictability, identified by Alford and O'Flynn (2009), within the life-cycle of public value, from its initial attraction, subsequent problematization and eventual socialization into the wider lexicon of concepts grappling with the issue of public administration in modernity. However public value must be historicized and placed in the political context of its emergence, dissemination and use. Public value rose to prominence under New Labour, an administration that was especially notable for its attempts at generating narratives of consensus by a range of consultative practices (Fairclough 2000). In some ways public value can be seen as the logical extension of the politics informed by the specific consultative practices that dominated the first two New Labour administrations (Rawnsley 2001 and 2010). Its dissemination was also closely associated with New Labour, whether its individual personalities, its think tanks or its policies. For example, the HLF's cultural value framework concerned itself with the impact of funding on social inclusion, an important concept for New Labour's social policy (Levitas 2005; Durrer 2008). Social inclusion is now a term that is almost entirely absent from Coalition discourse, which concentrates on more traditional notions of poverty and the poor.

Along with social inclusion, creative industries (McRobbie 2010) and evidence-based policy-making (Sanderson 2002) it may be prudent to see public value as closely associated with New Labour's approach to the question of government in the post-NPM era. Lee et al. (2011) see public value as a 'prime example' of New Labour's tendency to coin new terms, concluding that 'it will ultimately be seen by history as a short-lived policy curio of the New Labour administration' (Lee et al. 2011, 298). This is not to ignore the way that valuable work is ongoing outside of government, within academia, trade unions and the cultural sector itself, but rather the short- to medium-term prospects for public value in the UK are challenging.

Those proponents of public value who suggest it chimes with the more collectivist times required following massive state intervention to secure the banking and finance sectors of the economy (e.g. Talbot 2009) must contend with the radical shift resulting from the change of government in the UK, with the Coalition's focus on shrinking the state to deal with the financial crisis in the UK (Cabinet Office 2010) along with ideological commitments of both Liberal Democrat liberalism and Conservative commitments to ending the role of 'big government'. Although, superficially, the language of Moore's conception of public value would seem to have strong links to both Conservative rhetoric of the Big Society and the limits of 'big' government, alongside Liberal Democrat commitment to localism, there are clear limits to the possibility of public value gaining traction with the Coalition, because of public value's association with New Labour.

In addition to the political limitations of public value there are empirical limits to its ability to measure what is needed by central government. Talbot (2011) is open about the uncertainty surrounding the prospects for public value, as the Coalition's practices of public administration exhibit continuity with New Labour in some respects (O'Brien 2012), against the backdrop of strongly different ideological approaches to the role of the state. Talbot is also incisive about the role of HM Treasury in the UK, a role which may be the strongest determinate of the limit to public value as a framework for measuring and articulating the worth of public organizations. The lack of overt interest shown by the Treasury, even during the New Labour era, means that the forms of performance measurement favoured by central government have not been transformed by conceptions of public value, unlike organizations such as the BBC, ACE and HLF.

The experience of embedding public value illustrates the 'social life' of ideas (Law et al. 2011). Frameworks take on a life of their own, morphing and transforming as they move from context to context. Whilst the prospects for the language of public value may be pessimistic, its adaptation in the UK to concerns with immeasurable forms of value, rhetorical strategies of defending cultural funding as well as offering frameworks that have tried to engage with narrowly economic versions of technocratic policy-making, suggest the *lessons* of public value may have embedded themselves within the UK's cultural sector.

Public value returns us to questions that are at the root of the meaning of value. The term value encapsulates several complex meanings, ranging across moral positions (as values), prices (as value) and personal identity (O'Brien 2013). The case studies of the HLF, ACE and BBC have shown how public value has been used to understand value, in its many forms. Although in the UK to date, public value has tended to have more impact at an institutional, as opposed to a governmental, level, the differing uses of the term are all investigating the value of the institutions, an investigation that has never been more urgently needed.

There is, therefore, ambivalence at the root of public value in the present context. It would be proper for the contemporary cultural institution to consider that although public value can offer much to the public sector organization, its language is no longer the rhetoric or practice of government in the UK (O'Brien 2012).

References

Alford, J. and O'Flynn, J. 2009. Making Sense of Public Value: Concepts, Critiques and Emergent Meanings. *International Journal of Public Administration*, 32(3–4), 171–91.

Arts Council England. 2010. *Achieving Great Art for Everyone*. London: Arts Council England.

Benington, J. 2009. Creating the Public in Order to Creative Public Value? *International Journal of Public Administration*, 32(3–4), 232–49.

Born, G. 2004. *Uncertain Vision*. London: Secker and Warburg.

Bunting, C. 2007. *Public Value and the Arts in England*. London: Arts Council England.

Cabinet Office. 2010. *The Coalition Agreement*. London: HMSO.

Carey, J. 2005. *What Good are the Arts?* London: Faber & Faber.

Clark, K. and Maeer, G. 2008. The Cultural Value of Heritage: Evidence from the Heritage Lottery Fund. *Cultural Trends*, 17(1), 23–56.

Cowen, T. 2006. *Good and Plenty*. Princeton: Princeton University Press.

Coyle, D. and Woollard, C. 2010. *Public Value in Practice*. London: BBC.

Durrer, V. 2008. Theoretical Perspectives on New Labour's Cultural Policy: Art Museums as Vehicles for Social Inclusion. *Museological Review*, 13, 11–28.

Edgar, D. 2012 Why fund the arts? *The Guardian*, 5 January 2012.

Ellis, A. 2003. *Valuing Culture*. Available at: http://www.demos.co.uk/files/File/VACUAEllis.pdf [accessed 21 March 2012].

Elstein, D. 2004. *Building Public Value: The BBC's New Philosophy*. London: IEA.

Eriksson, L. 2011. *Rational Choice Theory*. London: Palgrave Macmillan.

Espeland, W. and Stevens, M. 1998. Commensuration as a Social Process. *Annual Review of Sociology*, 24, 313–43.

Fairclough, N. 2000. *New Labour, New Language*. London: Routledge.

Gray, C. 2008. Arts Council England and Public Value: A Critical Review. *International Journal of Cultural Policy*, 14, 203–15.

Gray, C. 2009. Managing Cultural Policy: Pitfalls and Prospects. *Public Administration*, 87, 574–85.

Hewison, R. 1995. *Culture and Consensus: England, Art and Politics since 1940*. London: Methuen.

Hewison, R. 2006. *Not a Sideshow: Leadership and Cultural Value*. London: Demos.

Holden, J. 2004. *Capturing Cultural Value: How Culture has Become a Tool of Government Policy*. London: Demos.

Hood, C. 2008. Options for Britain: Measuring and Managing Public Services Performance. *The Political Quarterly*, 79(s1), 7–18.

Horner, L., Fauth, R. and Mahdon, M. *Creating public value: Case studies* Available at http://www. theworkfoundation.com/downloadpublication/report/108_108_pv_case_studies.pdf [accessed 29 November 2012]

Jancovich, L. 2011. Great Art for Everyone? Engagement and Participation Policy in the Arts. *Cultural Trends*, 20(3–4), 271–9.

Jowell, T. 2004. *Why Should Government Support the Arts?* London: IPPR.

Law, J., Ruppert, E. and Savage, M. 2011. *The Double Social Life of Methods*. Milton Keynes: CRESC.

Lee, D., Oakley, K. and Naylor, R. 2011. The Public Gets What the Public Wants? The Uses and Abuses of Public Value in Contemporary British Cultural Policy. *International Journal of Cultural Policy*, 17(3), 289–300.

Levitas, R. 2005. *The Inclusive Society?* London: Palgrave Macmillan.

McMaster, B. 2008. *McMaster Review: Supporting Excellence in the Arts*. London: Arts Council England.

McRobbie, A. 2010. Rethinking Creative Economy as Radical Social Enterprise. Paper presented at 'Art and Labour' conference, Glasgow, November 2010.

Meynhardt, T. 2009. Public Value Inside: What is Public Value Creation. *International Journal of Public Administration*, 32(3–4), 192–219.

Miller, P. 2011. The Calculating Self. Paper presented at 'The Foucault Effect 1991–2001', Birckbeck College, London, 3 and 4 June 2011.

Mulgan, J., Potts, G., Audsley, J., Carmona M., de Magalhaes, C., Sieh, L. and Sharpe, C. 2006. *Mapping Value in the Built Environment: A Report for the Commission for the Built Environment*. London: Young Foundation.

NML. 2011. Museum Welcomes 250,000 Visitors. Available at: http://www.liverpoolmuseums.org. uk/mediacentre/displayrelease.aspx?id=964 [accessed 2 September 2011].

O'Brien, D. 2010. *Measuring the Value of Culture: A Report to DCMS*. London: DCMS.

O'Brien, D., forthcoming. Drowning the Deadweight in the Logical of Economism: What sport policy, free swimming, and EMA tell us about public services after the crash *Public Administration*.

O'Brien, D., forthcoming. Shaping cultural policy around practical utopianism. *Journal of Policy Research in Tourism, Leisure and Events*.

Power, M. 1997. *The Audit Society*. Oxford: Oxford University Press.

Rawnsley, A. 2001. *Servants of the People*. London: Penguin.

Rawnsley, A. 2010. *The End of the Party*. London: Viking.

Rhodes, R. and Wanna, J. 2007. The Limits to Public Value, or Rescuing Responsible Government from the Platonic Guardians. *The Australian Journal of Public Administration*, 66(4), 406–21.

Rhodes, R. and Wanna, J. 2009. Bringing the Politics Back in: Public Value in Westminster Parliamentary Government. *Public Administration*, 87(2), 161–83.

Sanderson, I. 2002. Evaluation, Policy Learning and Evidence-Based Policy Making. *Public Administration*, 80(1), 1–22.

Selwood, S. 2010. *Making Difference: The Cultural Impact of Museums*. London: NMDC.

Talbot, C. 2009. Public Value: The Next 'Big Thing' in Public Management? *International Journal of Public Administration*, 32(3–4), 167–70.

Talbot, C. 2011. Paradoxes and Prospects of 'Public Value'. *Public Money & Management*, 31(1), 27–34.

Throsby, D. 2001. *Economics and Culture*. Cambridge: Cambridge University Press.

Upchurch, A. 2004. John Maynard Keynes, the Bloomsbury Group, and Origins of the Arts Council Movement. *International Journal of Cultural Policy,* 10(2), 203–18.

Woodward, S. 2012. Funding Museum Agendas: Challenges and Opportunities. *Managing Leisure,* 17(1), 14–28.

11 Social Impact and Public Value: Perspective of a National Professional Association

SHARON HEAL

Introduction: What Value Museums?

The current period is one of uncertainty for museums in the UK. Unprecedented cuts in public sector funding have impacted on opening hours, public programmes, staffing levels and confidence. Changes to the bodies responsible for funding and setting the strategic direction for museums in England and Scotland have added to the uncertainty. Moves towards further devolution have fragmented the picture across the UK.

Yet at the same time more and more people are visiting museums of all types and engaging with culture at a local, regional and national level (DCMS 2012). From January to December 2011, 47.9 per cent of adults in England visited a museum or gallery, an increase from 42.3 per cent from 2005/6. According to the survey this is the highest proportion of participation recorded since 2005.

Despite these record-breaking visitor figures, increased pressure on the public purse has meant that museums are frequently asked to justify the funding that they receive. One of the ways they have sought to do this is by demonstrating the value of their services.

Over the past decade there have been many words published and many discussions had about the value of museums in the UK. From *Measuring Culture* by Sara Selwood (2002), to *Measuring the Value of Culture* by Dave O'Brien (2010, report after report has attempted to get to grips with the slippery subject of valuing culture.

Some of the debate has been driven by politicians and funders requiring organizations to justify the amount of money they receive, and some of it has come from within the sector as people who work in museums try to understand what value they embody and what value they could and should create in society.

Considering the amount of debate, it is surprising that public value, one of the leading methodologies for determining value in the not-for-profit sector, is little understood and much less practised.

The concept was introduced by Mark H. Moore in his book *Creating Public Value: Strategic Management in Government* (1995). It is a management theory that aims to put the public at the centre of what publically-funded organizations do. It views the public as active participants in decision-making rather than passive consumers.

VALUE FATIGUE?

However, over 15 years after its publication, interviews with more than 20 museum directors from a range of institutions across the UK conducted in January 2012[1] reveal varied understandings of the term and limited examples of its implementation in museums. Directors from a range of museums across the UK were asked how they would define public value, whether the concept was being used in their museum and whether they thought it had been adopted across the sector. Uncertainty about definition was common:

"Public Value is a very ill-defined term."

"We haven't sufficiently understood the language."

"The term is used and abused."

"The phrase is bandied about without much meaning."

"The danger this is that we all have a different definitions and no common language."

Less than half of the directors surveyed said they were actively using a public value approach in their own organizations and a majority said they thought that it had not been adopted across the sector as a whole.

Moreover, it is clear from the interviews that there continues to be confusion about the different methodologies for measuring the value of culture that have come and gone over the past decade and scepticism about the motives that politicians have in promoting one method above another.

Maurice Davies, the head of policy and communications at the Museums Association (MA),[2] says public value is not a concept that the MA has used or advocated and is of the opinion that the system for measuring value and distributing funding for museums lacks an evidence base compared to other areas of the public sector, which have national frameworks and targets. 'The rules change every few years, so as soon as people in museums get used to measuring things one way, it changes again.'[3]

Which public, what value?

In addition to this confusion, there is also room for debate about who the public are and who gets to make decisions about what they value. Bernadette Lynch, a museum

---

1   Unpublished survey and interviews with author conducted January 2012.

2   The Museums Association is the membership body for people who work in museums and galleries in the UK.

3   Unpublished interview with author conducted January 2012.

consultant, says in the past it has been people who work in museums who have decided what is good for the public.

> *My instant reaction is against a top-down definition. The question of value should be an ongoing discussion with people about what is valuable for them. A top-down approach means that people are turned into passive beneficiaries of what they are told is good for them.*[4]

Piotr Bienkowski is the project director of the Paul Hamlyn Foundation's[5] *Our Museum* initiative. He agrees that value is not something that museums should define themselves. He argues that museums should be asking themselves who their public are and how they are developing discussions with them. 'Public Value for one museum will be different to what it is for another. They have to go out to their public and ask them.'[6]

In order to navigate the confusion that surrounds public value it is necessary to examine the political and historical backdrop to the debate.

Government Cultural Policy

Vacillation in government cultural policy within and between different administrations over the past decade has added to the uncertainty about which method to use to value culture.

It was a commonly held belief amongst those who worked in the cultural sector that there was little sympathy for publically-funded arts during the 18 years of Conservative administration in the 1980s and 1990s. There was a feeling that elite national arts organizations were tolerated and local arts organizations in need of public funding were left, with dwindling resources, to manage as best they could.

This neglect was summed up in the Renaissance in the Regions[7] report on regional museums in England, published in September 2001. It concluded that there was a serious crisis in local museums, with low morale, constant financial pressure and that 'virtually all of the major regional museums and galleries and the smaller sub-regional bodies report serious problems' (Davies 2001, 19).

Change came with the election of a New Labour government in 1997. In part, it saw its mission as being to reform public administration and promote social inclusion. To this end, culture not only had to be efficient and to play a role in inner-city regeneration and bolster the creative industries – it also had to serve government agendas on learning, health and social cohesion.

Within a year of New Labour coming to power, Chris Smith, the Secretary of State for Culture, announced more than £100m of extra funding for national museums, on the condition that they fulfilled his manifesto pledge of scrapping entry charges. He made explicit his funding rationale:

---

4   Unpublished interview with author conducted January 2012.

5   A charitable grant-giving foundation.

6   Unpublished interview with author conducted January 2012.

7   Renaissance in the Regions is a central government funded programme of investment into regional museums in England.

I'll be more generous on the provision of good access for new audiences, new people coming in. I'll be generous on maintaining excellence of work because high artistic standards have to be maintained. And I will be generous where real managerial efficiency is put into place. This is not something for nothing. (http://news.bbc.co.uk/1/hi/uk/138658.stm)

There was also a large injection of central government funding into regional museums in England at this time – approximately £300m to date – but that didn't come without strings either – funding was linked to targets to increase audiences across the board and, in particular, education visits.

TARGETS AND IMPACT

Despite the extra funding, some in museums were frustrated that the money was tied so closely to the government's policy outcomes. However David Fleming, director of National Museums Liverpool, says a commitment to access and participation pre-dates New Labour policy.

Many people were working in an inclusive way before the Labour government came to power – partly because people from different backgrounds came into the sector and they were interested in engaging and working with people from different backgrounds.[8]

Rather than set the agenda, New Labour created an environment where social impact was deemed a desirable goal. Under their new funding agreements, the national museums were forced, sometimes reluctantly, to get on board.

Resistance to valuing social outcomes

Not everyone agreed, however, that museums should be measured or that the types of social outcomes that the government was demanding were anything to do with the real purpose of museums. In June 2003, the thinktank Demos organized a conference titled 'Valuing Culture'. According to John Holden (2006, 12):

It was convened because many people had become frustrated by the fact that culture seemed to be valued by politicians only in terms of what it could achieve for other social and economic agendas.

The debate polarized around the difference between 'intrinsic value', defined in part as the intangible benefits of arts and cultural heritage, versus the 'instrumentalism' or results-driven measurement agenda of New Labour's economic and social policies. This separation of value into two distinct categories was questioned by some. David Anderson, director of Amgueffda Cymru, National Museums Wales, says the polarization of value into intrinsic and instrumental is a 'cloak of deception'.[9]

---

8   Unpublished interview with author conducted in January 2012.

9   Unpublished interview conducted in January 2012.

What is intrinsic to one person is instrumental to another. The claim that certain activities of arts institutions have intrinsic value and others are merely instrumental has no discernible basis in theory or research and has never been justified on these grounds. We need more intellectual rigour than that, particularly from a group of people in the arts world who, when it suits them, so publicly declare their devotion to scholarship. In reality the wish of some to cast out 'instrumental' activities is another form of elitism rooted in political ideology.[10]

This debate about different types of value was a precursor to a change in government policy. In 2004 the English Culture Secretary, Tessa Jowell, published a discussion paper entitled *Government and the Value of Culture* in which she argued that the intrinsic value of culture should be recognized.

Too often politicians have been forced to debate culture in terms only of its instrumental benefits to other agendas – education, the reduction of crime, improvements in wellbeing – explaining – or in some instances almost apologising for – our investment in culture only in terms of something else. In political and public discourse in this country we have avoided the more difficult approach of investigating, questioning and celebrating what culture actually does in and of itself. (Jowell 2004, 8)

The culmination of this change in approach was the *McMaster Review: Supporting Excellence in the Arts – from Measurement to Judgment*, which was commissioned by James Purnell, the then English Secretary of State for Culture under New Labour. Published early in 2008, the report called for a move away from top-down targets towards a new way of evaluating the arts in England based on self-assessment and peer review.

In his introduction to the report, James Purnell said that artists and cultural organizations must be freed from 'outdated structures and burdensome targets' (McMaster 2008, 4).

The move from measurement to judgement ... is a vital one, and one that will allow all of us to articulate better the importance of the arts, how and where they add value to our society and why, now more than ever, they are deserving of public funding. (McMaster 2008, 4)

This move towards peer review was warmly received by many who saw it as a chance to break from DCMS directives and measurement targets and set their own course. However some in the sector saw a danger of museums assessing themselves. Mark O'Neill, director of research at Glasgow Life,[11] says the heart of the issue is the role of experts in a democratic society:

The McMaster report, which recommended peer review as the key measure of museum performance, was in effect a bid for complete professional autonomy, with no public accountability.[12]

---

10   Unpublished interview conducted in January 2012.

11   Glasgow Life is the trust which runs Glasgow museum service.

12   Unpublished interview with author conducted in January 2012.

In essence, peer review could be said to be the opposite of public value; letting the professionals decide what is excellent in the arts, a process in which the public has no, or very little, say. The reality is that many on both sides of the 'intrinsic' and 'instrumental' debate have ignored the role of the public, except as passive consumers of the arts.

How Does Government Value Culture?

No matter which method of measurement is used, all governments demand efficiency and value for money in public spending. The problem with the concept of intrinsic value is that it has proved difficult to measure. Although there were attempts to implement a peer review system in the arts sector after the McMaster Review, this has now been quietly forgotten.

In May 2010, the national election witnessed a change of government with a Conservative Coalition assuming office. Ideologically, the Coalition government in England seems more comfortable with one intrinsic definition of value – the 'art for art's sake' argument.

Jeremy Hunt, the then current Secretary of State for Culture in England, in his first keynote speech on the arts, referred to 'the basic truth that great art simply cannot be measured', and to government having the 'lightest touch' in determining a future direction for the arts sector (http://www.jeremyhunt.org/newsshow.aspx?ref=438).

However there is another side to this 'light touch' approach. Within the current government, there are perceptions that culture has been marginalized to the extent that other more powerful ministries and ministers see it as peripheral. Eric Pickles, in his first major speech as Secretary of State for Communities and Local Government, argued for the scrapping of 'non-jobs' and used the example: 'What does an audience development officer do?'[13] His lack of knowledge of a role that, amongst other things, can help increase participation in the arts by groups that don't normally engage, revealed something about how some politicians view the cultural sector.

PHILANTHROPY VERSUS PUBLIC FUNDING

One of the indices of value is the amount of public money which governments are willing to invest to ensure that culture is available and widely enjoyed by all. Since the Coalition government came to power, public funding has been cut and there have been numerous initiatives to encourage philanthropic giving. Jeremy Hunt, former Secretary of State for Culture in England, said in his one of first keynote speeches: 'For the arts to flourish we need different types of funding to flourish as well.'[14]

This mixed-economy funding model is based on the American concept where larger collections often have endowment funds and rely more on private income than they do on public subsidy. However, recent history has shown that a mixed economy has done little to protect museums in the United States from the bumpy economic ride that the

---

13   http://conservativehome.blogs.com/localgovernment/2010/07/eric-pickles-urges-councils-to-axe-nonjobs-and-share-back-office-functions.html.

14   http://www.jeremyhunt.org/newsshow.aspx?ref=438.

rest of society has suffered. Writing in the *Museums Journal*[15] in 2010, David Gordon, a former director of the Milwaukee Art Museum, confirmed that, though contrary to assumptions in Europe most US museums do get some funding from government (2010, 16), the mixed economy model has proved tenuous.

> *On average it [public funding] accounts for 24 per cent of revenues, predominantly from city, county or state, but with some federal money … Endowments can be a blessing when they provide a cushion of stable income. But the collapse of the stock market hit those institutions that had not sufficiently developed other sources of revenue. The biggest fell hardest. (Gordon 2010, 16)*

In the UK, the unevenness of philanthropic giving and corporate support has been problematic. In 2010, Andrew Scott, the former director of the National Museum of Science and Industry, said that outside London it had proved difficult to raise private funding.

> *A quick scan across several north of England city museum services suggests that individual philanthropy or corporate sponsorship grants of more than £50,000 in the past ten years are as rare as hen's teeth. (Scott 2010)*

An additional problem is that, in a time of cuts in public investment, philanthropic giving can also fall, with donors unwilling or unable to pick up the deficit in government funding. An Arts and Business[16] report published in February 2012 found that although private giving was up in 2010–11, business investment was down 7 per cent and over 80 per cent of individual giving went to London organizations.[17]

Wellbeing and the Big Society

Like the previous government, the Coalition government in England would prefer that publically-funded organizations reflect its big policy themes. Museum contributions to two of these, the *Big Society* and *Wellbeing*, have been seized on by some in museums as evidence of value in relation to government policy.

The *Big Society* is a flagship Coalition policy. Its aim is to empower local people and communities to get involved in and even take over the running of local services. Its key aims include giving communities more powers, increasing volunteering and transferring power from central to local government.

Many museums feel they 'fit' the *Big Society* agenda because they have a wide volunteer base and are embedded in their local communities. Indeed, one of the original pilot areas for the scheme was Liverpool, with National Museums Liverpool playing a key role. However the pilot quickly ran aground when Liverpool City Council withdrew from the scheme saying that government cuts were actually undermining the voluntary organizations that were central to the idea of the *Big Society*.

---

15 A monthly magazine published by the Museums Association.

16 A charitable organization that develops partnerships between the private sector and the arts.

17 http://artsandbusiness.org.uk/News/2012/Feb/private-investment-in-culture-figures-2010-11.aspx.

Wellbeing has long been championed by British Prime Minister David Cameron. Again some museums in England have been keen to associate themselves with the idea and it is seen as likely to influence future funding priorities. It is also a concept that can be experienced by individuals while collectively having a positive outcome in terms of community health. Mark O'Neill, the Director of Policy and Research for Glasgow Life, argues that there is now considerable scientific and medical evidence that visiting museums has such a powerful impact on people's wellbeing that they live longer as a result.

> *This evidence is distinct from the well-established findings on the benefits for health of art therapy and participation in creative activities, because it points to the fact that general museum visiting has a measurable health impact. (O'Neill 2010)*

In terms of current government policy in England, museums are experiencing unprecedented funding cuts and are struggling to get on the political radar. The case differs to some degree in the devolved nations of the UK where a clearer role for museum in contributing to government policies has been articulated.

Devolution and Value

Culture is a devolved responsibility in the UK. Northern Ireland, Scotland and Wales have each developed their own approach to cultural policy and the question of value. In all three countries national politics, cultural identity and geographical proximity to the seat of government have played a role in shaping the direction of the museum sector.

In Wales, the Assembly government requires all cultural institutions to develop explicit strategies to address child poverty, a key government objective that includes educational and cultural poverty. Writing in *Museums Journal* in March 2012, Huw Lewis, Minister for Housing, Regeneration and Heritage in the Welsh government, said that museums have a key role to play:

> *This is one of the biggest challenges we face as a nation. Crucially our strategy includes aims to reduce inequalities in educational outcomes, and this is the area where museums can make a positive impact. Good work is already going on, but needs to be more focused, and more joined-up. (Lewis 2012, 16)*

All three nations have also developed national museum strategies. Whilst they differ, they share commitments to public benefit, access, education and audience engagement.

The museum policy in Northern Ireland states that museums are uniquely placed to deliver public benefit on a number of fronts:

> *As well as their inherent cultural value and impact, museums can make a major contribution to economic and social regeneration and are a reflection of community confidence and health and well-being. Museums can make a very important contribution to a shared and better future for all based on equity, diversity, interdependence and mutual respect. (Northern Ireland Museums Policy, Department of Culture, Arts and Leisure 2011, 5)*

The Welsh strategy states that museums must contribute to 'living communities', and should 'promote the values of a fair and just society':

> Dismantling barriers to access, developing the learning potential of museums, and engaging existing and new users are critical issues to be addressed if museums are to fulfil their potential as organisations that contribute to their local communities. (A Museum Strategy for Wales, CyMAL, Museums, Archives and Libraries Wales 2010, 4)

It is interesting to note that the three strategies apply to all publically funded museums. There are no get-out clauses where some museums are allowed to carry on with their business as if a national strategy didn't exist.

The Welsh and Northern Irish strategies were published in 2010 and 2011. The Scottish strategy was published in 2012. In Scotland, Wales and Northern Ireland governments have shown a strong commitment to museums and see a role for them in the expression of national identity, their potential to contribute to clearly articulated national cultural policies and creating beneficial social impacts.

Measuring Culture Now

Where is the value debate now? In Wales, Scotland and Northern Ireland there is a broad consensus that museums exist for public benefit. In England the picture is less clear, with the Coalition government giving mixed messages about the type of value it wants to see demonstrated.

The unresolved nature of the debate was exemplified by the publication of two reports within a couple of months of each other. In December 2010, Measuring the Value of Culture by Dave O'Brien was published by the Department for Culture, Media and Sport. It argues that it is not enough for culture to claim to be a 'special case' and that the value of culture needs to be articulated using methods which align with government decision-making and measurement tools, particular those such as cost–benefit analysis. It recommends that the Department for Culture, Media and Sport create clear guidelines for measuring cultural value, based on economic valuation techniques.

In contrast, the Royal Society of the Arts published Arts Funding Austerity and the Big Society in February 2011. In it John Knell and Matthew Taylor argue for a 'new instrumentalism' and the setting of clear and explicit targets for the arts.

> We need to reinvent and strengthen instrumentalism breaking through some of the messy compromises and anaemic logic models that underpin the overall rationale for arts funding. (Knell and Taylor 2011, 8)

What the documents have in common is the focus on needing to demonstrate the value of culture in order to persuade government to fund it. It is also impossible to ignore the fact that the backdrop to the current debate about valuing culture is the economic recession and huge public sector spending cuts.

VALUE IN A TIME OF AUSTERITY

In 2011 the Museums Association carried out the first comprehensive survey of the impact of cuts on museums across the UK. It showed that cuts were leading to reductions in public service. It found that nearly a quarter of museums were reducing opening hours and over half of the museums that responded were cutting staff (*The Impact of the Cuts on UK Museums*. London: Museums Association).

Launching the results of the survey in July 2011, the MA said that local authorities that were cutting museum budgets by as much as 25 per cent were impoverishing their communities:

> *Services have been cut and opening hours restricted – there's a risk that, in some cases, the doors will be slammed shut for ever. Many local authorities haven't yet made a final decision so still have a chance to do the right thing for present and future generations by not cutting so ferociously. (http://www.museumsassociation.org/campaigns/funding-cuts)*

Cuts to public sector funding continue apace, making the question of having a clear basis for deciding what gets funded even more pressing. However John Holden from the think tank Demos believes the value debate is going backwards:

> *The debate is getting more simplistic than it was five years ago. Instead of trying to discuss the full range of value, we now seem to be reverting to looking only at how Whitehall and Treasury want to value culture – it's rowing in the wrong direction.*[18]

Cuts impact on culture

The issues around value have been further complicated because of structural changes within the sector. One of the organizations that fell victim to the first round of cuts was the Museums, Libraries and Archives Council (MLA), the strategic body for museums in England with a key role for funding regional museums. In 2010, the MLA became a part of the Arts Council England (ACE). And with this transfer came a further shift in policy.

For many people working in regional museums there was discomfort that ACE, an organization dedicated to artistic excellence and with an emphasis on the role of the artist, did not perceive the relationship with audiences and the public in the same way that museums do. This concern is echoed by Knell and Taylor (2011). They argue that the public and artists have different priorities:

> *Whilst it may be uncomfortable for the arts community it seems that the general public, local authorities and other parts of the third sector tend to place greater emphasis on access, reach, and tangible economic and social outcomes as the most important criteria that should drive public funding of the arts. In contrast artists, and those working in arts organisations without a particular social remit, tend to prioritise artistic excellence.*

---

18   Unpublished interview with author conducted in January 2012.

Iain Watson, the director of Tyne and Wear Archives and Museums, says there has not been enough debate about the value of museums and that

This has come more sharply into focus now because of the transfer to ACE. The arts sector is different because the role of the art and the artist is fundamental. For many museums it's the interaction with the audience that is fundamental.[19]

The Museums Association and Value

In this increasingly complicated funding, policy and administrative environment, the Museums Association has sought to define a new value agenda.

The Museums Association (MA) is a membership organization for people who work in museums and galleries in the UK. Its mission is to 'enhance the value of museums to society by sharing knowledge, developing skills, inspiring innovation, and providing leadership'.

David Fleming, director of National Museums Liverpool and a member of the MA's governing body, says it is crucial that the MA should have a clear position on the question of value: 'It should be asking questions about what value museums are producing and for whom. It should provide leadership for the sector on this.'

Maurice Davies, the head of policy and communication at the MA, argues that the debate has moved to the broader question of the social impact that museums can have.

This was reflected in the MA's response to the ACE's consultation on its strategic framework, *Achieving Great Art For Everyone*:

The key purpose of ACE funding and support for non-national museums should be to improve the impact and public benefit of museums and galleries, so museums and galleries give opportunities for inspiration, learning and enjoyment for the full range of people in England. (http://www.museumsassociation.org/download?id=327240)

The concept of the impact and public benefit that museums can have now informs the policy work of the MA. In February 2012 the MA launched its 2020 project, which aims to establish a vision for the future of museums and to look at the value and purpose of museums.[20]

Its July 2012 discussion document maintains that: 'every museum can do more to improve people's lives and play a part in meeting society's needs' (Davies 2012, 4). The starting point for the project is to look at the impact that museums can have.

Museums of all types have vast potential to make a difference to individuals, communities, society and the environment. Yet in most museums, much of this work seems marginal, perhaps not core business. The MA believes that having a beneficial impact is the core business of museums. The activities of acquiring, preserving, managing, researching, interpreting and displaying collections are all a means to an end. In the MA's definition of a museum (now over

---

19   Unpublished interview conducted January 2012.

20   http://www.museumsassociation.org/museums2020.

a decade old), that end is enabling people to gain 'inspiration, learning and enjoyment'. That's fine – but museums now know they can go further. (Davies 2012, 17)

It is something of a departure from traditional areas of museum work for a study of this kind to think first about social impact. Davies says that he hopes the findings of the 2020 project will be implemented in museums across the UK.

As a useful checklist, every museum needs: (1) A commitment in principle to redressing inequalities in cultural engagement; (2) acceptance that the population as a whole is as wise, clever and culturally experienced as museum professionals; (3) effective action to support more public learning and creativity; (4) participation and personalisation for priority groups in gallery development, collections work and public programmes; (5) extension and distribution of services beyond the institution into social communities; (6) sustained investment in learning, research and evaluation; … and (7) a refocusing of our thinking away from what we want to offer, towards what is needed for individual and community wellbeing. (Davies 2012, 19)

Conclusion: The Future of Public Value

The concept of public value has not been widely understood or adopted by museums in the UK, although evidence suggests that the broad idea of serving the public is central to what many in museums see as their core purpose.

Definitions of public value may be disputed and imperfectly understood, but museums want to provide value to the communities they serve. David Anderson from Amgueddfa Cymru – National Museums Wales thinks that though the theory of public value has not been adopted in museums, museums should start by asking what their purpose is and that means speaking to the public. 'We describe ourselves as a dialogical museum; we are constantly in dialogue with audiences, for example about the redevelopment of St Fagans.[21] That is an attempt to identify public value in practice.'[22]

Iain Watson from Tyne and Wear Archives and Museums says public value is written into his organization's vision: 'For me it's about an emphasis on people and our impact on people.'[23]

Tony Butler, the director of the Museum of East Anglian Life, says his organization doesn't use the term public value but

We define ourselves through our own values which are: social enterprise; partnership; stewardship and mindfulness – and all of them have some element of public value. We've tried to create a value-based organisation where everyone believes in the social value of what we do.[24]

The political framework in the UK is changing. After more than a decade of devolution the divergent cultural, social and education policies of the four nations means that there

---

21 The National History Museum for Wales, part of National Museums Wales.

22 Unpublished interview conducted January 2012.

23 Unpublished interview conducted January 2012.

24 Unpublished interview conducted January 2012.

are no longer shared government policies on cultural issues within the United Kingdom. And, after decades of different methods of measuring and valuing culture, value fatigue means that many organizations are wary of political interference, sceptical about ways of measuring value and, in many cases, content to apply their own purpose or mission.

Notwithstanding the uncertainty about what public value means in the British context, a new emphasis on social impact is emerging as a policy strand for the Museums Association. In part, this reflects the practice by museums closely aligned to their local communities that have been independently developing programmes dealing with issues of social justice and equality of access and participation. For some it is in this area that museums can really demonstrate their value to the public and to society as a whole.

For now the debate about value, benefit and impact continues. Public value could yet be a useful tool for museums but only where there is a genuine desire to work with and listen to the public, and where it is driven by the aims and objectives of the organization rather than the need to prove worth to funders.

Perhaps the debate should not be about which is the best method for measuring and valuing museums but a more fundamental discussion about what the role of museums is in society. Museums need to ask themselves: do they exist to preserve the status quo or do they exist to make a difference?

References

Arts Council England. 2010. *Achieving Great Art For Everyone: A Strategic Framework for the Arts*. London: Arts Council England.

Davies, M. 2012. Museums 2020 discussion paper. Available at: http://www.museumsassociation. org/museums2020 [accessed April 2012].

Davies, S. 2001. *Renaissance in the Regions*. London: Resource.

Department of Culture, Arts and Leisure. 2011. *Northern Ireland Museums Policy*. Belfast: Department of Culture Arts and Leisure.

Department for Culture, Media and Sport. 2012. *Taking Part Survey*. London: Department for Culture, Media and Sport.

Gordon, D. 2010. How are US Museums and Galleries Coping with the Recession? *Museums Journal*, April, 16.

Holden, J. 2006. *Cultural Value and the Crisis of Legitimacy*. London: Demos.

Jowell, T. 2004. *Government and the Value of Culture*. London: Department for Culture, Media and Sport.

Knell, J. and Taylor, M. 2011. *Arts Funding Austerity and the Big Society*. London: Royal Society of the Arts.

Lewis, H. 2012. Museums Can Help Address Inequality. *Museums Journal*, March, 16.

McMaster, B. 2008. *McMaster Review: Supporting Excellence in the Arts – from Measurement to Judgment*. London: Department for Culture, Media and Sport.

Moore, M. 1995. *Creating Public Value: Strategic Management in Government*. Cambridge, MA: Harvard University Press.

Newman, K. and Tourle, P. 2011. *The Impact of the Cuts on UK Museums*. London: Museums Association.

O'Brien, D. 2010. *Measuring the Value of Culture*. London: Department for Culture, Media and Sport.

O'Neill, M. 2010. Scientists Say: Get Out and Get a Life. *Museums Journal*, February, 14.

Scott, A. 2010. Potential for Giving is Limited Outside London. *Museums Journal*, November, 17.

Selwood, S. 2002. Measuring Culture. [Online]. Available at: http://www.spiked-online.com/articles/00000006DBAF.htm [accessed April 2012].

Welsh Assembly Government. 2010. *A Museum Strategy for Wales*. Cardiff: Welsh Assembly Government.

12 *Going Further: Public Value in Scotland*

JOANNE ORR

Introduction

The recently launched 'Going Further – The National Strategy for Scotland's Museums and Galleries' has creating public value at its heart and has unified the whole of the museum sector under a single vision:

> *Scotland's museums and galleries will be ambitious, dynamic and sustainable enterprises: connecting people, places and collections; inspiring, delighting and creating public value. (MGS 2012, 14)*

This has been achieved through collaboration between what Moore's (1995) model would refer to as the 'authorising environment' of the Scottish government and the 'operational environment' of a museum sector that is rooted in the communities and public of Scotland and represented by Museums Galleries Scotland (MGS). The National Strategy has emerged from an intense period of discussion and consultation with the sector in Scotland. It is also, unusually, a result of a direct intervention from the Scottish government who, perceiving that there were barriers and issues to museums moving forward, entered into a dialogue with the sector. This dialogue resulted in action, with the Cabinet Secretary for Culture and External Affairs first requesting the development of a National Strategy for museums in discussion with the sector, and then supporting and engaging in its progress to a successful conclusion. Throughout the process, the Secretary championed both the role of museums in creating public value and having this at the heart of the National Strategy. This is perhaps a rare example of what Moore envisaged in his public value model, as the National Strategy was developed in the context of a partnership between the 'authorizing environment' of Scottish government and the 'operational environment' of the museum sector represented by Museums Galleries Scotland. This collaboration has required both sacrifice and change, and continues to involve a complex set of negotiations and compromises to achieve the wider goal of a unified sector engaged with a National Strategy. This chapter offers some insights into the events that have led up to achieving a National Strategy, *and for those wishing to embark on a similar path, some consideration of the issues involved.*

Background

With over 340 museums (Scottish Museums Council 2002), almost every Scottish community has a museum or *is in close proximity to one*. Communities are highly engaged with their heritage, showing their commitment through their enthusiasm for *establishing* museums and through working within them as volunteers; the percentage of volunteer workforce is 52 per cent (MGS, formerly, Scottish Museums Council 2006). At least two-thirds of the museums in Scotland are run as independent charitable trusts staffed by volunteers, often maintaining a local history museum that elsewhere in the UK would be run directly by a local authority.

The public, be they resident in Scotland or visiting tourists, acknowledge the value of museums through their high visiting patterns. From a population base of just 5.2 million (Scottish Government 2011), Scottish museums attract more than 23.5 million museum visits (MGS 2010a) per year. When the National Museum of Scotland[1] reopened in the summer of 2011 after three years of closure for refurbishment, it received 1.29 million visits in the first six months, 'equating to 25% of the population of Scotland' (MGS 2012, 10).

Museums Galleries Scotland (MGS) is the development body for museums. It began life in 1964 as the Area Museums Council for the Scotland region. Initially established by a partnership of local authorities to create capacity to provide support for existing and new museums and to develop and improve the quality of their service, it has evolved over the years, reflecting the changes in policy relating to museums, themselves reflective of changes in government and the political landscape.

A CHANGING POLITICAL LANDSCAPE

Scotland is a devolved[2] nation and, since devolution in 1999, its cultural policy has taken a different route from the rest of the UK. The Scottish National Party (SNP) came to power in May 2007 and in November 2007 produced their first Economic Strategy. Progress on this Economic Strategy was monitored through a National Performance Framework (NPF). Until this point there had been little policy development focused on museums and this made it initially difficult to articulate museums' contributions to national outcomes within the NPF.

The museum sector: Diversity, fragmentation, challenge and change

Contributing to the difficulties in articulating museum contributions to the NPF was the fragmentary nature of the sector which lacked a clear and unified voice. The diversity of governance and funding structures made it difficult for potential stakeholders from outside the sector to find channels to engage with museums. A lack of regional museum infrastructure compounded this perception of fragmentation, with two-thirds of the

---

1   The National Museum of Scotland has free admission.

2   UK devolution created a national Parliament in Scotland, a national Assembly in Wales and a national Assembly in Northern Ireland. This process transferred varying levels of power from the UK Parliament to the UK's nations. http://www.parliament.uk/about/how/role/devolved/.

sector made up of small independent charities with few, large local authority services to support them. There are 32 local authorities in Scotland that vary greatly in their scale, from Dundee with a geographical coverage of 26 square miles to Highland Council which covers 12,437 square miles and population ranges from 20,000 in the Orkney Islands to over 600,000 in the Glasgow City Council area (COSLA 2012).

So although there are two levels of government in Scotland, national and local, some of the 'local' governments cover an enormous geographical region. Regional museum infrastructure within local government areas also varies. For example, although the Highlands region has a strong museums' forum that includes the majority of the Highland independent museums, this is not necessarily the norm. Compounding the perception of fragmentation there is also an increasing diversity in the types of governance models that are emerging in museums including charitable trusts, social enterprises, mutual societies and Scottish Charitable Incorporated Organisations (SCIO).

Policy development and funding is inevitably linked to existing infrastructure, and the majority of Scottish government funding for museums is allocated to the National Museums of Scotland and the National Gallery of Scotland, who both receive grant-in-aid in the form of capital and revenue support. The Scottish government grant to Museums Galleries Scotland is the next largest allocation followed by some revenue and capital funding for three industrial museums. The grant received by MGS partly supports its core operations while another amount is available as grants. The grant schemes have traditionally supported the development of museums using framework standards such as Accreditation and more recently the Quality Improvement System (QIS).

However, the distribution structure for funding museum development has arguably contributed to the fragmentation of the sector. The Recognition Scheme, in particular, contributed to factionalism.

At the request of, and with funding from, the Scottish government, MGS developed and administers the Recognition Scheme. Recognition was developed to identify and support collections of national significance. Museums can apply to the scheme to achieve the recognition of all, or part, of their collection and there are now 38 Recognized Collections in Scotland.

Applications for Recognition must supply evidence of the depth and quality of a collection which is then assessed by an independent panel. The Scottish government has been keen to support collections that have gone through this process of demonstrating their national importance and has established a Recognition fund of flexible project funding of around £1 million a year. Each year, this project funding is also supplemented with capital funding that MGS negotiates with government and which is channeled through the Recognition scheme.

Though a positive initiative in many ways, the Recognition Scheme also created problems which exacerbated divisions within the sector. Unlike other MGS grants which require 50 per cent match-funding, the Recognition Scheme has been a conduit for large amounts of Scottish government funding that does not require the museum holding the Recognized Collection to find any additional funds. In effect, the Recognition Scheme has created a two-tier funding regime giving those museums with Recognized Collections access to a larger and more flexible funding source than the rest of the non-national museums in Scotland.

Some of the earliest museums to be Recognized have been the university museums who make up 16 per cent of the Recognized Collections. With access to extensive research on their collections, they were quickly able to evidence their importance and breadth and make a case for their significance. The Scottish government was also keen to see that the industrial museums would benefit from this scheme and initially instructed some ring-fencing of Recognition funding, specifically for larger industrial museums who had achieved the Recognition standard. This rather contentious anomaly has since been resolved and three large industrial museums now receive revenue and capital funding directly from the Scottish government. Recognition has perhaps contributed to a situation where parts of the sector, such as the university and industrial museums, have a stronger lobbying voice with government through their respective forums such as the recently formed Industrial Museum Forum and the longer-established University Museums in Scotland (UMIS) forum. However, the Recognition scheme has also enabled larger local authority museum collections (such as Dundee, Edinburgh, Glasgow, Aberdeen) to successfully achieve Recognition status for their collections, opening up access to a fund that has provided a welcome boost at a time of unprecedented budget cuts.

These widespread budget cuts, particularly from 2009 onwards, have led to many authorities reviewing cultural services and have resulted in significant changes to how museums are funded and supported. These recent changes have further contributed to the perception of a fragmented sector. Where, formerly, museums were directly managed by the local authority, there are now 12 museum services (which can consist of multiple museum sites), out of a total 29 museum services that are either actively carrying out options appraisals or have already moved to a trust model. This means that museums, although still owned by the local authority, are operated and managed by new, arm's-length organizations.

The initial impetus for these changes appears to have been the budget savings that could be made on rates relief by creating an arm's-length management organization. The long-term implications of these recent changes are not yet known, but it is probably one of the most significant changes to the way museum services are provided through local authorities in Scotland.

As MGS takes on the new role of the National Development Body outlined in the National Strategy, its approach to funding will move from grants that directly support development to funds that enable investment for development to happen and, within this new context, the Recognition Scheme will need to be reviewed. But, in the meantime, the Recognition Scheme has set an expectation of funding and a pattern of dependency for the Recognized Collections that will be challenging to change.

Problem Solving: The Authorizing Environment's Approach

For Moore, the role of government is 'not just as a rule-setter, service-provider and social safety net, but potentially as a creator of public value and a pro-active shaper of the public sphere' (Moore and Benington 2011, 3). Activating this proactive role in relation to museums is evident in government actions that have unfolded in Scotland over the last three years.

In 2009, a new Minister for Culture, External Affairs and the Constitution, Michael Russell, came into his position with a brief to address perceptions of a divided museum sector, to develop common goals and to clarify how museums and galleries could be contributing to both community and government policy outcomes. The minister came to his portfolio with a strong background in culture and an active interest in museums in his own constituency of Argyll and Bute. He recognized that museums have both tangible and intangible value and he was particularly interested in the role that museums and heritage could have in exploring identity and citizenship.

In May 2009, the minister called for a Museum Summit to be held in Stirling and asked MGS to organize the Summit. The outcome of the Summit was the decision to set up a think tank to explore what the role of museums in Scotland should be and what support was needed to enable museums to fulfil this role. The minister was prepared to chair the think tank with membership to be drawn from the sector.

However, it rapidly became apparent that the think tank was comprised of some of the stronger lobbying voices discussed previously who tended to act as representatives for their area rather than focusing on the wider future for the sector as a whole and who were hampered by a lack of a strategic overview. Eventually, the Scottish government asked MGS to provide this strategic overview as well as much of the data that the group required to compile its report. Although there was a change in minister mid-way through the life of the think tank, the new minister, Fiona Hyslop, was equally committed to see progress made. In November 2010, the think tank reported and the minister quickly followed with her response to the report (Scottish Government 2010a, 2010b).

Drawing upon data provided by MGS, the think tank report first outlined the value of museums to Scottish society. It then recommended the development of a National Strategy to move the entire museum sector forward and, further, proposed that one National Development Body lead the strategy and provide support for the sector. Specifically, the think tank recommended that the new 'National Development Body should not be a membership body' (Scottish Government 2010a, 11), as they perceived this would be in conflict with its *national* role. MGS was referred to in the report as the most likely body to take up this challenge as it was already providing a development role for the majority of the sector. But, if MGS was to take up the new role of National Development Body, it would have to address the membership issue.

In December 2010, the minister, whose status had now been elevated to that of Cabinet Secretary (an indication of the Scottish government's support for and recognition of the importance of culture), responded to the think tank report. She invited MGS to produce a National Strategy and to make the transition to become the National Development Body, subject to a reform of its governance arrangements in line with the think tank recommendations.

The minister had practical reasons for approaching and inviting MGS to undertake this role. In the first instance, there was an active government policy to cut down the number of Non-Departmental Public Bodies (NDPBs) through amalgamations (such as combining the Arts Council Scotland with Scottish Screen to establish Creative Scotland) and to avoid establishing new ones. Secondly, it would have required lengthy legislation to establish a new NDPB.[3] A third reason involved the MGS's status as a charitable trust. Scotland differs from England and Wales in its special legislation under the Office of the Scottish Charity Regulator (OSCR) that prevents the board of a charity from taking ministerial direction. Therefore, the future status of MGS, though in receipt of a grant tied to a service level agreement based on the delivery of the National Strategy, was

---

3   The Public Service Reform (Scotland) Act that eventually established Creative Scotland, took almost three years to write and a total of almost six years to produce if all consultation is taken into account.

perceived as independent from government. The proviso to this invitation was that MGS would update its constitution in line with the think tank's recommendation and cease its membership function. This would prove to be one challenge among many.

The role envisaged for MGS, engaging the sector and the government in partnership with a joint, long-term goal in mind, was a complex one. In the first instance, MGS was asked to lead the development of the National Strategy by involving the sector and negotiating with government. Secondly, it would facilitate the sector's contribution to the Delivery plan to activate the Strategy. MGS would also monitor and evaluate progress on achieving the aims and objectives of the Strategy and report on this progress to both the sector and the Scottish government. Moore (1995, 38) states that 'politics remains the final arbiter of public value just as private consumption decisions remain the final arbiter of private values'. The Scottish government envisaged that the National Strategy would represent their policy on museums and actively promote a parliamentary debate that would provide a platform for endorsing the public value of museums.

All of this change was to be delivered within MGS's existing budgets with a deadline for the development of the Strategy of March 2012.

Museums Galleries Scotland Take the Lead

In this process, the intervention came initially from the Scottish government who, keen to see all parts of the museum sector in Scotland engaged with the process of developing the strategy, encouraged MGS to form a Museum Steering Group. With MGS as Chair, this Group began by including some of the largest providers of services – the National Museums, National Galleries and Glasgow Museums,[4] as well as two Scottish government civil servants. In March 2011, the Steering Group amalgamated with another MGS strategy group to form a single Museum Strategy Group. Led by the Chair of MGS Board, their remit was to support the development of a National Strategy and provide advice to MGS as the lead organization.

The process was beginning from a position of strength. Both the think tank report and the minister's response made it clear the Scottish government endorsed the important contribution that museums make to communities in Scotland. That museums deliver public value was put at the centre of the Strategy from the outset: 'Our museums and galleries are at the very heart of the development and transformation of society' (Scottish Government 2010a, 6).

By the time of MGS's conference 'Collaborating to Compete' in September 2011, an outline paper with options for the strategy, based on first-thinking and initial sector consultation was available to be circulated and used as a basis for further consultation. This venture was resource intensive; MGS deployed its entire staff capacity to achieve the comprehensive consultation considered key to future adoption and implementation. The investment produced encouraging results.

The engagement and response from the sector was overwhelmingly positive with over 200 responses to the survey and full attendance at events. This response meant

---

4   Glasgow museum service www.glasgowlife.org consists of several museums including St Mungos Museum of Religion and Art, Kelvingrove Art Gallery and Museum, Riverside Museum, People's Palace, Gallery of Modern Art, Open Museum, The Burrell Collection, Scotland Street School Museum, Glasgow Museums Resource Centre.

that the voice of the sector could truly be reflected in the National Strategy's content which is situated within the key issues and challenges that the sector consider important. These include 'keeping museums and collections relevant', 'sustaining collections' and 'remaining competitive in the context of a harsh economic climate', 'ensuring that workforce skills are shared' and 'brokering of collaboration and partnerships' (MGS 2012, 12). Using the same language, definitions and terminology, these consultation responses were used in the final strategy. Recognizing that museums do not operate in isolation, stakeholder groups such as the tourism and enterprise bodies of *Visit Scotland* and *Highlands and Islands Enterprise* also responded to the consultation process. It was clear that they could see how their work and funding streams could be aligned.

A first draft of the National Strategy was delivered to the Museum Strategy Group in December 2012 for comment and then given to the Cabinet Secretary in February 2012. There followed an intense period of dialogue with the Scottish government. The tone of the National Strategy was tightened up to reflect government expectations of an increased authority for the new National Development Body and the Cabinet Secretary brought to the draft an emphasis on skills development which she considered essential to the plan's long-term success.

Going Further: A National Strategy for Scotland's Museums and Galleries (MGS 2012) was launched on 30 March 2012. It was met with widespread enthusiasm from a sector that recognized the outcomes of the consultation process within its aims, objectives and direction of travel.

The Strategy picked up the key challenges that had come through in discussions with the sector and developed six aims to move the sector forward. The first aim looks to 'maximising the potential of collections' but also recognizes the intangible culture that surrounds them. The second aim focuses on participation, but also on the outcomes or public value that result from this, 'strengthening connections between museums, people and places to inspire greater public participation, learning and well-being'. Although the third aim focuses on developing the workforce, the importance of skills development and knowledge transfer is a theme that runs throughout the National Strategy. The fourth aim is about achieving sustainability through a culture of enterprise. The fifth aim focuses on collaboration, innovation and ambition and the sixth aspires to develop a global perspective in museum work. The National Strategy is illustrated throughout with examples of current best practice in museums which demonstrate how museums can, and are, already delivering on the aims and objectives.

Vision statements get to the heart of the matter. The vision statement for this Strategy had been the subject of much debate during the consultation but putting 'creating public value' at the heart of the National Strategy was readily accepted. To endorse this as a central concept is aspirational and requires a level of belief in the inherent value of museums and trust in the value that they generate.

The strategy uses the International Council of Museums (ICOM) definition of museums which acknowledges both the intangible and tangible heritage with which museums work. This definition was perceived to be best suited to the context of the museums in Scotland, where there is a close relationship with host communities and where museums are working with both material heritage and living culture. The public value of museums is 'clarified and authorised by the public' (Blaug et al. 2006, 42) and communities that have and support their museum provide this authorization. However Blaug et al. (2006, 42) also state that public value 'is made, increased and created by public service organisations'. Museums are the public service organizations that provide a focal point for the creation and increase of public value in the heritage arena. However in the context of Scotland and the broader definition of museums used in the strategy, the public are the active co-creators of the public value as well as the authorizers of the value. The museums curate the tangible heritage but they also facilitate and engage actively with the intangible aspects – the meaning and knowledge of that heritage – and the living culture in which it is located.

ADDRESSING THE MEMBERSHIP CHALLENGE

A collaborative partnership with government involved some challenging changes for MGS. In addition to delivering the National Strategy, MGS was also tasked with transitioning to become the National Development Body. It was to remain the same charitable trust, but had to make major changes to aspects of its operations.

The Scottish government confirmed a three-year funding settlement from 2012 to 2015. This agreement provided an increase in funding for the museum sector but at the cost of a decrease to MGS's operational funding. This required a restructure to MGS staffing by April 2012 and development of a new structure aligned to delivering the National Strategy.

To progress this, the MGS board set up a transition group that considered several models of operation for the future National Development Body. Working to a tight timeline which required the new structure to be in place by April 2012, it was decided that the new body should initially be based on a 'facilitator' model (like a hub-and-spoke model) but with an aspiration to work increasingly as a networked organization that would move to establishing multiple hubs that would network together. It was felt that the facilitator model would ensure that the National Development Body would be government as well as sector facing and would require MGS to develop new skills such as commissioning, brokering partnerships and moving to an investment and enabling model rather than just providing grants and advice.

As well as operational changes, MGS made changes to its governance structure. These were in line with modern governance and the Office of the Scottish Charity Regulator (OSCR) best practice. In order to make these changes the existing membership needed to vote on a special resolution to update the Memorandum of Articles.

This resolution was presented to the membership in April 2012. The resolution consisted of two elements: a revising of the charitable objectives to place museums in the wider context of culture and heritage, and a change to membership. This change was a restriction of membership to just the members of the board of MGS who were legally accountable for MGS. Under the existing constitution, membership of MGS was open to all accredited museums in Scotland who could then vote a representative onto the board. The resolution meant that voting rights would be restricted to the MGS board and not open to the sector. The new board for the National Development Body would be openly recruited, rather than be representational of different parts of the sector.

This change raised many questions. It was clear that there were misunderstandings and concerns about what the changes entailed. Because the Scottish government was not replacing lost income from membership, the future sustainability of the National Development Body depended on generating income from the services it would be offering. Although membership and the associated membership income would be lost, the Scottish government had agreed that moving to a subscription model would be acceptable. The subscription would be based on a new service offer that was linked with the roll out of the National Strategy and, therefore, had not yet been fully developed. For the first year of transition it was agreed that subscriptions would mirror existing membership rates with a small discount to give time to work up a menu of services in consultation with the sector. It was testimony to the sector's loyalty and trust in MGS that they voted through the changes to the constitution with an 82 per cent majority in May 2012.

With the main operational changes to the constitution and structure now in place, MGS still faces many challenges. It has to develop its service offer in partnership with the sector to ensure it remains relevant and responsive to its needs and so that it can facilitate change and development. The sector is currently united by its enthusiasm for the National Strategy, but it now needs to move to practical implementation and involvement in the Delivery Plan. One of the biggest challenges will be developing systems that monitor progress on meeting the aims and objectives of the strategy and which will require the collection and evaluation of data without burdening the sector with new bureaucracy.

The Scottish government has endorsed both the National Strategy and the National Development Body as ways for museums and galleries to not only show that they deliver value but to also drive the creation of public value. Whatever evaluation systems are developed, they will need to draw on existing evidence mechanisms such as Accreditation and QIS, tourism visitor attraction ratings and industry standards. MGS will not have a membership but subscribing museums will be the direct customers of the National Development Body.

It is envisaged that the sector will develop relationships with the National Development Body on multiple levels – so, although a museum may be a subscriber, they may also be contracted to deliver services on behalf of the NDB. MGS is clear that the National Development Body should facilitate and support the sector to achieve the strategy's vision and aims, and that subscription should not be a barrier to achieving this. The main role of MGS as the National Development Body is to lead on taking the strategy forward. It is currently at the stage of engaging the sector in the development of the Delivery Plan and will work up a pilot plan for six months before moving into a two-year cycle which will take it to the next comprehensive spending review.[5] MGS is committed to regularly reviewing both the National Strategy and the Delivery Plan to ensure that it is continuing to work towards achieving the Vision.

The Scottish government, the 'authorizing' environment, has endorsed the view that museums are of public value. To create the National Development Body, it has worked with the 'operational environment' principally through the existing infrastructure of MGS to engage with the museums' sector in Scotland. The MGS model of a charitable trust is at arm's-length from government. It needs to be entrepreneurial and imaginative in its approach to generating funding, but still report to the Scottish government on the outcomes of its grant. This is a challenge and much will depend on the skill of MGS in managing and continuing to negotiate the various relationships with the Scottish government and the museums sector.

A key function for MGS in the past has been as the voice and advocate of the sector. It is likely that the smaller volunteer-led museums in particular will continue to look to

---

5   The comprehensive spending review happens on a three-year cycle and is the government's complete review of its spending and setting of the new three-year budget 2015 to 2018.

MGS for this advocacy role. The Scottish government was at first nervous of this as it did not want to support a lobbying organization. However, MGS persuaded the government that advocacy was an important role for the new National Development Body and that the National Strategy was a tool that could be used to gain support for the sector from other government portfolios such as health, education and skills. This is perhaps evidence of the maturing of the relationship with the Scottish government, but also reflects a different way of working. It could also be viewed as an example of what Moore (1995, 15) refers to as 'entrepreneurial advocacy' or 'what a public manager needs to do to maximise the chance that his or her preferred policy will be authoritatively adopted and solidly backed'. Through the development of the Delivery Plan, museums will have a mechanism to promote their public value to major stakeholders, potential supporters of the sector and to the Scottish government.

Moore (1995) and Holden (2004) both advocate the notion that what is of public value is partly shaped by the public. As the majority of museums in Scotland are managed by their communities, their involvement in the Delivery Plan for the National Strategy is directly engaging the public in creating the future of Scotland's museums. In this context it would seem appropriate that the model chosen for the National Development Body is that of a non-government organization (NGO) and charitable trust.

Other dimensions of public value

Museums in Scotland reflect the culture and identity of the nation and much of that is expressed intangibly through a strong tradition of oral culture such as music, song, storytelling and Gaelic and Scots language. Museum projects often incorporate an element of the intangible and it pervades many aspects of the communities' relationship with their museums. MGS, through the museums it serves, has a close connection with the communities of Scotland.

This connection has recently been recognized from an unlikely source, with MGS becoming the first UK NGO to be accredited by the United Nations Education Science Culture Organisation (UNESCO), as an expert advisor on the safeguarding of intangible cultural heritage.

To achieve accreditation, MGS described the work it does with museums and their communities, and in doing so demonstrated a relationship that encourages communities to actively participate in the safeguarding of their heritage. The 2003 UNESCO Convention for the Safeguarding of Intangible Heritage clearly places the responsibility for the intangible cultural heritage at community level. Governments and public service organizations can support the safeguarding process by providing training and awareness raising or by supporting the infrastructure to create inventories of intangible cultural heritage.. It is not governments, but communities that decide whether a tradition or example of intangible cultural heritage continues to be practised – they are the creators, practioners and the authorizers.

To achieve accreditation NGOs have to demonstrate that they are working closely with communities in an empowering and partnership manner. By engaging with intangible cultural heritage, MGS has found a mechanism to remain connected with the public and to have a conduit for channelling that into the National Strategy. Perhaps the most important aspect of the 2003 Convention is that it captures and promotes a way of working with communities that is centred around partnership, empowerment and ownership, all important values for the new National Development Body.

Conclusion

In a short space of time, MGS has changed, delivered and balanced conflicting demands. However, it still faces many challenges.

MGS, between the authorizing environment of Scottish government and the operating environment of the museum sector, has as Moore (1995, 189) says, walked 'a fine line between, on the one hand, exercising too little influence over the judgment of overseers and the actions of co producers to be effective in achieving attractive public purposes and, on the other, exercising so much authority that they risk the quality of democratic governance and the freedom of citizens'.

The National Strategy has raised high expectations within the museums and the communities they serve. There is enthusiasm from the sector to participate in building the Delivery Plan and MGS now needs to work with this new and unifying enthusiasm. MGS and the sector need to take on some of the active roles of brokering new partnerships and attracting new resources from outside the sector. Delivery has to be a true collaboration if it is to achieve and bring the added value to which the National Strategy aspires. For the first time, there is one vision uniting the sector and the National Strategy sets out a way of moving forward together. This is an incredible opportunity that everybody involved in museums in Scotland appears to be ready and willing to grasp.

References

Blaug, R.L. and Lekhi, R. 2006. *Public value, politics and public management: A literature review.* London: The Work Foundation.

Council of Scottish Local Authorities (COSLA). 2012. *Scottish Local Government.* Available at: http://www.cosla.gov.uk/scottish-local-government [accessed 30 July 2012].

Holden, J. 2004. *Capturing cultural value: How culture has become a tool of government policy.* London: DEMOS.

Moore, M. 1995. *Creating Public Value: Strategic Management in Government.* Cambridge: MA: Harvard University Press.

Moore, M. and Benington, J. (eds) 2011. *Public Value: Theory and Practice.* London: Palgrave Macmillan.

Museums Galleries Scotland (MGS). 2010a. *Realising the True Impact of Museums And Galleries in Scottish Tourism 2010.* Edinburgh: Moffat Centre for Travel and Tourism Business Development.

Museums Galleries Scotland (MGS). 2010b. *Choices for Change.* Available at: http://www.choicesforchange.info/toolkit/ [accessed 23 July 2012].

Museums Galleries Scotland (MGS). 2012. *Going Further: The National Strategy for Scotland's Museums and Galleries.* Edinburgh: Museums Galleries Scotland.

Population of Scotland Scottish government. 2011. Available at: http://www.scotland.org/facts/population/ [accessed 24 July 2012].

Scottish Government. 2007. *The Government Economic Strategy.* Available at: http://www.scotland.gov.uk/Resource/Doc/202993/0054092.pdf [accessed 24 July 2012].

Scottish Government. 2010a. *Report by the Museums Think Tank: Scotland's Museums and Galleries* Available at: http://www.scotland.gov.uk/Publications/2010/12/06145220/0 [accessed 23 July 2012].

Scottish Government. 2010b. Response by Fiona Hyslop Minister for Culture and External Affairs to the Report by the Museums Think Tank. Available at: http://www.scotland.gov.uk/Publications/2010/12/15144150/1 [accessed 1 August 2012].

Scottish Museums Council. 2002. *Scotland's National Audit*. Edinburgh: Scottish Museums Council.

Scottish Museums Council. 2006. *A National Workforce Development Strategy for Scotland's Museums*. Edinburgh: Scottish Museums Council.

Index

Page numbers in *italics* represent figures; page numbers in **bold** represent tables.